[英国] 安德鲁·戴维斯 著　胡毅 译

牛津通识读本·

# 项目管理

## Projects

### A Very Short Introduction

译林出版社

**图书在版编目（CIP）数据**

项目管理 ／（英）安德鲁·戴维斯（Andrew Davies）著；胡毅译.
—南京：译林出版社，2023.7
（牛津通识读本）
书名原文：Projects: A Very Short Introduction
ISBN 978-7-5447-9756-6

Ⅰ.①项… Ⅱ.①安… ②胡… Ⅲ.①项目管理 Ⅳ.①F27

中国国家版本馆 CIP 数据核字（2023）第 098137 号

著作权合同登记号　图字：10-2019-588 号

**项目管理**　［英国］安德鲁·戴维斯 ／ 著　胡　毅 ／ 译

责任编辑　陈　锐
装帧设计　景秋萍
校　　对　戴小娥
责任印制　董　虎

原文出版　Oxford University Press, 2017
出版发行　译林出版社
地　　址　南京市湖南路 1 号 A 楼
邮　　箱　yilin@yilin.com
网　　址　www.yilin.com
市场热线　025-86633278
排　　版　南京展望文化发展有限公司
印　　刷　江苏凤凰通达印刷有限公司
开　　本　890 毫米 ×1260 毫米　1/32
印　　张　9.875
插　　页　4
版　　次　2023 年 7 月第 1 版
印　　次　2023 年 7 月第 1 次印刷
书　　号　ISBN 978-7-5447-9756-6
定　　价　39.00 元

版权所有·侵权必究

译林版图书若有印装错误可向出版社调换．质量热线：025-83658316

# 序　言

宁　延

作为一名资深粉丝，我很荣幸能向国内读者推荐这本通识读物，也是安德鲁·戴维斯教授在国内面世的第二本中文译作，而且是一本面向非专业背景读者的独立著作。作为国际著名的项目管理专家，安德鲁·戴维斯教授引领了多个项目管理理论的发展，其研究兼具理论发展启示和实践相关性。他的著作我是一篇不落地做了认真研读，并在教学和研究工作中广泛引用。

在这里，我仅从自身对项目管理研究的体会谈几点粗浅的认识。

## 理解项目管理，要从历史开始

虽然中国古代有大量卓越的项目，但大家普遍认为现代项目管理的起源主要是从20世纪四五十年代美国的国防项目开始，当时的项目计划技术获得了成功，后来传播到不同的领域，并促成了专业协会的成立，进而形成了早期的标准化项目管理知识体系。到了20世纪七八十年代，计算机和软件领域得到了飞速发展，但随着软件复杂程度的不断提高，软件项目普遍出现预算超支、不符合实际需求和延期等问题，进而催生了敏捷开发等新的项目管理方法。本书展现了项目管理在大时间跨度里的发展，并通过多个典型实例对理论的发展进行了生动的说明，如美国国防项目、奥雅纳工程实践、伦敦的朱比利地铁线等。

从历史维度看，项目管理理论的发展与社会经济的发展紧密相连，具有鲜明的时代性。随着价值多样化要求和技术进步等引发的社会大变革，项目管理理论也将迎来大跨步发展的机遇。

## 负责任的项目管理研究

虽然项目管理方法与工具在实践领域取得了较大成功，但项目管理理论的发展与传统的管理和组织行为等相比仍存在差距，管理学科的学术期刊中项目管理相关的论文还很少，项目管理领域的研究者也难以拓展到主流管理学科领域。项目管理成为一个研究领域，既要有与其他领域的紧密关联，也需要有其独立存在的条件。可喜的是，也有一些方面取得了进展，如临时性组织得到了项目管理以及主流管理学领域的广泛关注，并被大家所接受和认可。

当然，发表在不同级别的杂志只是学术圈对研究成果的评价，更为重要的评价标准是，项目管理研究结论要能够经得起实践的检验，有助于改进实践并促进社会经济的发展。同时，项目管理理论也需要基于实践持续修正和完善。在本书中，我们可以清晰地看到作者如何诠释了项目管理理论与实践的充分融合。

## 作为一个实践性研究领域，项目管理研究成果需要更多的传播途径

项目管理研究者是一个非常庞大的群体，也产出了大量研究成果。但是，如何将理论研究更好地传播到从业人员和大众仍是一个值得探索的问题，我们需要更多的连接理论成果和从业人员的桥梁。虽然早些年在研究领域对项目管理的知识体系有不少批判，但在行业中，与研究成果的传播相比，认证和培训工作似乎更有效地推动了从业人员对项目管理知识体系的接受。通识读物可能是传播理论知识的一种有益尝试。当然，写作通识读物对研究者也提出了极高的要求，一方面需要具有精深的理论功底，如用词、表达的精准，另一方面又需要兼顾不同类型读者的喜好。

## 项目管理概念的清晰界定

一个成熟的研究领域要拥有一些被广泛认同并清晰定义的核心概念。在项目管理领域，由于其强实践导向，在行业中时常听闻一些"俗语"。虽然这些俗语朗朗上口，但对有效的专业性传播带来一些障碍。本书中项目管理相关概念的阐述极为讲究，界定得恰到好处，无不体现出原著的精良和缜密。本书的翻译也很好地照顾了项目管理理论体系的要求和中文阅读习惯，无不体现译者的用心。

总而言之，在这本通识读物里，原著者用简单的语言系统地介绍了项目和项目管理的发展历史，充分展现了项目管理理论和实践的融合。中文翻译也极为用心和恰到好处，是项目管理研究者和从业人员可选的一本上乘读物。

献给我的妈妈和女儿们

# 目 录

前 言 **1**

第一章　引 言 **1**

第二章　美国对未知的探索 **18**

第三章　从曼哈顿到月球 **36**

第四章　奥雅纳公司的灵活机构与理论视角中的项目 **59**

第五章　精益、重量级和颠覆性项目 **80**

第六章　伦敦的超大项目生态 **100**

第七章　重返未来 **123**

索 引 **131**

译后记 **144**

英文原文 **147**

# 前　言

　　正如我们在工作和日常生活中所做的许多事情一样，本书的写作也是一个项目。它开始于一个想法。虽然已有许多关于项目管理的优秀图书，但是它们大多只是提供"如何成事"的指南，以及有关最佳实践工具、技术和程序的简单技巧。每个项目都被视作一项"孤立的"尝试，它可以与其计划和实施的环境相脱离的方式进行管理。我近来加入了伦敦大学学院的巴特莱特建筑环境学院，担任项目管理专业的教授，期望能够向更为广泛的读者介绍有关项目组织方式的新思想。这一理论方法有时被称为项目研究，它试图理解项目如何适应复杂、不确定和快速变化的条件，并对丰富且不同的组织、制度和历史情境中的项目进行考察。我将自己的想法写成了一份建议书，提交给了潜在的资助方牛津大学出版社，经过修改以后，我获得了一份符合资助方规范要求的图书出版合同。虽然像其他许多项目一样，这一项目也出现了进度延误（我数次超出了交稿要求的期限），但是，它还是在预算要求内完成了（它的价格是固定的）。从长远来看，这一项目的成果并不确定，因为它有赖于能否给身为客户的您（读者）带来持久的效益和价值。

虽然这一成果的文责在我，但是像大多数项目一样，这个项目也涉及了一个协作的团队。我要感谢马克·道奇森、戴维·甘恩和戴维·穆森，是他们鼓励我撰写了这部牛津通识读本。同时，我还要感谢牛津大学出版社的珍妮·纽吉和她的同事们，即便是在我超过了交稿要求的限期时，她们对这个写作项目的实施还是给予了耐心和支持。我还要感谢那些在项目导向型组织和知名项目中与我合作的经理人，以及那些在伦敦大学学院及他处的同事和学生，他们继续做着这一回报丰厚和激励人心并已成为我职业生涯中心的主题。我要感谢那些提供了有关如何完善此书的详尽评论和宝贵建议的同事，包括：马克·道奇森、蒂姆·布雷迪、萨姆·麦考利、乔纳斯·瑟德隆德和西尔万·朗夫勒，以及近年来与我进行论文合作以及紧密工作的合作者们，尤其安德烈亚·普伦奇佩、珍妮弗·怀特、努诺·吉尔、尼尔斯·诺德哈文、拉斯·费雷德里克森、延斯·勒里希、欧金妮亚·卡恰托里、斯蒂芬·曼宁、伊尔泽·基夫莱涅采和保罗·奈廷格尔。我还要感谢伦敦大学学院的同事们：唐娜·凯奇、布赖恩·科林斯、尤利亚诺·丹尼尔科尔、安德鲁·埃德金斯、吉姆·米克尔、斯蒂芬·米拉利亚、贝丝·摩根、彼得·莫里斯、亚历克斯·默里、纳塔利娅·谢尔盖耶娃、赫德利·史密斯和韦德兰·热里亚夫，因为他们澄清了多处问题并为具体问题的解决提供了帮助。感谢马克·瑟斯顿、蒂姆·德巴罗、约翰·佩尔顿和萨姆·麦考利的创造性工作和相同的乐趣，我们为伦敦横贯铁路项目开发了一个创新计划。我还要向汉斯·约尔格·格

2

明登和卡拉·梅西科默表示感谢,因为他们对项目研究学术圈成员们的引领、支持和激励。我要向对理论和管理实践有着深刻理解的学者彼得·莫里斯、雷蒙德·莱维特、傅以斌及亚伦·申哈尔致以特别的敬意,因为他们对我的项目思考产生了巨大的影响。

前
言

# 引 言

我们依靠项目来改造自然环境、创建人造世界。自人们最初生活和工作于早期农耕社会的村庄、集镇和城市起,我们就开始参与项目了。项目是用于协调临时性团队成员参与到一次性任务中,其范围从狩猎、居所建造等小型非正式活动,到精心谋划的壮举,比如军事行动、海外探险(每次新的航行都是一个项目)以及房屋、道路、港口和整个城市建造等。世界上最古老的项目,例如埃及的金字塔,伊拉克的灌溉工程,罗马帝国的神庙、水道、公路和桥梁,中国的万里长城,以及哥特式风格的大教堂等,都是规模巨大的,涉及难以计数的人力,耗时数年、数十年甚至更长时间才能完成。

在今天,项目实际上无处不在。复杂的、一次性的新技术尝试,比如耗资一千亿美元的国际空间站、第一部完全采用3D全景式镜头拍摄的电影《阿凡达》,以及上海时速五百公里的磁悬浮列车,都是显而易见的项目实例。我们日常生活所使用的各种产品,诸如汽车、相机、智能手机、量产药物等,在大批量生产之前都

1

是以项目的形式开始的。我们所做的许多事情,比如组织变革、产生并实践新的想法(如提供3D打印定制服务的新创企业)或是应对危机(比如非政府组织在世界上战争地区提供人道主义援助)都是项目。尽管它们在目标、规模和范围上有所不同,跨越不同行业,但是每个项目都是用于召集具有不同知识背景的人员,完成某项临时性工作,解决某个复杂的问题或实现某个新的想法。

## 何为项目?

现代意义上的“项目”这个词直到20世纪才被广泛使用。在此之前,它有多种不同的含义。《牛津英语词典》表明这个词在公元2世纪曾被使用过。在古典拉丁语中,动词“prōject”是指前抛或投射。在15世纪,这个词是指构思想法、提出计划、将某事付诸实践或是对未知事物的探险等行为。丹尼尔·笛福曾在其《论项目》一书的标题中使用过这个词,用以描述一个“项目化时代”:当时,出现了海外扩张、贸易计划及科学、艺术与生产制造的创新性改进想法,这些想法通过项目的方式实施来获取利润,并“担负着能否成功的风险而探索”。

本书将“项目”定义为:通过临时性组织和过程对人员与其他资源进行组合配置,以实现一个确定的目标。是什么使得项目区别于生产制造和服务等其他组织活动呢?这就在于项目有着明确的时限,从数小时、数天、数周到数年,有时甚至要数十年。与被视为持久性的生产制造企业或服务企业不同,项目组织是有意设计成临时的、一次性的。每个项目都需要聚集必要的人员和资源以实现目标,但在工作完成后就不复存在。比如说,当庞巴迪、西门子和东芝等企业着手准备某一城际高铁列车合同竞标时，它们会建立一个项目型组织，用以协调其员工和分包商网络所承担的工作。该组织的计划生命周期仅有若干年，并会在工作完成后解散。

项目规模有小有大，小至数人的团队，大至大型国际合资企业，以及由公共机构和私营组织组成的临时联合体。每个项目都有一个从始至终的生命周期。每个项目实施都有一个明确的顺序性阶段或活动，用以构思和推介想法、准备建议书、制订计划，以及实施和完成工作。这些顺序性阶段或活动时常也会并行。例如，瑞典移动通信产品制造商爱立信，着手准备全球性移动网络运营商（比如沃达丰或德国电信）的某一合同竞标时，它会组建一个有着不同专业背景的专家团队（比如技术、服务和销售等），其人员都是借调自公司不同的部门。该团队致力于搜集信息并预测运营商对下一代移动通信系统的需求，这些工作甚至在运营商招标之前就会开始进行。当运营商发布正式的招标邀请给投标人时，这个在招标之前建立的小组就会被解散。其中的许多成员都会回到各自的部门，而一个新的团队会被组建起来准备实际的投标建议书。一旦投标建议书提交，建议书撰写团队也会被解散，而另一个新的团队又会被组建来执行项目。某些人员会随着项目进展参加各个陆续建立的团队，但是其他的专家则只会参与一两个阶段的工作。

定义清晰的项目目标及其进展，时常是通过成本、进度和质量三项限定予以考核的，即所谓的项目管理"铁三角"。项目经理的工作就是按照进度、预算及质量和性能规范的要求完成项目。为了实现项目目标，需要在进度、成本和质量之间进行权衡（图1）。比如：尽管可用于建设伦敦2012年奥运会场馆的工期

"我们必须走捷径！"

图1 我们总是面临着项目权衡管理的挑战

是确定的，即有着一个"不可变动的完工日期"，但是能达到预期效果的成本和质量是可以调控的。尽管如此，此类权衡大多没有考虑其自身对"用户满意度"——第四项限定——及长期战略目标的影响。

现在我们认识到，项目成功是有多个维度的，并会随着时间发生变化。其他维度还包括：项目能否提升相关人员、团队和组织的知识和技能，以及它能否对某一组织的商业成功、利润和市场份额有所贡献。即便是有些项目在短时间内不太成功（按照成本、进度和质量予以考核），但是它们可以提供有关技术、产品、服务和客户需求的新知识，从而开拓未来的商机。正如悉尼歌剧院所示，那些伟大的项目按照三重限定模型考核可能会被视为短时间内的失败，但是如果它们能为业主、用户、社区，甚至是整个国家创造额外的效益并提供一份可长久流存的遗产，那么它们会在更长的时间里取得成功（方框1）。

4

**方框1　悉尼歌剧院**

悉尼歌剧院项目在1957年初步估算时投资仅为700多万澳元，并计划于1963年1月完工。该建筑最终于1973年10月启用，比最初的计划晚了十年，其成本达到1.02亿澳元，超过预算的14倍左右。在计划和建设时，该项目遭受了众多的反对和批评。项目启用时，据说该建筑并不具备大剧院的功能，因为最初的设计为满足新的要求、成本上涨和工期延误进行了多次变更。从进度、成本和质量目标来衡量，该项目被视为令人沮丧的失败，可能创造了糟糕绩效的世界纪录。然而在今天，有着好似明亮风帆般屋面结构的悉尼歌剧院，被赞誉为全世界最具特色的建筑之一。在1980年出版的《大规划的灾难》中，彼得·霍尔指出，"它就是悉尼"，并"让这座城市置于世界伟大城市的某种心理地图之上"（第138页）。

项目经理负责制订清晰确定的计划并管理计划，直至项目结束。他们制定项目目标，确定检查点、工期、计划进度和资源要求。他们管理、激励并赋能项目成员个体，促进沟通，打造激发团队活力的共识，并鼓励创新、风险承担和创造性。艾伦·伦道夫和巴里·Z.波斯纳提出了十条简要的原则，以帮助项目经理计划和管理项目（见表1）。当项目处于复杂、难以预测和持续变化的状态时，计划必须要灵活且项目要能在最初无法预见的情形下进行调整。担任不确定项目的经理必须要往复进行计划/管理、计划/管理的工作，直至达成目标。

**表1  项目计划和管理的原则**

<table>
<tr><td colspan="2" align="center">项 目 计 划</td></tr>
<tr><td>1. 确立明确的项目目标</td><td>从终点开始并倒推工作。确立项目目标,包括出资方、项目经理、项目团队及项目用户。</td></tr>
<tr><td>2. 确定项目的具体目标</td><td>制定详细的具体目标,帮助项目成员理解他们的贡献是如何与整体目标关联的。</td></tr>
<tr><td>3. 建立行动计划和时间估算</td><td>建立行动计划,详细说明何种工作将要执行并如何根据项目完工时间监测其进度。</td></tr>
<tr><td>4. 绘制项目进度计划图</td><td>绘制项目蓝图或项目进度表,可视化项目活动、活动间关系及时间估算。</td></tr>
<tr><td colspan="2" align="center">项 目 管 理</td></tr>
<tr><td>5. 引导个体人员成为项目团队</td><td>构建强大的合作者团队,鼓励他们从经验中发现和解决问题。</td></tr>
<tr><td>6. 增强团队承诺</td><td>鼓励人员参与项目,使他们拥有主人翁感并致力于项目成功。</td></tr>
<tr><td>7. 保持全员的紧密联系</td><td>克服沟通障碍,定期向人员传达信息,使他们倾听和使用从团队成员处获得的信息。</td></tr>
<tr><td>8. 建立激发团队活力的共识</td><td>项目要求协调多项任务,整合不同单位和人员。冲突也可成为激发想象力和创造性的动力。</td></tr>
<tr><td>9. 赋能自我和其他项目成员</td><td>项目经理需要具备与正式授权等同的个人能力。高效执行项目的经理会分享权力。</td></tr>
<tr><td>10. 鼓励创新、风险担当和创造性</td><td>为创新而计划。分享理念和创造性需要支持与沟通。创新可以通过目标、预算和期限得以强化。</td></tr>
</table>

项目管理

　　针对环境变化进行调整的必要性,可以解释为什么能达到目标的某个项目却最终失败。比如,摩托罗拉公司投资50亿美元的铱星项目采用了固定总价合同,即最初确定的合同总价至合同完成时也不会发生变化的方式，用以构建一个卫星群，提供卫星电话语音和数据通信服务。它可以被认为是个成功，因为它按时完成，没有超支，符合技术规范要求，但是从商业上来看则是个失败。在项目实施时，摩托罗拉公司的管理团队没能预见到，当前我们所依赖的、快速扩张中的地面移动电话网络会完全颠覆铱星项目的商业模式。

比如新的消费品、建筑或城市地铁系统被创造出来，意味着一个项目自身的完成。它可能成为持续进行的集群项目的一部分，通过关联项目之间的资源共享和协调，实现共同的目标，比如手机通信系统在全国范围内的示范性应用。项目组合的构建可以为处于计划、编制和排序进程中的一组项目分配资源，实现组织的长期战略目标，比如苹果公司产品数字化中心和iTunes在线服务平台（第五章）。

## 项目与运营

项目与运营存在区别。项目通过执行创新性、不可重复、一次性的任务，为个体消费者产出独特的、一次性或定制的成果，比如建筑、变革计划或新机场。运营则通过执行持续性重复任务，为大众消费市场生产标准化的产品和服务，比如小汽车、电脑和快餐食品。项目是一种灵活的、适应性强的组织方式，可以在动荡、快速变化的条件下进行组织，处理个体客户需求并推动创新；而运营则是在稳定、可预见的环境中执行标准化惯例的一种设计。我们还会发现：项目虽然在复杂性、速度和不确定性方面有所差异（第四章），但它执行的任务既有独一无二的，也有重复的（第六章）。

7

项目的产出和成果也是有区别的。产出是项目所创造的有形和无形的事物，比如建筑、信息技术系统或组织过程。成果则是在项目开始运营以后，为出资方、客户和使用者创造的效果或价值，比如提升的绩效、既有产品的改善及开拓的新市场。

项目和运营之间存在过渡，比如类似于新建有轨电车线路的产出在移交以后，会转变成为运营性成果——运营中的城市电车系统。随着项目临近结束，构件和子系统将会集成和测试，客户在项目运营前将会学习如何使用项目的产物（如硬件、软件和服务等）。

许多复杂项目的失败是由于不成功的过渡所造成的。如果这个项目是由强有力的出资方主持，且运营者在初始阶段就开始介入、明确其要求并深入参与到启用前的各项准备工作中，那么实现准时、无缝衔接的运营过渡仍是有较大可能的。以2008年5月伦敦希思罗机场五号航站楼的启用混乱为例，大量航班取消，行李处理缓慢且无序，这一情况一直持续了十二天。通过吸取一次性开放整座航站楼失败的教训，机场运营方决定筹划希思罗的下一项重大项目，即二号航站楼的"柔性启用"。在2014年6月4日项目启用的两年前，一支专门的"运营筹备"团队就被嵌入到项目组织中。通过分阶段开放航站楼，移交得以一次性成功实现，其包括了涉及1.4万名志愿者的180次试运营、1700期培训、基于数字化"虚拟航站楼"的登机处理软件评估、一次航班实测以及阶段化流程，最终将每家航空公司转移到了新运营的航站楼。

若干项目会延伸到运营服务的提供过程中，并持续多年。例如：阿尔斯通交通公司（以法国为基地的阿尔斯通分支机构）

在1995年获得了一项总价为4.29亿英镑的私人融资计划,用以更新伦敦地铁北线的线路车辆。与明确的具体线路规模相比,伦敦地铁对相关成果的要求如下:它要求在二十年内,每天须有96列车辆可用于服务。为了完成这一目标,阿尔斯通生产了106列车辆并建立了专门的运维组织为其服务。项目需求包含了服务的提供,以鼓励IBM、阿尔斯通及劳斯莱斯这类项目导向型企业改变自身的整体商业模式,从而使得它们能够同时设计和集成系统并提供它们的运维服务。

　　所有组织或多或少地都会参与项目,但是某些组织和行业的活动几乎完全是项目驱动的,比如空中客车的飞机业务、IBM的信息技术解决方案,以及扎哈·哈迪德的建筑设计实践。对于项目导向型组织而言,每个客户订单都造就了一个新的项目。与此同时,索尼、三星和星巴克等大批量生产商以及庞大的政府部门在正常运作以外,也会依靠项目去实施战略、开发新产品、造就组织变革、建造新资产和系统,以及处理一次性问题或机遇。

## 项目简史

　　阿尔文·托夫勒在其著作《未来的冲击》(1970)和《第三次浪潮》(1980)中广泛地使用了"灵活机构"一词,用以描述一种后工业化组织的新物种,即临时性、专门的、适应性项目小组和团队。托夫勒论述道,农业的产生与第一次浪潮有关,但被18世纪末英国工业革命引发的第二次浪潮所终结,由此造成了后来的大批量生产在美国和德国的兴起。起始于20世纪中叶的第三次浪潮,是源自后工业信息社会的突变性新原则。托夫勒认为,计算机发明所造成的临时项目结构和信息渠道,将会突破之前的社会制度安排，并会抵制标准化的任务、科层制、层级制及其他第二次浪潮的价值和利益。

农业时代的许多建设项目是由某位"巨匠"所完成的。综合了建筑师、工程师和工匠的角色、知识和实践经验，"巨匠"负责产生新的想法并将其转变为现实、设计有关建筑并雇用工匠建造它。举例来说，在1666年伦敦大火之后，克里斯托弗·雷恩爵士被任命为首席建筑师，负责调查受损区域，规划新的城区，设计圣保罗大教堂等建筑并管理建造过程。

大概在工业革命前后，设计和施工之间的联系开始割裂；此时的工程和建筑大多从其他的建筑行当中分离出来，演变为专门的科学和精英化职业。在17世纪末期和18世纪，精英化的职业土木工程团队在法国建立，工程师除了承担桥梁、道路和其他政府项目的设计、规范制定和采购的职责，还要负责明确项目实施中的承包商任务。此后，专业土木工程师也开始在英国出现。在1818年英国土木工程师学会成立后，以托马斯·特尔福德和伊桑巴德·金德姆·布鲁内尔为代表的负责设计道路、水道和铁路的工程师们，开始从组织和合同上与建造人员相分离。例如，托马斯·布拉西的总承包企业建造了大部分的英国铁路网络。在1834年英国皇家建筑师学会成立后，建筑设计被确认为一门职业，建筑师们被禁止参与营利性承包交易。随后，建筑设计师就开始与工程和建筑日常实践相分离。近几年来，比如弗兰克·盖里、奥韦·奥雅纳和托马斯·赫斯维克等建筑师、土木工程师和产品设计师开始尝试重新塑造"巨匠"式的职能来主持项目，通过合作性流程来加强设计和施工的联系（方框2）。

**方框2　项目缔造者和"巨匠"**

　　托马斯·赫斯维克的伦敦设计工作室是一个"项目缔造者"。它试验新的材料，提出新的想法，产生从产品（比如伦敦新的节能巴士）到标志性建筑设计（2010年上海世博会英国馆）等不同规模的创新，并塑造未来的城市。正如赫斯维克所强调的那样，产生新的想法和实现它们，意味着每个项目都是"一种强烈的混合物，包蕴着确定与怀疑、突破与终结、紧张与欢愉、挫折与进步"。这个工作室像项目集合体一样运作；每个项目都是根据某个客户问题所形成，并由工作室的资深成员负责。受到"巨匠"这一历史性人物的影响，赫斯维克认为，分别由建筑师、工匠、工程师和设计师承担的分工应当由协作型团队进行综合，从而使产品或建筑的设计能够与其实现过程形成紧密的关联。

　　直到20世纪中叶，应用最为广泛、先进的项目管理方法依旧是在工程建设中。但是，行业协会的学者和从业人员忽视了项目自身也是一种组织方式。相反地，他们主要关注于理解那些最初源自铁路建设和现代公司制度诞生的运营改进，是如何导致大型、分层级的常设组织崛起的。作为德国社会学者及其时代最主要的理论创建者，马克斯·韦伯宣称：只存在一种最优化的大规模人员队伍的组织方式。有关工作分解、自上而下的权威及大型科层制结构的规则被设计出来，用以完善标准化的运营程序并改善稳定环境中的绩效。弗雷德里克·W.泰勒的科学管理与亨利·福特的T型车生产流水线，将其中部分的想法变成了现实。大批量生产对福特、标准石油（美孚）、卡内基钢铁及可口可乐等公司而言，成为其实现增长并在竞争中生存的关键。大批量生产商不仅从后端集成了原材料来源和部件化制造，还从前端集成了分销商购买和大众市场渠道控制。

管理理论与实践似乎很少涉及项目，这个具有完全不同组织逻辑的对象。在经济学历史上，曾有过一篇令人激动的关于项目研究的论文，菲利普·斯克兰顿在其中指出：铁路建设所具备的模式，是值得其他组织仿效的；但是它们如何经营获利的问题，掩盖了它们起初是如何建设的问题。这一点是令人惊讶的。因为如果没有那些以项目形式进行组织的大量努力，英国和美国工业革命是不会出现的。那些项目包括承担着大量原材料、人员、信息和货物运输的运河、铁路、电报和电话网络的建设，大批量生产相关的工厂、车间和机器，能源、照明、供水、排水及其他市政系统，以及满足快速城市化社会的建筑环境。几乎所有的事物都被发包给多个独立机构，以临时性组织的方式共同开展作业，并在任务完成后解散。项目造就了一次性、独特的事物，而运用已完成的成果则是一种持续的运营作业。

关键的历史转折点发生在第二次世界大战期间及之后，此时的管理学者和专业管理者开始认识到国防和航空航天领域中项目的重要性（第三章）。在进行美国技术最为先进的武器系统开发时，尤其是像生产原子弹的"曼哈顿项目"，以及"宇宙神"和"北极星"弹道导弹计划这类项目时，其所面临的挑战需要一种突破式创新且更为成熟的方式，用以管理这类复杂项目。为这些项目所创造的"系统方法"鼓励管理者聚焦于对系统整体的理解，包括构件之间的界面和相互关联。开发新形式的项

12

目组织、流程和工具,可以整合、调度和协调科学家、工程师和管理者,以多学科项目团队的方式进行工作。

项目管理系统方法在20世纪60年代和70年代,被扩展应用于美国及世界各地的多个其他行业中。在论述美国战后技术项目的《拯救普罗米修斯》(1998)一书中,托马斯·休斯将项目管理系统方法的重要性表述如下:

> 在弗雷德里克·W.泰勒及其追随者的倡导下,科学管理在20世纪初期开始扩展其应用。然而,相较于项目活动,泰勒信仰者们主要是在持续的制造运营中应用科学管理技术。

到20世纪80年代,许多曾关注于运营改进的组织发现很难适应日趋动荡、不确定和快速变化的环境。有些组织开始寻求更灵活的方式应对无休止的变化,而不是寻求对它的控制。正如托夫勒在《适应性公司》(1985)中所写,灵活机构的涌现是由于:

> "一次性"或临时性的问题需要"一次性"或临时性的组织去解决。对于处理一段时间后就不会存在的问题而言,建立完备的临时结构是低效的。其结果是必然会涌现出各种模块化、临时性、自我消亡的单元,比如特别任务组、攻关团队、专责委员会和为特定的临时性目标所建立的其他队伍。

在《追求卓越》(1982)一书中,汤姆·彼得斯和罗伯特·H.沃特曼期望:灵活机构会扩展到新的行业和环境,因为它们正变得更加不确定、复杂并呼唤创新,甚至影响到那些20世纪最为庞大、成功的科层组织,比如IBM和通用电气。在后工业信息社会中,企业和市场之间的中间地带会日益扩张,对此,曼纽尔·卡斯泰尔予以强调道,生产的单元成为"基于网络的商业项目",而不再是由公司个体或多家公司的正式集合所构成。

从20世纪90年代开始,个人电脑、互联网、万维网、智能手机、社交媒体和其他数字技术开始重塑各种形式的工作,项目形式的应用也开始加速。比如,波音公司采用了基于电脑的"无纸化"方式进行设计、测试、生产并集成波音777型客机项目(第五章)。数字技术正开始广泛应用于支持整个项目生命周期所进行的活动中,并时常拓展到资产的运营维护中。在我们基于互联网的世界中,几乎所有类型项目的协作参与方只要拥有智能手机或笔记本电脑,就可以实现数字信息的实时共享。

在21世纪,项目是使一个组织的现有活动得以继续的载体,但它在全球竞争性市场中具有更为基础性的功能,能够像创新引擎那样去实现从想法到商业化的转变。世界上最具竞争力的企业利用项目开发新技术,设计创新产品、流程和服务,引入组织变革,发起企业内部创业并实施商业战略。随着产品生命周期变短,公司不得不在现有产品淘汰之前,加快新的多样化产品和服务的开发,尤其是在快节奏、高度竞争的消费品市场中。大公司逐步将自身改造成项目的巢穴,试图创造以创新为焦点的灵活性、问题攻关导向型的结构。某些大批量生产商正在将其纵向集成运营业务中的大批量生产部分外包出去,并聚焦于成为面向新产品开发的,由外部制造商和供应商所组成的网络的"项目协调者"。宝马公司和雷诺公司都将每个新产品平台——下一代汽车产品基础——视为一个项目。耐克公司不再生产跑鞋，而是管理不同的鞋类项目。可口可乐公司外包了饮品的装瓶和营销业务，其当前的运作更像是一个多项目的集合。

政府采购政策的变化、私有化和开放国有部门的竞争，导致公共项目的数量和类型极大地增长，这些项目包括大学研究、高速公路维护、学校、住宅、医院、机场、音乐厅、城市轨道交通系统、污水、防洪及可持续能源项目。这些变化为公共和私营组织创造了新的机遇，常常是以合作的方式承担公共部门的风险和责任，履行社会义务、资源节约和环境保护的要求（方框3）。

## 方框3 公私合作模式

20世纪90年代，英国在公共项目中试点一种新的合同模式。私人融资倡议（Private Finance Initiative，简称PFI）要求私营部门承担项目的设计、建造、融资和运营，并获取其若干年内或数十年间形成的运营收益作为回报。与通过私营部门进行项目融资并承担大部分风险的PFI相比，公私合作模式（Public-private partnership，简称PPP）的项目资金仅部分来自私营部门，同时政府会分担部分风险或提供相关的担保。比如，英国国家医疗系统在2013年就有130多个PFI/PPP项目，总值达到120亿英镑。其中最大的PFI医院项目就被授予了一个名为"首都医院"的私营联合体。在这份价值11亿英镑的合同中，首都医院负责在皇家伦敦医院和圣巴塞洛缪医院的旧址设计、建设、更新和运维两所新的伦敦医院，直至2048年终止。

在近期出版的一本书中,罗尔夫·伦丁及其合著者描述了始于20世纪60年代的一个趋势,即组织中运营的比重开始下降,项目的比重开始快速增加。世界银行发布的2015年固定资产投资完成数据(包括建筑活动、机器及设备的开销)可以提供了一个大概的指数参考,有助于了解主要以项目方式开展的这一类型经济活动:在全球生产总值的114万亿美元中,固定资本形成总额占到了23%;在某些新兴工业化国家中,这一数字超过了30%,譬如印度为31%,中国为46%。这些投资大多数是以超大项目的方式实施的,即大型复杂的、高风险的科技、工程或基础设施项目,其成本达到10亿美元或以上(按照2003年价格计算)。随着全球超大项目每年的开支达到6万亿至9万亿美元,傅以斌认为这是"人类历史上最大的投资繁荣"。

项目组织方式应用的增长,可能比这些数字所体现的情形更为普遍。它的应用超越了新产品开发以及那些常常提供一次性、定制化产品和服务的传统项目行业,比如国防、航天、建设、咨询、软件、传媒和娱乐业等,几乎拓展到了后工业社会的每一个角落。消费品供应商、政府组织、大学、学校、非政府组织、"快闪"时尚或零售商店、志愿者团体、慈善组织以及许多其他类型的组织,现在都通过项目来形成创新,打破既有模式,解决复杂问题,以及探索创业机遇。

## 项目绩效

21世纪的组织正持续通过精益生产、商业流程再造、质量管理、六西格玛管理以及其他管理创新来提升它们标准化的运营水平。它们并不擅长成功地实现项目。尽管通过经验式学习,绩效改进的数字和机会可以获得增长，但是项目仍时常面临着难以达到其成本、进度、质量和长期目标的局面。

若干有影响力的研究表明，20世纪50年代末以来大量项目面临糟糕的绩效。通过对1959年至1986年公开报告中的项目超支情况的回顾分析，莫里斯和霍夫发现：在全球范围内的多个行业中，约3500个项目中都出现了40%~200%的超支。申哈尔和德维尔对不同国家的私营部门、公共部门和非营利部门中600多个项目数据的研究发现：85%的项目未能满足它们最初的进度和成本目标，其进度延迟率为70%，成本超支率为60%。糟糕的绩效不仅会影响项目参与方，某一项目的失败还会影响其所在城市和国家的兴盛。比如，2004年雅典奥运会导致的成本超支和债务是如此庞大，以至于严重影响了希腊的经济。

正如我们将在这部通识读本的其他部分所发现的一样，大多数绩效糟糕项目的共同点在于它们未能适应其环境。项目出资方、高管和经理们必须确定其目标，在其开始时重视其限制条件，比如复杂性、不确定性和完成任务所需的时间，并适应项目进展中未预见到的情形。项目都有需要学习的历史和有待塑造的未来。它们常常被孤立地看待，与之前的项目及其自身的构想和实施所处的广泛历史和组织情境割裂开来。

在第二章中，我们将会发现，大规模的工程壮举在正式的项目管理工具、语言和领域形成之前就已经实现了，通常也非常成功。

# 美国对未知的探索

正如今天超大项目的经理们所认知的那样,美国19世纪初最具雄心、规模最大的工程项目的实施面临着巨大挑战。然而,在构思这一项目时,美国并没有具备相关知识的专业土木工程师或经理,可用以组织如此大型复杂的工程壮举。正是这一项目创造了知识,尽管在此之前并不具备相关能力,同时还要面对和克服许多未知的条件。它不仅成为其自身项目经理的工程学校和培训场所,还成为美国工业未来的关键。这个项目就是伊利运河。

该项目的目标是创造世界最大的内陆水道,以连接纽约和伊利湖。这个项目在好多年里被认为是极不现实的。1809年,托马斯·杰斐逊总统认为这条穿越美国内陆荒野地带的运河建设"近乎疯狂"。彼得·伯恩斯坦曾写道,如此大规模的人工内陆水道,将连接国家的东部和西部边疆,"就如同向月球发射火箭一样令人激动"。该项目需要克服大量的地理空间挑战,比如19 穿越河道、密林、疟疾流行的沼泽、深谷和岩崖。尽管它创造了多项第一,但是其建设资金在1817年被批准后的好些年里,它仍旧受到许多的质疑。尽管存在这些障碍，但是该项目依然按时完工，与最初的投资估算相差不大，并于1825年10月26日开始运营。

伊利运河建立了一条通道，使得越来越多的原材料、谷物和农产品输往哈得孙河畔的东部城市奥尔巴尼，并且几乎能够无限地将货物和人员送达尼亚加拉河畔的西部城市布法罗。这条内陆水道长363英里（584公里），是美国最大运河长度的13倍多。该运河深4英尺（1.2米），宽40英尺（12.2米），设有83个石材建造的水闸，可使船只能够升降达675英尺（206米），穿过沿河道全程分布的18条水渠。它激发了总长3300英里运河网络的建设，成为美国首个面向公众的交通基础设施。

该项目是在私营运河企业失败尝试之后，才由政府进行投资、设计和管理并获得成功的。纽约的民选政治家团队为项目确定目标、设定政治舞台、保障资金支持并监管运河的设计和建设。他们任命了缺乏土木工程经验的人员担任测量师，但是他们具有学习意愿和创新的才能，从而能识别路径、进行设计、估算成本、解决技术难题、计划并监管作业。通过今天被我们称之为公私合作的方式，项目得以由一个临时性公共机构管理，通过竞争性招标所选定的私营承包商予以实施，并在政府聘用的工程师指导下建造运河各小段。

## 构思与推进

这条连接哈得孙河和伊利湖的运河内陆线路的构想，利用了唯一穿越阿巴拉契亚山脉的水路——莫霍克河峡谷。在1817年开始建设之前，纽约政治家们和富有的投资者们很早就提出

20

了这一构想。一旦运河能够建成，它将释放美国西部巨大的自然资源，通过货运驳船将它们送抵纽约城，而其成本仅为陆路运输线路费用的一小部分。在最初的一份建议书中，纽约市市长亨利·穆尔爵士就提出：希望改善这一线路的沿线内河航运；但正如许多后来的建议书一样，它没能获得必要的政治支持得以继续发展这一构想。

西部内陆船闸航运公司成立于1792年，致力于改善莫霍克河的状况。尽管该公司缺乏必要的工程专长，以克服沿河地带较大的自然屏障，但是它所开展的工作表明：一条穿越阿巴拉契亚山脉的内陆河道是可行的。许多后来参与伊利运河项目的顶尖工程师和重要政治家都是为该公司工作的。尽管该公司的私人融资不足且管理糟糕，但是它为后来参与伊利运河的人员提供了重要的一课，即：如此大规模的项目必须要由政府管理和融资。

伊利运河最早的具体建议书可以追溯到纽约谷物商人杰西·霍利在1807年和1808年撰写的十四篇文章。霍利探讨了不同的运河设计、技术方案和路线。他还考虑了可能的资金支持渠道并建议：运河应当采用联邦资金进行建设，而非私人融资。他摒弃后一方案是由于它的不充分性、垄断性及自利性。基于欧洲主要运河的规模、复杂性、建设进度和成本资料的研读，他预计运河建设将要花费500万美元。完成于1681年的米迪运河连接了大西洋和地中海，穿越了法国南部和西部。这条运河表明：大规模的运河建设是可行的，尽管伊利运河的长度将会是这一法国运河长度的两倍多。数月后，在研读法国的米迪运河和苏格兰的格兰奇运河资料后，他将数字修订为600万美

21

元，以涵盖他选中的设计构想的额外花费，即：一个将26道水闸按照伊利湖到莫霍克河之间的落差逐级布置的倾斜设计。霍利对于运河成本和效益的估算被证实是极为准确的。十年后开工的这一项目最终由政府出资，按照几乎等同的成本估算，沿着与其建议的类似路线进行。

这些运河项目的推动者注意到，纽约作为商业中心的优势正在受到威胁。穿过阿巴拉契亚山脉巨大地理屏障的西部旅途是艰难的，而较容易的路线则需要通过较远的南部。巴尔的摩、费城以及其他的城市正在快速发展，因为它们通过从匹兹堡到费城的收费公路以及到巴尔的摩的国家公路相连。从密西西比河和俄亥俄河到墨西哥湾的贸易线路发展迅速，会形成一个将商业中心转移到新奥尔良的威胁。伊利运河的支持者们坚信：这条内陆水道是必需的，它将会使得纽约成为通向美国西部市场的大门。

在有关运河建造立法的第一步中，联邦政府提供了并不宽裕的600美元，用于调查哈得孙河和伊利湖之间的最可能线路。该项调查由詹姆斯·格迪斯于1808年进行。他是一名年轻但经验不多的测量师，后来成为伊利运河西段的总工程师。他在1809年完成的报告预计了伊利运河的未来布局和设计，包括一系列的水闸和漫长的堤岸，蜿蜒流过林木茂密的山岗，这一地区后来成了洛克波特市。

在霍利文章的启发下，德维特·克林顿于1810年开始支持伊利运河项目。在他长期的政治生涯中，克林顿曾担任美国参议员、市长和纽约州州长。他将自身的政治能量投入到项目上并用职业生涯冒险，将项目从梦想变为现实。1810年4月，克林顿被任命为纽约州运河委员会委员。他的角色对于这个项目如此重要，以至于有人称其为克林顿的"大渠"。

在极其不确定和争议性的政治环境中，克林顿和其他委员对伊利运河项目予以声援。而代表着南方多个州和城市的政治家们则坚决抵制这个计划，因为它将加强纽约的商业优势。作为最终的最大获利者，许多纽约政治家和沿线的居民在运河开放服务之前也抵制它。委员们不得不与许多沿河的相关方进行沟通，说服这些公开反对运河建设的人，包括手握实权的政治家们、居民及纽约的媒体。委员们通过争取民众支持，在幕后为项目营造声势，减少对于项目的反对。1815年和1816年，克林顿在纽约城为运河支持者们组织了大规模公众游行，并发起了一场民粹主义运动，收集了数以千计的签名，以支持项目审批所需的立法备忘录。

委员们为项目审批和资金支持而付出的努力，取决于对路线的详细调查和建设成本估算。1811年夏季，委员们任命本杰明·赖特作为测量师。他之前在西部公司工作时累积了些运河建设的经验，之后又被任命为运河中段的总工程师。1816年，赖特和格迪斯对到伊利湖的备选路线进行了深入的调查，考察了不同的设计构想，为来年的建设做准备。在这些调查的基础上，委员会将整个运河建设的总成本从500万美元增加到600
23 万美元。

委员们在获得授权后，开始寻求国会的资金支持，以将其作为针对国家道路和河道项目的基础设施投资计划的一部分。联邦资助之所以被优先考虑，是因为诸如西部内陆船闸航运公司的其他私营运河企业都以失败而告终。但是，联邦政府不太愿意资助如此庞大的、代表着纽约利益的公共项目；尤其是在经济不稳定时期，公共开支不断增加，并且英美战争引发了贸易限制。尽管在国会获得了政治盟友和支持，但是伊利运河仍未能获得联邦政府的资助，因为总统詹姆斯·麦迪逊于1816年动用其宪法权利否决了这项提案。在这一方案行不通后，委员会不得不寻求纽约州政府的资金支持。州立法机构要求委员们给出提议，确定如何筹集运河修建所需的600万美元。这在当时是一大笔钱，相当于纽约州所有银行和保险资本的三分之一。

委员们的报告出版于1817年2月，包括了完整的地图和概况。报告建议了北线的运河方案，它全长353英里，有77个船闸（比最终交付的线路短，且少于实际船闸数）。他们否决了倾斜设计的方案，决定采用与米德尔塞克斯运河同样的规模和外形。米德尔塞克斯运河连接梅里马克河与波士顿，长27英里（44公里）。此外，没有任何其他美国先例，可以为如此巨大复杂的尝试做准备。按照每英里1.38万美元的建设估算，他们将总成本估算从600万美元降低到略低于500万美元，从而使得这笔开支能更容易为纽约立法者所接受。

随着运河预算议案被纽约州政府通过，伊利运河的建设最终于1817年4月15日被批准。一组包括克林顿在内的五名新任 24 委员负责监管运河的建设，其资金主要来自向公众和以英国投资者为主的海外金融市场出售的州政府债券。正如项目巨大的技术成就那样，运河基金作为公共融资领域的创新被广泛用于其他运河项目的融资。在建设过程中，吸引其他资金支持的努力仍在继续。到1824年时，州政府和委员们售出了近750万美元的运河债券。

## 设计与建设

在获得政府审批和资金保障后,此时的运河支持者必须确定如何实现1817年《运河法》的立法目标。作为纽约州州长,克林顿同时兼任委员会主席,直至1824年才卸任这一职务。他是项目的主要倡导者,负责争取资金和克服项目实施过程中遭遇的政治阻碍。两位执行委员被任命管理项目的日常活动:塞缪尔·扬担任委员会秘书,迈伦·霍利则为委员会财务主管。本杰明·赖特和詹姆斯·格迪斯成为总工程师,负责运河的设计和建设。由于缺少正式的工程师专业训练和运河建设知识不足,他们不得不边干边学。

委员们1817年的报告总结了之前的调查和设计考量,由此成为伊利运河的建设蓝图。这条363英里长的运河建于1817年至1825年间,分为三段,由不同工程师和承包商实施。运河中段从莫霍克河延伸至塞尼卡河,长约94英里(151公里)。工程始于1817年7月4日破土动工仪式。由于自然阻碍较少,这一相对平缓的河段建设于1820年10月完工。到1819年时,项目建设转移到同步开始实施的极为困难的运河东段和西段,此时证明了中段建设所获取的经验和新技术是有价值的。沿着莫霍克河的运河东段长110英里(177公里),于1823年秋季完工。当160英里(257公里)长的运河西段于1825年完工时,整条运河整合为一个完整的系统,准备投入运营。

赖特和格迪斯组建了一支经验不太丰富的年轻人队伍,进行运河各段的详细调查。其中知名的有约翰·杰维斯、内森·罗伯茨和坎瓦斯·怀特,他们后来成为美国顶尖工程师和

25

运河建造者。他们必须确定各河段的设计规范，估算建设成本并确定工作的进度。初步方案、设计和路线布置，必须根据项目实施过程中遇到的困难进行调整。根据克林顿的要求，怀特于1817年自费访问英国，研究运河、隧道、水下混凝土和高架水道。在走访北威尔士托马斯·特尔福德的庞特斯沃泰水道桥，以及架设在迪河上高达100英尺高的拱形铁架之后，怀特懂得了大胆创新的工程设计是如何征服极其困难的自然障碍的。当他于1818年重回项目时，他具有的运河工程知识之丰富，几乎超过了当时在美国的任何人，对伊利运河各部分的船闸、堤坝、桥梁的设计和建设都贡献颇多。

尽管运河中段的主要工作是简单的开挖，然而运河东段和西段的处理则需要更为先进的工程方案。在东段，较低的莫霍克河谷要求在超过30英里（50公里）范围内分布27道水闸，并在科霍斯瀑布和利特尔瀑布等一系列的天然激流中逐步爬升。在西段，一座802英尺（244米）高的石拱桥要承载运河穿越罗切斯特的杰纳西河。一个更大的、需要克服的自然障碍，存在于 26 运河西段末端。委员会邀请了多位工程师提交方案，用以测量尼亚加拉断崖的岩石山脊。他们选中了内森·罗伯茨的设计，即经过五个水闸的两条线路，包括运河东段和西段各一条，用以爬升通过矗立于洛克波特新城镇的66英尺（20米）高的石灰山脊。经过四年的建造，这个地标式结构成为整个伊利运河上最令人叹为观止的工程壮举。

委员们于1817年6月会面，设计项目组织和合同模式，以聘用和管理运河建造者。他们决定将施工作业分包给多家私营承包商。三段工程的各个部分被分解成更小、更便于管理的单元，这是现在大型工程项目广泛采用的实践操作。某一承包商在州政府聘用的运河工程师监管下,受雇建造运河的某个标段,短的仅有0.25英里(约400米),长的也不超过3英里。以小标段分包工作的方式曾在米德尔塞克斯运河项目中小范围地使用过,但是伊利运河推广和完善了这种实践。各承包商能有效地负责建造运河的一小段,与运河两侧其他承包商承建的小标段保持较大的独立性。以小标段建造运河的方式意味着:在运河建造中雇用经验不足承包商的风险,可以被控制在各份合同所约定的有限尺度内。这被委员们视为一种风险,但在公共建设项目资源有限和经验不足时,这种冒险是值得的。

现在政府项目中普遍采用的竞争性招标,曾被视为一大创新,当时的传统方式是政府直接雇用运河项目劳动力。对于工作范围变更(比如对于高架河道采用石料取代木料的决策)或处理意外问题的额外工作(比如1817年的大洪水),承包商会获得相关风险补偿,并收到超支的额外支付。他们只有在完成工作并通过工程师的审查后,才能收到付款。很少有承包商拥有财务资源,用以垫付工程实施所需的工具、给养和马匹。因此,委员会提供给承包商每月不超过2000美元的预付款,并从完工结算款中扣除。保障措施也安排到位,以确保有承包商被发现存在腐败或掩盖过失行为时,能严格执行中止进度款支付的措施。若某承包商未能按时开工、按时完工,或是未达到规范要求时,将会被要求偿还预付款及利息。也有一些不太知名的承包商对无法拒绝的额外工作提出了争议性索赔,希望寻求获得额外的利润。然而,大多数时候,委员们和承包商的关系并不太正式,大多是比较融洽的。由于任何工作范围变更都可以通过公开友好的方式协商、记录并形成正式书面合同变更，承包商们完工结算的难题最终得以解决。

　　竞争性招标帮助项目保住了进度，但是建造若干挑战性较大的运河部分的成本超出了最初的估算。在1820年完工的时候，运河中段花费约100万美元，仅超出了预算10%左右。更为困难的杰纳西水道桥完工于1823年9月，进度上晚了十一个月，超出最初成本估算8.3万美元。然而，到了1821年，委员们之所以能够降低运河建设的总成本，是因为大量承包商降价来竞争项目工作。当一些承包商失败的时候，其他能成功地发展和磨炼自身技能的承包商会一个又一个完成项目合同。例如，约翰·理查森作为运河项目签署的第一个承包商，后来成为整个项目最大的承包商之一。

　　雇用私营承包商的政策也存在例外。"大深挖"的开挖工作需要沿着洛克波特市的山脊自南向西穿过3英里的硬石灰石和4英里的岩石和泥土混合物。这一工程最初就被划分为四小段，分包给了私营承包商。它被视为运河西段最为困难的部分。工程开始于1821年，但是进展缓慢。到了1823年9月，委员们决定：这一任务超出了私营承包商的能力，于是不得不将其作为一项公共工程项目来实施。数以千计的人员被州政府雇用，在运河工程师的直接控制下爆破和截断岩石来开路。

　　为了从最低价中标授予的合同中获利，承包商不得不开发出许多创新，比如新的流程、工具和材料等，以有效地完成项目并处理可能导致延迟或超支的意外问题。许多创新是由训练和经验极其匮乏的工人们所开发的，他们愿意不断重复地做试验，直至成功实现为止。一些新工具在运河中段开工后不久就被开发出来了。1817年特大洪水使得工作比预想更为艰难，于是承包商们开发出一种新的运河开挖技术进行应对。这种"犁式刮刀"由三人和一队马或牛操作，可用于切割和清理小树根。1818年开发的"倒树机"可由一人操作，用于清除大面积的树林。与传统的用斧或锯砍树的方式相比，"掘根机"被开发出来，它由七名男子和马匹操作，被用以清除剩余的树桩树根。

　　穿越困难地形和山岭障碍的运河西段建设则需要更大胆的创新。由于用手推车的方式连续清除由"大深挖"形成的大量废料不太切合实际且效率低下，被称为"起重挖掘机"的新装备被29开发了出来。这种大型木架起重机能够通过绳索和滑轮升降大吊篮，可以快速挖掘废料，其速度与废料堆垒速度同步（图2）。

　　罗纳德·E.肖写道，发明防水水泥之所以被视为伊利运河建设的划时代成就之一，是因为它开创了美国水泥业。坎瓦

PROGRESS OF EXCAVATION, LOCKPORT.

图2　用于开挖伊利运河的洛克波特"大深挖"段的新式起重挖掘机

斯·怀特常常因为发现在水里可以硬化的生石灰水泥而被称道，这种水泥是通过当地生石灰的不同配比重复试验而获得的。由于原料丰富且容易制备，这种防水生石灰被用于建造整条伊利运河，同时成本更低，减少了对欧洲进口水泥的依赖。怀特在1820年取得了原创发明的专利，并在1821年取得了其改进的专利。最初伊利运河委员们将这一发现视为他们的知识产权，鼓励承包商们供应这种水泥，且不肯付专利使用费。但是，怀特最 30
终成功地赢得了诉讼并驳回了他人购买专利的尝试。

## 启用与成果

在运河启用时，整个国家都在庆祝美利坚对于自然的掌控力。作为一种进步的标志，它实现了政治领导、民兵、贸易商、实业家及普罗大众的联合。克林顿在1822年选举中未能连任，于是在1824年离开了运河委员会。但是，当运河快要完工时，他从运河项目中收获了巨大的惊喜以及不断增长的民众声援。他再次当选为纽约州州长，并恰好主持了在曼哈顿举办的盛大启用仪式。当时，他将一小桶伊利运河的水倒入了大西洋，标志着1825年11月4日是"水流的婚礼"。

伊利运河是当时世界上最长的运河，是在相关经验极其匮乏的情况下建成的，其收益远远超出了最初的最佳预期（图3）。用今天我们评估项目绩效所用的话语来说，它绝对是成功的。它于1825年10月26日如期完成，花费了710万美元，惊人地接近其最初的估算，且在建设过程中没有经历重大的失败或延误。考虑到穿越突兀陡峭的地形、改造高耸的尼亚加拉悬崖，以及在大范围林区清除和开掘所涉任务的创新性和不确定性，最初估算的准确性是极不寻常的。设计大多都按计划精准地实施,多项创新也都成功地部署,保障了项目按照计划和预算运作。不到十年,州政府的债务就还清了。

伊利运河项目并不仅仅是建设了一条363英里长的河道,连接了西部和纽约,它的价值远非如此。它推动了美国作为工业国的崛起。东西部贸易的数量在运河开通运营后的第一年就超过了之前的两倍。从布法罗到纽约城的货物运输成本从每吨100美元降到了不足10美元。运河的经营收入很快超过了其运营成本。到1833年时,运河通行收费已经还清了运河的建设成本。运河所带来的经济增长超出了推动者的期望,还加快了西部的移民,促进了运河沿岸的城市开发,并为货物和人口流入中西部、大量谷物原料流向纽约和欧洲打开了新的市场。得益于美国第一条东西贸易纽带,纽约很快成为一个新的世界强国的"帝王之州"及商业中心。

图3　1825年完工后的伊利运河"大深挖"

伊利运河项目对于某些工程师而言，则意味着一种学习式体验；他们在此之后继续着19世纪美国运河和铁路的设计建造工作。由于美国工程专业训练的匮乏，运河建设被称为"伊利工程学院"，赖特和格迪斯则是院长。赖特在加拿大、古巴和美国建设运河和铁路确立了声誉。在其逝世后，他因为在伊利运河的工作于1969年获得了美国土木工程师学会授予的"工程之父"荣誉。格迪斯则继续他在俄亥俄州、宾夕法尼亚州和加拿大的运河设计工作。"伊利工程学院"最著名毕业生的一部分人成为美国19世纪最伟大的工程师。坎瓦斯·怀特在伊利运河完工之前就离开了，并成为宾夕法尼亚联合运河的总工程师。约翰·杰维斯和内森·罗伯茨则从运河项目步入美国铁路的设计。

## 对项目管理的启示

伊利运河提出了大型、复杂、不确定性项目管理的根本性问题。项目是从某一构想、愿景或是建议书开始的。随着构想的不断发展，项目出资方会界定目标、考察多个方案设计、估算成本收益、保障资金支持、识别项目的不确定性并思考如何予以应对，以及安排目标苛刻但仍可行的工作进度。在保障资金来源和获得审批以后，组织必须对多个承包商实施的工作进行协调和计划。在大型项目中，工作被划分为若干可管理的部分（我们现在称之为"工作分解结构"），分阶段实施并依次序完成，但也可重叠或是并行实施。项目结束后，运营活动会从新建成的设施提供服务时开始。

伊利运河显示了彼得·莫里斯所强调的东西，即：某一项目获得较大概率成功的前提是，其出资方（资产的业主和运营者）

33 将时间花在项目前期——"前端"——界定目标、解析收益和风险并形成战略方针。出资方必须和众多相关方（例如政治家、用户、承包商、当地商户和公众）进行磋商,因为项目绩效和成果将对他们的利益、期望和要求产生积极的或是负面的影响。设定目标作为一项艰难的任务,会涉及出资方、项目经理和最终用户之间的对话,以确定何为他们的项目诉求。

尽管我们不应当低估德维特·克林顿所扮演的重要角色,但是伊利运河正如大多数工程项目一样,其成功要归功于集体领导所形成的判断力和洞察力,而不是某一个人。项目拥有多位领袖式人物:提出这一构想且富有远见的思想家,成就项目、保障资金支持及面对强烈政治阻力时仍完成审批的委员们,管理和推动项目完工的执行委员们,以及能够克服项目所面临的巨大技术挑战的工程师们和承包商们。

伊利运河是大型工程壮举的范例,我们今天称之为"超大项目"(第六章)。在努力争取审批和资金支持时,出资方常常低估了成本、风险和完工时间,并过于夸大超大项目的收益。傅以斌及其同事指出:低估成本的倾向,即"乐观偏差",能够在规划阶段通过向其他同类项目学习而予以避免。尽管当时世界上没有其他的运河项目像伊利运河那样庞大、复杂,但是对于其他运河的研究和线路调查仍有助于实际成本估算和关联风险分析。最终的成本确实是被有意低估了——这就是傅以斌所说的"策略性虚报",从而使得项目成为对纽约立法机构更有吸引力的

34 投资。最终,项目得以按时交付,几乎没有超出预算。也许更重要的是,其收益远远超过霍利、克林顿及其他推动者极其乐观的期望。

即便仍有机会向自伊利运河以来的过去二百年里的大规模工程壮举学习，但是今天的超大项目大多还会出现超工期、超成本，且未能实现最初的目标。在一项对于全球60项大型工程项目的研究中，米勒和莱萨德发现：40%的项目在成本、进度和技术绩效方面表现低下，超过18%的项目投资严重超支，接近27%的项目进度严重滞后。在一项对于258项铁路、跨海大桥和道路的超大工程研究中，傅以斌及其合作者发现：成本超支40%是常态，超支80%也不少见。在一篇2014年发表的论文中，傅以斌发现：十分之九的超大项目成本超支接近50%。表2提供一个存在严重成本超支的超大项目清单，且让我们深入考察其中一个实例吧。

美国波士顿中央干线/隧道建设是当时美国规模和投资最大的土木工程项目。波士顿"大开挖"原计划于1998年建成并启用，其成本估算约为26亿美元。该项目全长7.5英里（12公里），是一个包括桥梁和隧道的新建高速公路系统，其目的是提升从波士顿地区到洛根国际机场的交通流量。项目设计和建造工作由国有的马萨诸塞州收费公路局所管理，由柏克德工程公司和柏诚集团公司组成的联合体负责协调参与项目的多家承包商。随着项目的进展，这些组织遇到了许多开始并没有预料到的技术、地理、政治和环境问题，需要予以调整，并采用创新的方法解决。中央干线/隧道原计划于2007年12月完工，但延迟了八年，其成本约合150亿美元：考虑到通货膨胀的调整，超支约为220%。

前期规划不足、策略性虚报、乐观行为，以及在不太乐观形势下的追加投入，是造成超大项目执行得如此糟糕的部分原因。

35

**表2 大型项目的灾难性成本超支历史（引自傅以斌，2014）**

| 项　目 | 成本超支百分比（%） |
|---|---|
| 埃及的苏伊士运河 | 1900 |
| 苏格兰的国会大厦 | 1600 |
| 澳大利亚的悉尼歌剧院 | 1400 |
| 加拿大的蒙特利尔夏季奥运会 | 1300 |
| 英法的协和超音速客机 | 1100 |
| 美国的特洛伊和格林菲尔德铁路 | 900 |
| 美国和瑞典的神箭智能导弹 | 650 |
| 加拿大枪支登记处 | 590 |
| 美国的普莱西德湖冬季奥运会 | 560 |
| 美国的医疗交易系统 | 560 |
| 挪威银行总部 | 440 |
| 瑞士的富尔卡基线隧道 | 300 |
| 美国的维拉札诺大桥 | 280 |
| 美国波士顿"大开挖"干线/隧道项目 | 220 |
| 美国的丹佛国际机场 | 200 |

资料来源：引自 B. Flyvbjerg, Project Management Institute Inc., *Project Management Journal: What You Should Know About Mega Projects, and Why: An Overview*, 2014. 45（2）：6—19。版权所有。本书的材料得到美国项目管理协会的复制许可。

36

但是，超大项目之所以也会失败，主要是因为相关组织在实施过程中，未能对意外情况变化和出现的新机会进行计划调整和革新。艾伯特·赫希曼引入了"遮蔽的手"原理，来解释在规划大型项目时如何将创新资源引入其中，处理没有预知到的不确定性。尤其是在前期规划时间很长的项目中，当没有预料到的问题在后续过程中产生时，则需要更多认真的努力来解决它们。正如赫希曼所指出，富有挑战性的项目之所以被实施，是因为我们误判了"该任务的性质，将其视为我们印象中较为常规简单的工作，低估了真正的创造性应有的样子"。不了解其真实成本似乎更好。一只看不见的手将困难从我们的眼前遮蔽了起来，推动了这些项目的启动。

我们现在知道：对于超大项目而言，后续的创新能力是可以解决前期规划者忽视的问题，"遮蔽的手"原理似乎过于乐观了。但是，它也帮我们认识到：正如伊利运河所展现的那样，在项目生命周期中不同时间的创新应用，是有潜力提升超大项目完成效率的。前期阶段的创新既可以通过学习其他行业来实现，也可以通过学习世界其他地方的类似项目如何设计、融资和组织来实现。因为超大项目很少能够按照最初规划的样子去实施和完成，各参与方必须根据其进展寻找解决问题的方法并进行创新。

伊利运河标志着工程与项目管理开始了彼此之间长期而紧密的联系。欧洲和北美的快速工业化国家依靠运河、铁路和电报通信的大型技术系统来发展。没有高度成熟的工程和项目管理能力的共同协作，它们是无法设计和建造的。在伊利运河项目开始时，土木工程在法国和英国已被确立为一项专业，它在美国也很快获得了类似的地位，而作为被正式认可的学科，并很快在美国的大学教育中广泛推行。项目管理则一直等到20世纪60年代才获得类似的关注和认可。

37

38

# 从曼哈顿到月球

巴拿马运河、亨利·福特的红河汽车生产厂、胡佛水坝、田纳西河谷管理局综合大楼和帝国大厦是20世纪初伟大项目中的一部分，影响了美国的后来发展。如同伊利运河一样，这些项目在项目管理成为一个正式学科之前，就达成了它们的目标。然而，大型复杂项目的管理和组织的真正突破，可以追溯到第二次世界大战时期的曼哈顿项目及战后的宇宙神项目。前者开发了原子弹，后者产生了洲际弹道导弹。在几乎没有先例可资参考的情况下，新的结构、流程和工具必然会被创造出来，用以协调、安排和集成这些项目所涉及的庞大人员、资源和组织网络。为了加快进度，多种系统"平行"开发，研究、设计、测试和生产的阶段同时或"并行"实施，而非按次序进行。科学家通过跨学科团队与工程师和管理者进行紧密的合作。为了各项目的实施，拥有"项目管理者"和"系统工程师"的专门组织得以建立。在20世纪50年代和60年代冷战时期，由于苏联的威胁加剧，日趋复杂和先进的技术系统必须进行快速的设计和生产。在应用于

39

阿波罗空间计划之前，一种起源于宇宙神及后续导弹项目的新的系统方法被开发出来，用于管理快速扩张的技术项目。

## 曼哈顿项目

曼哈顿项目的目标是生产出原子弹，它可以比传统的战争方式更快地实现第二次世界大战的成功结束。到1945年夏季任务完成时，1940年2月批准的用于启动裂变链式反应研究的经费从最初6000美元增加到22亿美元。项目以前所未有的方式聚集人力和物力资源，专门用于生产单一的产品，其规模可以与美国汽车业相比拟。在其高峰时，这个地点分散的由政府领导的项目雇用了约13万名科学家、工程师、管理者和工作人员，在总统富兰克林·D.罗斯福和几位高级别内阁官员的指挥下，以极端保密的方式实现紧急的目标。

1939年，艾伯特·爱因斯坦写信给罗斯福总统，督促他支持开发"极端强大武器"，并担心美国可能在原子能的军事用途开发上落后于德国。这一想法是指，如果可裂变物质（铀-235或者近期发现的钚-239）能够用于触发核反应，那么巨大的能量会被释放。这种巨大能量的释放是在可裂变物质发生分裂（裂变）比其聚合逃逸更快的条件下产生的。相应地，罗斯福总统建立了一个咨询委员会，监管可用于核爆的可裂变物质燃料的生产。

曼哈顿项目正式确定于1942年6月，此时能够清楚确定的是：为了生产原子弹，需要在多个地点建设一大批的实验室、生产厂家和反应堆。大部分的前期研究是由哥伦比亚大学承担的，美国陆军在其所在的纽约曼哈顿区建立了"曼哈顿工程区"。因此，该项目就成了众所周知的"曼哈顿项目"，尽管其地

40

点遍布美国多地，包括田纳西州、华盛顿州、新墨西哥州的多家工厂，以及位于哥伦比亚、芝加哥、弗吉尼亚和伯克利的多所大学研究实验室。

1942年9月，莱斯利·格罗夫斯将军获得领导该项目的委任。作为一名富有经验的工程师，他在不久之前就曾监管过当时世界上最大的建筑国防部五角大楼的建设。美国陆军工程兵部队有着丰富的大型建设项目经验，承担了材料采购、工程设计及工厂设施建设。斯通·韦伯斯特公司于1941年春天被任命为项目的总承包商，带来了它在工程、咨询、融资及大规模建设方面的知识。1942年12月28日，罗斯福总统批准了超过20亿美元的预算，用于建设全套的加工厂进行大量铀钚核爆原料供应和原子弹设计。如伊士曼柯达公司、杜邦公司、通用电气公司和西屋公司等大型工业企业也都签署了正式合同，承担相关实验室、工厂、反应堆和核原料生产系统处理设备的设计、建造和运营。

由于资金充裕，在三年内完成项目远比节省经费更重要。在起步阶段，不太可能预见到何种技术将会是适用的。军队所期望的原子弹生产线也不太现实。由于可裂变物质供应有限，所以只能够制造一枚或两枚原子弹。为了尽可能快地完成项目，格罗夫斯和他的顾问委员会决定：两枚原子弹设计（铀弹和钚弹）及可裂变物质生产的三项流程应当同时进行。正如格罗夫斯所提出的："整个工作是基于可能性的，而非或然性的。"此时，也不太确定哪种原子弹设计是有效的，或是哪种可裂变爆炸物质是两种原子弹所需的。

两项用于铀-235同位素分离的工艺流程——电磁扩散和气体扩散——最初安装于田纳西州橡树岭。由于供电、供水和铁

41

路连接的要求，占地70平方英里（180平方公里）的橡树岭建筑群是经过审慎选择的，且地点偏僻有利于保密。由于这两项工艺流程的进展未满足要求，格罗夫斯决定考虑第三项工艺流程——热扩散，而且这项工艺流程最终被确定用于铀的初步分离。

唯一可用于生产钚的工艺流程是铀反应堆和石墨块。钚的研究是由芝加哥大学冶金实验室承担的。为了安排生产进度和确定工厂产量，格罗夫斯需要知道两个原子弹各需要多少用量的钚。但是在1942年秋季，他发现芝加哥科学家并不清楚钚物质的具体用量，同时将其处境比作"一个餐饮商家被告知要为10到1000位之间任意数量的客人提供服务"。由于科学技术数据如此有限，格罗夫斯决定"开足马力"推进钚物质的生产，尽管这可能会招致失败。1942年12月，杜邦公司承包了生产钚的反应堆和分离设备的设计、建设和运营。1943年2月，格罗夫斯获得了另外一个大型的偏远场地，它位于华盛顿州帕斯科附近的汉福德工程厂区，可用于建设三个大规模的生产堆或反应堆及四个承担钚物质分离的工厂。杜邦公司面临着一项挑战，需要根据芝加哥实验室所提供的试验性的和不完整的数据确定工程设计并继续进行施工（高峰时达4.2万人）。42

在等待可裂变的铀物质和钚物质时，原子弹设计尝试也在同时进行。1942年，物理学家罗伯特·奥本海默被任命为洛斯阿拉莫斯科学实验室的主任，负责领导科学家研发团队。这个团队既负责可实现核爆的可裂变物质融合，又负责设计可从飞机上投放并在目标上方空中引爆的原子弹。奥本海默于1942年7月组织了研讨会，提出了多达五种的不同的原子弹设计。各种设计方案也在同时进行探索，直到选择了两种设计：铀弹的"枪爆式设计”和钚弹的“内爆式设计”。为保持科学家之间的开放性沟通和独立工作的习惯，洛斯阿拉莫斯实验室最初采用了按照学科领域组织的职能型结构。然而到了1944年春天时，测试表明枪式组装的钚弹设计失效，项目陷入了危机。奥本海默注意到更为复杂的内爆式设计进展过于缓慢，于是决定创建一个专注于终端产品的专门项目组织，改善沟通、促进跨职能集成并加强紧迫感。

少量的铀物质和钚物质最后分别从橡树岭和汉福德运抵到实验室，内爆式设计在1945年2月予以定型，两枚原子弹在同年夏季时组装完成。由于缺少充裕的核物质用于测试，采用枪爆式设计、名为“小男孩”的铀弹，直接被运到了太平洋地区，用于军事行动。由于钚物质充足，可以测试被温斯顿·丘吉尔称为“胖子”的钚弹，以及另一枚用于打击日本的原子弹。由于对钚弹的性能和内爆式方法的可靠性信心不足，所以进行了实地测试。世界首枚原子弹于1945年7月16日在新墨西哥州阿尔伯克基附近的测试基地进行了试爆。

该项目实现了生产原子弹的主要目标，并使战争很快走向了尾声。铀弹于1945年8月6日投到了广岛。它的威力杀死了7万人，并在1945年底造成了另外7万人的死亡。钚弹则于1945年8月9日投到了长崎。它杀死了4万人，到1946年1月，死亡人数达到了7万人。日本于1945年8月10日宣布了投降。

在格罗夫斯将军看来，项目确实是“成功的”，虽然它引发了灾难性的后果。这是由于它有着清晰界定的使命（尽管在刚开始时对于如何实现目标几乎一无所知），相关工作划分为多项具体的任务，权力被合理地授予各个责任层级。曼哈顿项目通过开发两枚原子弹设计和多项可用于可裂变物质并行生产的工艺流程，为战后导弹项目的并行开发提供了范例。它主要获益于大量试错式学习，包括备选技术和设计的并行测试、持续克服不确定性，以及利用项目实施过程中的意外进展等。

## 宇宙神项目

第二次世界大战后，美国和苏联进入了军备竞赛，开始逐步开发强大的武器系统。美国在1953年收到苏联导弹项目及其氢弹爆炸的报告后，开始了洲际弹道导弹研究。一枚洲际弹道导弹包括火箭发动机、装载燃料的巨大圆筒状弹体，以及携带核弹的弹头和制导控制系统。其设计要求以每小时1万英里的高速实现约5000英里（8000公里）左右射程的弹道（重力轨迹）飞行，并在距离目标5000英尺（1500米）范围内发射核弹头。

1953年，美国空军建立了由精英科学家和工程师组成的、昵称为"茶壶委员会"的顾问专责小组，督导洲际弹道导弹研究。小组人员包括了西蒙·拉莫和迪安·伍尔德里奇，他们创建了系统工程企业拉莫-伍尔德里奇公司。该公司在宇宙神项目中扮演了重要的角色。该委员会建议：导弹应当开发到"技术所允许的最大极限"，并于1954年2月向总统德怀特·D.艾森豪威尔提出了即刻启动洲际弹道导弹项目的正式建议。洲际弹道导弹开发有着国家最高的军事优先级，由美国空军实施，且几乎没有对资金支持的限制。

美国洲际弹道导弹计划有赖于工程与项目管理领域的进展，这二者之间的联系愈发紧密且比之前的壮举更加关注"系统问题"。洲际弹道导弹项目产生了三种导弹，即"宇宙神"、"泰坦"和"民兵"。在1957年最为紧张的设计阶段，整个计划涉及1.8万名科学家、工程师和技术专家，22个行业的7万名人员和17个总承包商及200个分包商。"宇宙神"和"泰坦"导弹的首次测试于1958年进行，并证明了5000英里射程的可行性。"民兵"导弹于1958年启动，并在1962年完成布置，并最终取代了"宇宙神"和"泰坦"导弹。

1954年7月，在洛杉矶附近英格尔伍德的一个空置教堂内，美国空军建立了西部研发部。"特别项目办公室"在准将伯纳德·施里弗（在任命后不久就被提拔为将军）的领导下，负责开发洲际弹道导弹。施里弗之所以被公认为"项目管理之父"，是因为他在西蒙·拉莫及其他顾问的帮助下，为"宇宙神"导弹开发所创造了系统方法，这一方法被广泛地用于管理许多其他的军事、航天和民用项目。

施里弗花费了大量时间管理"系统之外"的外部相关方并进行跨组织的工作，从而保障资金投入、获得高级决策者的沟通渠道，并确保他的管理措施不会被缓慢的行政审批流程所扭曲。但是，施里弗所面对的最紧迫任务是，决定何种组织才能够提供美国空军所需的技术和系统工程专长，协调宇宙神项目中庞大的行业、政府和大学参与者之间的努力。"茶壶委员会"建议：创建"类曼哈顿式"的项目组织，但是施里弗拒绝了这一建议。这是由于这一任务被认为比原子弹更为复杂，无论是美国空军还是科学家们，都不具备管理洲际弹道导弹所需的技术能力。

美国空军采用了第二次世界大战期间的习惯做法，委托某一弹体制造商作为总承包商，进行设计工作并协调参与洲际弹道导弹开发的分包商。但是，施里弗并不认为有哪家制造商具

项目管理

备所需的系统工程和物理科学的全面能力，可以构建广泛的技术基础，实现从弹体制造到电子计算设备总装。在考虑了各种方案后，施里弗及其顾问们决定，需要建立一种新的革命性组织来协助西部研发部。拉莫-伍尔德里奇公司被指定为担当"系统集成者"的角色，为美国空军提供项目管理所需的系统工程和技术建议。

导弹系统的配置造就了项目的组织（图4）。一种并行结构被创造了出来，用以促进美国空军项目办公室人员和拉莫-伍尔德里奇公司项目经理们的紧密互动。"宇宙神"导弹的各个子系统，比如推进系统和导航系统，被分配给其自有的项目办公室人员和项目经理们。正如西蒙·拉莫所描述的那样，所有参与方都"被嵌入洲际弹道导弹和系统的单一集成式项目和单一集成式设计中"。大楼建筑的平面物理布置反映了两大跨学科队伍之间的紧密协作。拉莫和施里弗以及他们的代表会经常会面，而他们的办公室都在拉莫-伍尔德里奇大楼内，距离很近。

拉莫-伍尔德里奇公司和美国空军一起工作，而且他们一起选定"关联承包商"，协调他们的作业，并监督他们的表现。已在开发"宇宙神"远射程导弹的联合伏尔提飞机公司（简称"康韦尔"），获得了弹体总装的合同。然而，康韦尔公司的导弹并没有进行试飞，之后数年里也一直没有生产。施里弗和格罗夫斯将军及奥本海默讨论了从未被验证的洲际弹道导弹技术开发的挑战，并决定采用曼哈顿项目所采用的系统式并行开发做法。格伦·L.马丁公司于1955年10月获得了采用替代性弹身技术备用系统——"泰坦"导弹——的总装合同。"宇宙神"导弹和

"泰坦"导弹各个主要子系统,包括弹身系统、导航系统、推进系统、弹头系统和计算机系统,也都由相关承包商同步开发,以激发替代性技术方案的探索,并保障某一承包商的失败不会造成项目延误(表3)。

作为宇宙神项目的系统集成者,拉莫-伍尔德里奇公司的人员包括了100多位民用工程师和科学家,他们能够看到整个系统不同部分的相互关联。在共同愿景的引导下,他们负责系统的整体优化,包括对可能降低组件之间的可靠性、射程或导弹的精确性问题进行权衡。比如,开发更轻的弹头就涉及对于降低洲际弹道导弹推进系统要求或推进力要求的权衡。拉莫-伍尔德里奇公司的系统工程师负责准备背景研究、形成初步设计,并制定各个子系统及其之间界面的性能规范要求文件。设计在最终定型之前都会被视为"初步的",它们定型后会成为工作图纸并用于导弹组件和系统的原型。当组件或子系统的规范要求在项目过程中变更时,拉莫-伍尔德里奇的工程师会对导弹

表3 "宇宙神"和"泰坦"洲际弹道导弹项目的相关承包商

| 子系统 | 宇宙神 | 泰坦 |
| --- | --- | --- |
| 弹身系统 | 康韦尔公司 | 马丁公司 |
| 导航系统 | | |
| 无线电惯性导航 | 通用电气公司 | 贝尔电话公司 |
| 全惯性导航 | A. C.斯帕克·普拉格公司 | 美国博世公司和麻省理工学院 |
| 推进系统 | 北美人公司 | 洛克达通用公司 |
| 弹头系统 | 通用电气公司 | AVCO公司 |
| 计算机系统 | 柏洛兹公司 | 雷明顿兰德公司 |

资料来源: T. P. Hughes, *Rescuing Prometheus* (New York: Pantheon Books, 1998)

项目管理

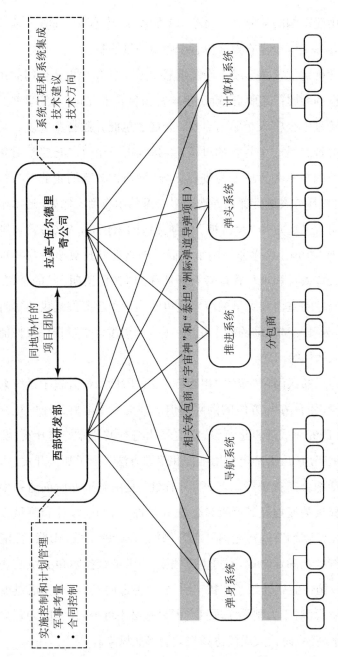

图 4 西部研发部和拉莫—伍尔德里奇公司组织

45

系统中受影响的部分进行修改，以确保与之相匹配。此后，他们会对导弹工作情况的测试和运作环境予以控制。

在确定规范并形成工作图纸后，拉莫-伍尔德里奇公司的系统工程师会履行其职责，确定宇宙神项目技术方向，和施里弗的项目管理办公室人员紧密合作，选定承包商并监督其表现。承包商的选择是一个冗长的过程，要持续近三个月。它包括对备选企业的技术和管理能力进行评分、邀请评分高的企业参与投标、对投标方案进行评估并选定最合意的承包商。例如，通用电气公司就被选定为"宇宙神"导弹弹头的承包商，AVCO公司则被选为"泰坦"导弹弹头的承包商。施里弗和拉莫坚持与其项目办公室人员和项目管理者召开被称为"黑色星期六"的会议，在一间控制室内利用早期数字化电脑显示承包商们提供的实时信息，处理测试期间的成本超支、里程碑进度计划延误以及性能要求未达标等问题。

施里弗认为，传统的"串行"方法按阶段依次开发子系统太过缓慢，不能在与苏联的洲际弹道导弹竞赛中取胜。在串行开发中，研究完成后再进行设计，之后再进行武器原型的开发、测试和生产，最后再制定使用维护和培训方法。为了加快开发，每项活动都会搭接进行。名词"并行性"是由施里弗所创造并用于解释相关流程及其必要性。在并行性计划中，设计和测试设施会在计划细节确定之前开工。例如，在导弹尺寸、形状、性能和操作规范确定之前，位于佛罗里达州卡纳维拉尔角的组装和发射设施作业就开始了。数年后，施里弗证明：当优先考虑进度时，并行性对于大型系统项目之所以是必不可少的，是因为它复制成本高昂，而且大规模协调失效会形成风险。

协调组件和子系统的并行开发和测试，是宇宙神项目所面临的最困难任务之一。因为只有在确定系统组件的初步规范要求之后，子系统和界面设计才能确定，所以进行系统的计划和进度安排是必要的。只有当对子系统个体及其之间的交互管理进行大量研究和测试之后，才能确定规范要求。拉莫–伍尔德里奇公司的系统工程师会开发可以逐步实现设计定型的程序，减少可矫正且成本高昂的设计变更的涟漪效应。配置管理流程也会予以创建，以保证任何设计变更建议都会由变更控制委员会予以评审和中止，并会与所有受影响的参与方进行沟通。

康韦尔公司在宇宙神项目中的角色表明了，承包商是如何从专门项目组织转变为新的矩阵型结构组织的。1954年，康韦尔公司建立了航天部门，执行宇宙神项目的相关工作。项目上的人员数量从1953年的300人增加到1958年的9000人，最后到1962年的3.25万人。在20世纪50年代大多数时间里，康韦尔公司以单一项目组织方式来执行宇宙神项目。但是，当它开始开发不同版本的"宇宙神"导弹，并发起比如相位比较电子追踪系统等新的子系统项目时，其职能部门型结构很快就遭遇了优先事项问题和授权冲突。为解决这一问题，航天部门创建了矩阵型组织，各个计划都配备了总监，与项目经理、职能经理一起计划任务进度和解决事项优先级问题。到1963年，航天部各个重要的新计划都采用了矩阵型组织方法来运作和管理日益增长的子项目（方框4）。

在施里弗、拉莫等人的倡导下，为宇宙神项目所创造的系统方法帮助实现了计划目标——赢得了与苏联的竞争，开发了首枚可用于发射的洲际弹道导弹。在威廉·F.拉伯恩将军的领导下，一个类似的故事也发生在美国海军北极星项目中。美国海军设立了特别项目办公室，用于开发和集成可用于潜艇上的"北极星"舰载弹道导弹。然而，与宇宙神项目不同的是，北极星项目的系统集成是由海军特别项目办公室内部完成的。北极星项目也创造了其自身的重要项目管理创新，比如项目评审技术

---

### 方框4　职能型、项目型和矩阵型组织

传统的"职能型组织"被证明并不能应对洲际弹道导弹项目中日益增长的新项目。跨越相互分离的工程部、制造部、销售部和其他职能部门的沟通路径过于冗长，难以为许多大型复杂项目提供有效的管理协调。

康韦尔公司和马丁公司等承包商最早建立了"项目型组织"，将制造部、工程部、研究部、销售部、财务部及其他职能部门的人员整合到专注于单一项目的队伍中。项目经理可以控制和集成所有必需的职能资源，完成各个项目的目标。然而，20世纪50年代末洲际弹道导弹工作的增长则需要更进一步的组织创新。

在新型二维"矩阵型组织"中，每名员工既隶属于某一职能部门，又被分配到某个或多个难以通过单一部门完成的项目上。此时，项目人员需要向项目经理和职能经理同时进行汇报。当他们的任务完成时，他们会回到原职能部门。矩阵型结构设计加速了信息流，更高效地在多个项目中分配资源，并避免了职能"土壤"中的人员狭隘地看待问题。

图5提供了三种项目组织结构的简要说明。

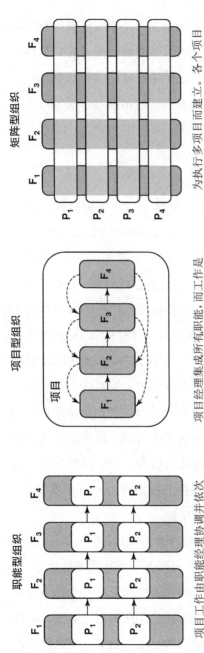

**职能型组织**

项目工作由职能经理协调并按次序从一个职能部门到另一个职能部门完成

**项目型组织**

项目

项目经理集成所有职能，而工作是依次地和并行地在专门，彼此独立的结构中完成（例如：20世纪50年代的康韦尔公司和马丁公司）

**矩阵型组织**

为执行多项目而建立。各个项目由一名职能经理和一个项目经理协调（例如：20世纪60年代的康韦尔公司航天部门）

关键：

$F_1 - F_4$　职能部门（例如：研发部、工程部、制造部和运营部）或者学科（比如：科学和工程专长）

$P_1 - P_4$　设立在组织内的项目

——→　不同阶段的项目作业依次开发

----→　并行式开发中从后续阶段到前置阶段的反馈

图 5　职能型、项目型和矩阵型组织

（PERT）网络规划工具。该工具从1957年起，就可以运行于电脑上，显示和提供一系列规划活动的进度估计及其完工日期估计。然而，项目评审技术对于北极星项目成功的贡献甚微。它主要用于保证技术开发进展不会被外部政治家和官员的过度干预所阻碍。

## 阿波罗登月

系统方法的影响很大程度上得益于1958年美国国家航空航天局（简称"NASA"）的建立，以及1969年7月20日的第一次阿波罗登月。当1961年尤里·加加林被送入太空时，苏联宣布它将赢得与美国的"太空竞赛"。美国总统约翰·F.肯尼迪在当年5月份的回复中提到，"这个国家应当在未来十年内，致力于实现一人登陆月球并使其安全返回地球的目标"。从对人类在失重状态下如何正常行动的近乎一无所知开始，美国国家航空航天局设计和建立了一个融入了多项新技术的系统，包括火箭、太空飞船、测试设施、生命支持系统及计算机控制跟踪和通信网络等。该系统将会使人类在十年内登上月球。最终的月球登陆成本超过了200亿美元，与最初的130亿美元预算和70亿美元应急备用金比较接近。通过电视转播的视觉冲击，"阿波罗"号将项目管理系统方法的优势推向全世界。

作为美国国家航空航天局整个太空计划的负责人，詹姆斯·E.韦布认为，第一次阿波罗登月任务与曼哈顿项目相比，面临着更加巨大的管理挑战。美国国家航空航天局必须协调分布于80个国家的2万家承包商和200所大学的30万名员工。阿波罗项目由美国国家航空航天局所领导，并与七家大型承包商的太空系统部门进行合作，包括通用电气公司、洛克希德公司和波音公司。在承包商们实施子系统开发工作的同时，美国国家航空航天局自身也需要具备系统集成能力，才能比任一承包商都54更好地掌握这一壮举的整体状况。

经过宇宙神项目、北极星项目和其他导弹项目的尝试，有关项目管理的想法和实践都被移植到阿波罗项目中，这是由于参与这些项目的人员加入了美国国家航空航天局。1963年9月，曾任职于汤普森-拉莫-伍尔德里奇公司（TRW）的乔治·米勒，成为美国国家航空航天局空间航行管理办公室主任。米勒在主要设计方案确定之后加入了项目。但是，他很快发现，在1970年之前实现月球登陆的概率不到十分之一。米勒创建了一个矩阵型结构来提升计划的沟通和监管：工作按照计划控制、系统工程、飞行运作、测试、可靠性及质量等职能进行划分，并由承担载人任务的三个中心实施（亨茨维尔、休斯敦及卡纳维拉尔角）。他放弃了采用大量飞行测试和差异化装备配置的冗长筛选流程，转而决定开发所有的组件，并准备用"阿波罗"号飞行全设置模式进行"全面测试"。

认识到美国国家航空航天局在计划和管理大型项目方面能力不足，在施里弗的建议下，米勒招募到了准将塞缪尔·C.菲利普斯，将其职务从时任的"民兵"导弹项目总监调整为阿波罗项目总监。菲利普斯和米勒需要保持必要的灵活性，跟踪未预见到的问题，同时引入专业的系统化管理（比如配置管理、变更控制委员会、计划评审技术和系统工程），从而加快整个项目的进度和控制成本，并在1969年最终期限内实现人类的月球登陆。项目开发规划于1965年1月被引入美国国家航空航天局，用以识别如何管理和组织整个项目的进度和阶段，由此成为系统化项目管理的重要工具之一。

在1969年出版的《太空时代的管理》一书中，韦布写道：美国国家航空航天局的月球登陆之所以成功，是因为所创建的管理项目的组织兼具灵活性和适应性，具有"能够适应难以预见的、间或动荡的环境并在其中前进的能力"。美国国家航空航天局认识到，关于"阿波罗"号的技术和运作环境的多项预测将会被证明是错误的，它必须"在项目开始时对所有已知的要素进行最为审慎的分析，同时对实际条件与最初所预见的不一致情况做好调整的准备"。韦布建议，由美国国家航空航天局实施的70%或80%的任务是具有相当的确定性，能够掌握并予以提前准备，而剩下的20% ～ 30%则是一个不确定性地带，需要在项目过程中通过适应和创新予以解决。韦布总结道：需要在大型复杂项目中已知和可预测部分的"秩序性和稳定性"与其变化和不确定部分的"激发创新的程序"之间实现平衡。

由于涉及多种技术不确定性，所以美国国家航空航天局并不能完全依靠国防部所青睐的固定总价合同。固定总价合同对所需实施的任务规定了明确的货币限额。他们仅将注意力集中在项目起始和结束的两个时点上，前一时点是确定规范要求说明并达成合同协议的时候，后一时点是确定接受或否决技术的时候。但是，他们忽略了项目过程中对于未预见事件的适应性需求。美国国家航空航天局承认，固定总价合同只有在确定和可预测的条件下才是有效的，但是它更倾向于采用激励性合同进行新技术开发，激励那些完善初步规范要求、解决预测外问题以及抓住机会的尝试性努力。例如,波音公司采用了激励性合同生产五艘航天器,以承担月球拍摄的五项任务,它包括对于 56 成本、进度和航天器入轨后性能的奖励。这种柔性合同鼓励了合作方在条件变化和搜集到新信息时调整任务和进度(第四章)。

## 项目管理舍弃根本

到了20世纪50年代末,新的系统想法和实践通过非正式的方式开始传播。随着参与了洲际弹道导弹项目和北极星项目的人员持续走上了其他项目的领导岗位,这一方法被保留了下来。当工程师、管理者和学者正式地定义和整理这一新方法时,一个名为"项目管理"的新学科已经奠基了。相关论文开始出现于管理学期刊,同时第一本项目管理教材也出版于20世纪60年代,它们都是以系统方法为基础的。当罗伯特·麦克纳马拉于1960年开始担任国防部长时,他重组了军事采购并建立了以系统化为基础的项目和计划管理。

在20世纪70年代,系统化项目管理很快传播到了欧洲的航天项目以及全世界范围内的其他行业和政府部门中。项目管理的影响促成了美国和欧洲的专业协会的成立,即1967年成立的国际项目管理协会(IPMA)、1969年成立的美国项目管理协会(PMI),以及1972年成立的英国项目管理协会(APM)。项目管理支持者(方框5)强调了它的实践性,以及人员接受项目管理训练的必要性,由此可以针对各种项目、集群项目和项目组合实施相应的标准化指引、流程和知识体系,譬如美国项目管理协会的《项目管理知识体系指南》(PMBoK)。 57

**方框5　项目管理标准化**

美国项目管理协会的《项目管理知识体系指南》2013版界定了项目生命周期的阶段，提出了客户和相关方需求的流程，以保障项目可以在工期和预算内完工，并达到相关要求。

一个项目开始于基于范围说明的计划，它包括确定工作包的工作分解结构（WBS）、组织分解结构（OBS）、网络进度图、预算及相关资源。"基准计划"明确了项目如何实施的部分细节，提供了可用于评估项目团队绩效的明确目标。风险管理计划则假定了事前所识别的项目不确定性，并形成与之相匹配的应急计划。

项目一旦开始实施，其绩效将会根据基准计划进行测度。计划的变更应当控制在最小范围内，或是被视作意外，需要予以纠偏。项目的实施只有与基准计划保持一致时，才会获得成功，即使该计划的主要假设在环境改变时可能会失效。

尽管有了宇宙神项目和阿波罗项目的成就，但是系统化项目管理在20世纪70年代及其之后也遇到了困境，许多政府资助的军事和航天项目陷入了严重的工期延期、成本超支及实施成果糟糕等困境。虽然有些项目通常会被批准并获得资助，但是它们既没有充分考虑资金许可条件下的技术预案，也没有进行其各子项目的成本、进度和绩效的切实评估并确定合理的目标。譬如航天飞机和国际空间站这一类被发起的项目就具有太多的未知,难以准确地预测其成本、完工时间、绩效、人员生命风险、市场需求及实用性。

美国国家航空航天局航天飞机项目最初于1969年被提出,当时整个国家仍处于成功登月的激动之中,并满心期待能在80年代实现人类的火星登陆。在这一成本高昂的初步建议书并没有获得支持之后,美国国家航空航天局试图利用可重复使用的系统和成品构件,开发一种性价比更高、太空适应性更强的航天飞机,以获得政府的批准。这种航天飞机是一种可回收的系统,被设计用于发射可返回地球且能重复飞行的载人飞行器。政府决定将其所有资源集中于这种航天飞机的研发上,以淘汰一次性发射装置等替代性技术。正如西蒙·拉莫所说的那样,乐观偏差(第二章)造就了那些争取航天飞机项目审批及资金支持的努力:

> 美国国家航空航天局将对成本、进度和绩效的所有估计都建立在最为乐观的可能性之上。由于这种极度乐观,航天飞机项目与其困境几乎是同时开始的。随着技术问题被严重低估和可用于完成必要步骤的时间过短,航天飞机的进展很快就出现了进度延误。

如果参考航天飞机最初的真实预算和预测,那么这个项目不大可能会获得资助。在尽可能压缩成本的压力下,美国国家航空航天局不得不放弃了建立一个小型测试飞行器的最初计划,这一装置用以保障所有技术在全面装备飞行器之前得到检验。航天飞机陷入了成本严重超支之中,同时其飞行也在1986

年"挑战者"号事故之后被取消了，这一事故导致了七名航天员的身亡。该事故的起因通过各种尝试被调查清楚后，航天飞机项目于1988年9月再次重启。2003年2月"哥伦比亚"号又造成了七名机组成员身亡。在这一事故之后，美国国家航空航天局的航天飞机舰队一直被搁置到2005年7月，并于2011年完成了最终任务。

到了20世纪60年代末，产生了一种普遍的看法，即为宇宙神项目和阿波罗项目所开发的系统方法，可以用于重建美国快速衰败和拥挤的城市群。但是，这一想法并未能实现，它被证明不能应对大型城市区域中众多的社会、政治和环境问题。许多人认为，美国的城市更新建设项目比将人类送抵月球更为复杂和难以应对。伦纳德·R.塞尔斯和玛格丽特·K.钱德勒在对阿波罗项目激动人心的研究中指出：与美国城市项目相比，"美国国家航空航天局是一个简单的生命体。美国国家航空航天局是闭环的——它设定自己的进度，设计自身的硬件，采用自己的齿轮。它既是资助方，也是使用方。太空是不属于任何人的领域"。与这种"封闭的系统"相比，在人口稠密城市区域的项目则是"开放的系统"。比如，在波士顿中央干线/隧道（第二章）的设计过程中，许多不同的声音和城市中的相关方——联邦政府、州政府、当地政府以及关注贫困、伦理和环境的当地利益团体——都拥有影响项目的话语权，造成了项目延迟数年及严重超支。

管理大型航天项目所创造的系统方法在20世纪60年代末之所以日趋受到质疑，是因为它不仅在解决美国城市问题时遭遇失败，而且与越南战争中失败的军事行动存在关联，还导致了冷战期间军备竞赛升级。民权运动者、反越战运动者、环境保护主义者和反核主义者，都将危及自由价值、伤害当地社区、破坏自然环境的责任，归咎于政府不辨是非地滥用军事和大规模技术。许多参与美国公共资助项目的管理者、工程师和科学家，开始不再相信高度理性的、计划的、协作的系统分析和管理，称它是由麦克纳马拉为了军事毁灭目的而开发的。托马斯·休斯表明：20世纪60年代是项目管理历史上转折的十年，当时的美国 60 高级研究项目局网络项目——建立面向互联网的计算机通信系统——开始表现出这一时代的反主流文化价值观。美国高级研究项目局的创建者更偏好扁平化管理结构，其成员都是协作性的、精英化的，并以协商一致的方式进行决策（参见第四章灵活机构）。他们拒绝等级性、科层制及专家控制的方式，这些都曾在20世纪60年代之前的宇宙神项目和北极星项目中使用过。

项目管理的系统模型假定：项目所面对的不确定性可以在其开始时识别，当其在项目实施过程中出现时，可通过落实与之相应的应急计划来予以应对。这种方法适用于常规性简单项目，忽略了真正创新和复杂项目中的适应性需求。例如在国防、航天和城市建设项目中，一系列有着明确顺序计划的行动并不总是可能的，因为它们延期的进度、太多的技术未知，以及持续变化的条件、限制和压力。由于大多数大型复杂项目同时包含着可预测的部分和不确定的部分，在项目实施中，刚性的和柔性的项目计划以及秩序惯例和创新之间需要平衡。西尔万·朗夫勒和克里斯托夫·洛赫近来呼吁：项目管理要回归到其已舍弃的、蕴藏于适应性方法的本源，而不是它现在变成的这个样子——秩序化、理性的系统方法；而适应性方法曾在曼哈顿项目、宇宙神项目以及北极星项目中尝试过。

在第四章，我们将考察在20世纪60年代和70年代，适应性项目结构的传播是如何鼓励管理学者开发新的组织思维方法的。

项目管理

# 奥雅纳公司的灵活机构与理论视角中的项目

　　奥韦·奥雅纳是20世纪的杰出结构工程师之一。他与全球最伟大的建筑师贝特霍尔德·莱伯金、伦佐·皮亚诺及理查德·罗杰斯等在不同的项目中紧密合作。在勒·柯布西耶的工程之颂扬和瓦尔特·格罗皮乌斯所主张的艺术与技术融合理念的影响下，奥雅纳所确立的"全面设计"实践的愿景，要求建筑师和工程师在项目伊始就进行紧密的合作。他于1946年创建的企业——奥韦·奥雅纳及合伙人公司，就体现了这一设计哲学。

　　作为该企业的突破性项目，悉尼歌剧院创造了一种项目团队中建筑师和工程师合作的新模式，用以创新和解决挑战性问题。悉尼歌剧院拥有着令人叹为观止的屋面设计，是一个空前复杂的工程项目。最初的设计是基于几张令人印象深刻的草图，由西班牙建筑师约恩·乌松在没有工程顾问的情况下所创造出来的（图6）。奥雅纳公司和乌松建立了紧密的合作伙伴关系，以寻找将想法转变为现实的方式。奥雅纳公司的工程师们率先尝试采用计算机来模拟屋面结构和设计大型预制混凝土装 62

图6　悉尼歌剧院的前期草图之一, 1956—1957

配式壳体建筑。

尽管奥韦·奥雅纳于1988年就已辞世，但显而易见，他协作解决问题的方法仍留存于奥雅纳公司当前的项目中。今天，奥雅纳公司是一家总部设在伦敦、雇员超过1.3万人的全球性专业服务组织，并在37个国家设立了90个办公室。在任一时刻，都有工程、建筑、设计、规划、项目管理、经济和其他领域的专家在一万多个项目上工作。每个项目都需要满足客户对于某一系统、建筑、基础设施或是整个城市的要求。客户会改变想法，建筑的要求会变更，规范会更新，且政治环境也时常变化。所有这些持续变化的形势、不确定性和交织的活动，都必须通过奥雅纳公司内外的多学科专家队伍来予以解决。

从悉尼歌剧院到巴黎蓬皮杜艺术中心，再到英法海底隧道铁路，奥雅纳公司参与了多项挑战性项目，为其自身开辟了新的市场。近来，奥雅纳公司备受瞩目的项目之一是2008年完成的被称为"东滩"的中国生态城的先锋城市设计，它位于上海的崇明岛上。根据2050年达到50万居民的预计，东滩项目的目标是成为全世界首个专门建设的可持续生态城，通过高效供水、可再

图 7　奥雅纳公司的东滩东城和东湖的生态城效果图

64

生能源和回收系统及零碳排放或零微粒排放的城市交通车辆，尽可能地接近"零碳"目标（图7）。奥雅纳公司与上海实业有限公司签署了东滩项目合同，随后又在伦敦签署了生态城项目的合作协议，这一协议的签署是在中国国家主席胡锦涛和英国首相托尼·布莱尔的共同见证下进行的。

通过将拥有建筑、城市设计、项目管理、环境咨询和经济不同专长的人员聚集到一起，一支由非常积极和有经验的人员组成的小型团队建立了起来，领导东滩项目和构思总体方案设计，其人员包括罗杰·伍德、亚历杭德罗·古铁雷斯及董山峰。奥雅纳公司在当地的东滩项目合作团队基地就设在业主方上海总部办公室。项目发展成为一个大型多学科并具有多元文化的组织，高峰时曾达到150人。它包括了出生于20个不同国家的人员及分布于全球的12个办公室，并最终成为一个独立的新业务部门"集成化城市规划"的一部分，由彼得·黑德领导。新部门包括了30个专家团队，每个团队包括了3~4名从奥雅纳公司各部门借调的人员，用以应对新生态城的社会、经济、环境和物理的交叉单元。

通过奥雅纳公司的矩阵型方法，专家团队（如水、废弃物、物流交通和文化策划的新领域）会与多学科队伍的其他人进行合作，促进设计问题的快速解决。虽然这种方法可以激励创新，但随着东滩团队在承受巨大压力下需要快速地交付设计，以满足高要求客户持续变化的优先事项和需求，它也引发了自身创造性的紧张点。在没有先例可供参考的情况下，用于管理快节奏项目的一种突破性的可持续城市设计和流程几乎是从零开始建立起来的。正如一位奥雅纳公司的高级设计师在一次访谈中所表述的那样,"我们在一年里做了正常要四年才能完成的工作"。奥雅纳公司必须满足未来居民、商业、政府机构及其他相关方并不确定的偏好,并实现具有挑战性的目标——可持续的绩效。<sup>65</sup>一个新的数字化建模工具——集成化资源模型——被创造出来,用以识别集成化城市系统中多个技术和组织部分之间的紧密依存性。

尽管东滩项目被《经济学人》称为"梦想之城",最终也未实现零碳开发的建设,但是该项目为奥雅纳公司提供了生态城设计的基本经验,获得了在这一快速增长市场中备受信赖的声誉。东滩项目团队成员被分配到其他的竞标中,赢得和实施了多个生态城设计项目。在这一极其重要但未曾实现的项目中获得的知识被整理成册,同时还开发了新的数字化计划和项目管理流程,用于中国和全球的后续项目中。

当奥雅纳公司于20世纪60年代参与悉尼歌剧院设计时,其他企业也发现了项目工作组织的适应性方法,美国项目管理协会、英国项目管理协会及其他专业团体制定并推广了相关指南、流程和知识体系,并发展成为项目管理领域的标准(第三章)。工业社会的观点认为,单一最优的组织方式是存在的。也许是受到这一观点的激励,他们开发了一种优化明确的单一模式,按照可预测和精密受控的阶段计划实施项目。这种方法假定:项目管理与其环境中的变化是相独立的。它在技术和市场被清晰合理地理解时是有效的,计划可以用于应对项目实施过程中已知和可预测的条件。然而,正如奥雅纳公司案例所展示的那样,标准化方法对于不确定、持续变化和复杂项目而言,并不完全适用。

在本章余下的部分，我们将会讨论组织学者们所引入的理论见解和观点，帮助我们思考项目在动态变化环境中的灵活适应性结构。

## 组织理论与灵活机构

尽管项目早在20世纪50年代就已广泛应用于国防工业中，但是直到20世纪60年代中期，研究者才首次注意到这一新物种——临时适应性组织。几乎是与此同时，一群有影响力的学者开始挑战当时的观点，即存在着适用于所有环境的一种最优化的组织方式。在后来被称为"权变理论"的雏形中，他们声称：包括项目导向型组织在内的成功的组织设计，反映了技术和市场环境变化中的复杂性、不确定性和变化速度。

传统工业组织有着"机械型"结构，以执行标准化的运营（例如大批量生产的消费品和服务），并解决相对稳定环境中的常规问题。它在很大程度上是将可预测任务按照职能化作业进行分解。个体处于某一劳动部门中清晰界定的岗位，并融入一个垂直的层级结构，沟通是从在顶层的领导到最底层的工作人员进行的。与这种刚性与持久性不同，汤姆·伯恩斯和G.M.斯托克提出：在不稳定和持续变化的环境中，适应性组织有着"有机的"结构。这种柔性组织模式取决于同事之间的水平沟通或"侧向"沟通，这是同侪们专注于解决创新性复杂问题时发生的，而这类问题需要对其子任务进行持续的调整和界定。

沃伦·本尼斯创造了名词"有机适应性"，用以描述临时性问题解决组织中专门项目团队数量的增长，他们往往集合了金融、工程和营销等多个职能部门专家。在他看来，这可以使组织能更好地胜任，以适应日趋动荡的环境。机械式组织是设计用以满足生存和发展的长期需要，而项目则是一种临时组织：它将 在目标完成时或特定的结束状态下予以终止。各种拥有熟练技能但彼此之间对各自技能不太熟悉的人员被召集到一起，承担相互独立的任务并在给定的时间内实现某一具体目标。琼·伍德沃德表明：近似有机型结构的组织既包括了那些经常改变他们产品的组织，又包括了航天、国防、造船、音乐录制和电影制作等形形色色行业中的"单件式生产者"，他们以项目的方式为客户提供独特的、一次性或高度定制化产品。

　　詹姆斯·汤普森引入了我们常用的一些概念，来理解组织如何协调项目中相互依存的任务。在"集合式依存性"中，工作被分解成简单的任务，分别由某一职能部门予以实施，它们很少或几乎不需要其他的输入。标准化的规则和程序可以保障任务由某一职能部门独立实施，并与其他部门的贡献相区别，且不会影响其他部门的活动。

　　在"序列式依存性"中，项目任务之间存在着直接的串行关系，即某一项目阶段产生的输出（信息、材料和组件）会成为下一个阶段绩效所需的输入。序列实施的任务会在严格界定的阶段中予以计划和确定进度，从而实现预定的项目目标。正如我们在第三章中所读到的那样，这种情况发生在串行开发中，此时的某一项目职能队伍（例如工程部）会先完成其任务，再将已完成的工作移交给后续的队伍（例如制造部）。在传统项目管理的"瀑布模型"中，一个项目的序列阶段会通过严格的结束和开始标准予以界定，以使彼此之间相互区别。后续的阶段只有在之前的阶段达到某些条件之后，才可以开始。

在"交互式依存性"中，每项任务都与其他任务相交叉，而多项任务之间必须相互调整，以匹配其他任务的变化。这种情况出现在由专门项目组织进行的武器系统并行开发中（第三章）。设计规范是导弹生产（技术规范说明）的输入，而导弹系统的生产则是设计（组装、测试和发射设施的性能要求）的输入。在获得项目目标、技术和市场的新信息以后，处理交互式依存性需要通过任务间的"相互调适"进行往复式沟通和协调。

多个项目的优先级可以根据任务依存性及其相应的协调程度予以确定。许多项目会形成集合式依存性，某些则形成集合式依存性和序列式依存性，而最为复杂和不确定的则会形成集合式、序列式和交互式三种依存性。在稳定和可预测的环境中，项目可以提前定义、计划并安排进度（采用美国项目管理协会确认的流程），以处理集合式依存性和序列式依存性。与美国国家航空航天局的"不确定性地带"（第三章）类似，在不太稳定和快速变化的条件下，相互调适的协调是必须的，它可以满足不可以预见的互动，响应源于经验的反馈，并对环境和目标的变化进行实时调适。

保罗·劳伦斯和杰伊·洛尔施帮助我们认识到，一个项目组织中的各方成员只有融合或"集成"，才能就如何响应环境需求的问题达成一致。当项目复杂且相互依存时，各种联络岗位或"链销"是必需的，可用于横向协调工作，并实现项目团队和职能单元各自的内部协作及二者之间的协作。作为集成者，项目经理要发挥联络能力、劝导能力和协调能力展开行动，解决矛盾冲突。这些矛盾冲突是在不同知识及不同利益、观点和实践背景的人员聚集在一起时，他们在跨职能、多方参与的项目中发

挥作用时产生的。杰伊·加尔布雷斯描述了美国的航天公司是
如何创造了矩阵型结构的（第三章）。作为一种二维汇报关系
的集成机制，它可以实现职能线职权和项目线职权的权力平衡。
正如宇宙神项目中伯纳德·施里弗所成功扮演的角色那样，集
成者可以清楚了解不同的或相互竞争的内部团队的诉求，并对
外部组织和人员产生影响，这是由于他们具有支持或限制项目
的职权和权力。

正如我们在宇宙神项目中所发现的那样，有机型结构的项
目团队成员常常身处于同一物理地点，即在项目期间于同一间
办公室共事，以便集成多位参与方并满足交互式依存性的要求。
在关于研发项目的著作中，托马斯·J.艾伦表明：即便是最低
程度的分散，比如将人员布置在同一建筑的不同楼层，都可能降
低项目团队所需的紧密互动和协作。同事之间的亲密性和日常
的实际存在，有助于增加更多频次的沟通、建立信任、塑造紧密
的人际关系和非正式互动，并能加强团队成员之间的社会联系。
项目团队中常常会存在着若干关键人物，为其他人提供信息。
这些人被艾伦称为"技术守门人"，他们擅长转译和表达多种的
职能知识语言，并通过跨越组织边界的方式进行技术信息沟通。

20世纪70年代，权变理论的观点和概念被用于识别项目组
织的主要特征。在1979年出版的《组织的结构化》一书中，亨
利·明茨伯格借用阿尔文·托夫勒（第一章）的"项目"一词，
将"项目"确认为一种新的组织形式，它将不同专长的人员融合
在过渡性项目团队中，以解决复杂的非结构化问题，并在完成任
务后解散团队。这种组织基于有机型结构，主要面向单件式生
产，可以实现问题导向的解决方案创新，并具有面对面相互适应

式协调和水平式集成机制。当信息在跨职能团队人员之间进行水平的自由流动时，学科之间的界限会逐步变得模糊。团队成员的选择倾向于以个人专长和协作能力为依据，而不是他们在管理层级中的位置或级别。团队所汇聚的知识和经验是形成创新和持续开发新知识的基础。

灵活机构可能是临时性的，也可能是常设性的。在临时性灵活机构中，一个独立组织会组建起来，执行某一项目，并在完成时解散，比如，一部电影制作、一次候选人的竞选活动、建设和承办奥运会的机构组织，以及协调诸如波士顿中央干线/隧道等重大项目的联合机构。

在常设性灵活机构中，多个项目会嵌入两种类型的母体组织中。一类是"运营性灵活机构"，主要为外部客户实施项目，比如建筑实践、工程咨询、建造承包商、电影制作方或者广告公司。运营性灵活机构几乎没有真正的稳定。正如奥雅纳公司的东滩项目一样，多种策略会在满足客户需求过程中涌现并演化。灵活机构会随着项目变化和新项目的出现，持续地进行调整适应。它会从一个项目延续到下一个项目，直到没有新项目时才会消失。为了保证稳定且平稳的项目流入，运营性灵活机构的经理们会花费大量时间与潜在的客户发展关系并与其沟通合同事宜。

另一种常设性实体是"行政性灵活机构"，它仅为其自身实施项目，而非外部的客户。由于运营任务与所属组织的其他部分相对分离，因此，行政核心通过项目团队的形式予以组织，可以自由地专注于问题解决和创新。例如，阿波罗项目中许多研发活动和整体系统集成活动，都是在美国国家航空航天局内部

71

执行的,但是其部件和子系统的开发以及服务和专业技能的提供,则被外包给了一个外部的供应商网络。

## 项目组织的新思考

明茨伯格的"灵活机构"的适应性和创新能力取决于项目团队功能的顺畅发挥,并由于团队组成、规模和范围而有所差异。部分项目会由组织内小型项目团队中彼此相熟的人员实施。像奥雅纳公司的东滩项目显示的那样,其他的项目则会包括许多来自世界各地的具有不同背景和观念的人员。许多大型项目被分解成一些小的子项目,每个子项目都由一支独立的、多方参与的团队实施。例如,伦敦希思罗机场五号新航站楼建设就是作为一个集群项目予以组织的,它被分解成16个主要项目和147个子项目。其中,小项目的投资不低于100万英镑,希思罗快线地铁站等大项目则达到3亿英镑。每个项目都由一个多方参与的集成化集群项目团队予以实施,其成员主要来自业主方和承包商组织(第六章)。

近期的研究表明:经典研究过于强调项目团队的有机适应性特征。项目常常会融合有机性和机械性单元,以及共同地点和分散地点作业的单元。部分团队具有可应对动态变化环境的灵活性,而其他的则具有相对稳定的结构。

在一项针对美国、欧洲及亚洲计算机公司的产品开发项目研究中,凯瑟琳·艾森哈特和贝南·塔布里兹提出了两个可以用于加快开发节奏且差异明显的模型。"紧缩"策略被设计用于 72 已熟知且清晰定义的流程中,减少和压缩完成序列性步骤所需的时间。适应性的"体验"策略则有赖于即兴的、灵活的试错学习,从而处理不确定且快速变化的流程。该研究发现:成功的新产品开发需要微妙地融合这些机械性和有机性流程。多职能团队在强有力的项目领导者领导下,可通过计划好的里程碑来缩短时间并设定节奏,但是当条件变得难以预测时,他们也依赖于通过设计迭代和测试所进行的即兴的和实时的学习。

基于对权变理论的见解,埃米·埃德蒙森对稳定的项目团队和灵活的项目团队进行了区分。稳定的项目团队将相关人员召集起来,在合理组合其技能和经验的基础上,给予时间建立信任,可为现有客户及完全清楚的情况完成简单、可预测的任务。成员身份被清晰地界定:每个人或小组都知道将要执行的具体任务,没有人必须超越学科的边界去应对意外事件或是承担全新的工作类型。

相对地,灵活的项目团队则是为了满足复杂、不确定且快速变化的情况要求,比如产品设计、研究、救援行动及战略开发。新队伍由富有经验的老手和新手成员组成,不断地应对特殊的一次性问题。来自各个学科的人员和其他外部专家会服务于在同一地点共事、持续时间长短不一的多个团队,他们会持续变换身份,跟踪实现动态的目标。因为工作是临时性的,且团队组成会跨越职能、地理位置和组织边界,项目团队成员几乎没有时间去建立信任和习惯,以适应彼此的工作风格和优缺点。按照依存性层次对任务进行划分是必须的,这也同样适用于相互适应式协调,以保证计划灵活性。项目团队边学边干,调整作业节奏,满足紧张的期限要求,并对产生的问题和创新机会做出响应。

在埃德蒙森称之为"团队化"的流程中,灵活的团队依赖领导者来强化目标，进行心理安全建设，包容尝试过程中的不可避免之失败。此外，当有着不同价值观和竞争优先性的人员组成变动和多样化团队开始共事以后，所产生的冲突和沟通不畅也有赖于领导者的接纳。奥雅纳公司为北京2008年奥运会设计和建造的水立方水上运动中心项目，表明了团队化是如何实现的。这一复杂的任务无法通过传统的项目管理计划和努力将多项任务划分为序列性阶段来完成。其团队召集了来自四个国家二十个领域的人员以及外部专家，并随着工作进展以分组协作的方式进行工作。这些分组会随着所识别的多个问题而建立，并在问题解决后解散。

越来越多的公司使用数字通信技术（比如邮件、音频、手机和网络服务）和面对面的例会，组织远程的全球性项目，协调任务并加强团队成员的协作（第五章）。诸如IBM、通用电气和SAP等公司都已创建了能力中心，从不同的地方招募具有相关专长的人员，并通过分布式项目团队执行具体任务。分布式项目团队成员在地理位置上分布在多个城市、国家和大陆，来自不同的专业，讲不同的语言，生活于不同的国家，具有不同价值观、利益和信念。

在空间分布式的团队中合作，会比在同一工作地点中更为困难。物理空间距离可能会成为和睦亲密的障碍，导致信任减少，无力寻找共通点，并造成协调和协作障碍。一个分布型项目或"虚拟"团队的成员，可能必须适应多种工作模式，并根据多个时区的差异重新组织进度。如果团队成员不能常常一起讨论问题或者说明任务必须如何进行调整才能予以解决，某些易于在面对面会议中解决的情况就会变得失控，并会导致挫

74

折、分歧和矛盾。

在诸如软件开发等某些全球性行业中，空间分布式的团队则比在同一工作地点的团队表现更佳，这点众所周知。在同一办公楼中的团队常常会低估合作的障碍，比如必须爬段楼梯才能见到同事所产生的不便。相对地，分散在世界各地的软件开发团队常常对于合作中存在的困难有更多的认识，并会付出额外的努力去改善沟通和互动。团队面对面的例会有利于提升团队凝聚性，形成对当前任务的共同理解，并支持非正式沟通。比如"和团队成员出外喝啤酒"的非正式沟通，有助于在虚拟合作开始前建立共通点和"沟通规则"。

## 项目的权变维度

基于权变论的观点，许多学者现在认识到项目在不确定性、复杂性和紧迫性上存在着很大的程度差异，并建议各个维度的管理要与组织、流程和管理方法的特定形式相对应。阿瑟·斯廷科姆和卡罗尔·海默对北海石油和天然气项目的深度研究，是最早将权变理论应用于大型项目的尝试之一。他们认识到，一次性项目所遇到的高度不确定的和出乎预料的不利环境必须通过创新的适应性流程予以应对，但同时也强调，项目融入了许多持续的、机械的、稳定的结构特征。项目中的多方合同融入了构建管理层级所要实现的部分功能，比如应对不确定和变化的条件所需要的激励和控制。

不确定性是指关于项目目标、任务和环境的信息状况，正如我们在曼哈顿项目中所见，对于不确定性的认知并不多，尤其是在项目开始时所知甚少。不确定性可能是可预知的，也可能是

75

不可预知的；这两种情况需要采用不同的项目管理方法。

"可预知的不确定性"是指在项目计划时可以识别的某一事件或风险——"已知的未知"。风险管理是一项用于识别、评估和控制可避免或可转移的不确定性的技术。风险注册表（即所识别风险的记录）需要在项目实施前完成，并识别技术事件（如测试或界面问题）、合作伙伴选择、客户要求（范围变更）及其他风险。处理这些风险意味着将其简单地作为不可避免的麻烦接受它们，或是采取预防行动避免它们，包括应急方案（包括准备金和进度缓冲安排）。如果风险发生了，应急方案可以指导其处置。

"不可预知的不确定性"是指在项目开始时无法识别的某一事件、影响或未预见到的互动。有时被称为"不可知的未知"，这种不确定性常常会发生在下列的任一项目中，譬如开发新技术，开辟没有充分了解的新市场，或是应对未预见到的危机或灾害。传统的风险管理工作不能够处理这些突破性项目，或在快节奏、竞争激烈环境中实施的项目。在这些项目中，不可预知的不确定性是不可避免的，或被视作一项值得承担的风险，例如奥雅纳公司的东滩未来生态城设计。

项目必须应对多种不确定性；按照来源和影响，它们可分为经济类、制度类和生态类。亚伦·申哈尔和多夫·德维尔将技术和市场的不确定性专门挑了出来，将其视为最为广泛的、持久的和具有挑战性的无法预测和未知的因素，它们会影响项目实施中的目标和任务。技术不确定性涉及四种类型项目——低技术型、中技术型、高技术型和超高技术型。各类项目都将不同程度的新技术融入最终产品及其生产流程（参见第五章使用数字化技术开发波音777型客机的有关内容）。融合大量新技术的项目（例如国防、计算机和航天项目）需要团队成员中的更多互动、多次设计迭代、往复式学习和原型开发。一个项目采用或开发的新技术越多，成本、时间和质量超限以及未达成预设性能目标的风险的可能性就越大。

市场创新性是指项目试图达成目标或成果的不确定性。它是指购买方对产品和潜在用途的熟悉程度，以及对新产品或改进产品要求的明确程度。例如，航空旅客的时尚和喜好——譬如对低成本航空或长途旅行的需求——可以在航空公司对波音公司或空中客车公司设计和制造新飞机的要求中体现出来。根据第五章对于创新分类的详细论述，申哈尔和德维尔对衍生型项目、平台型项目和突破性项目进行了区分。产品越是新颖，在项目设计阶段识别客户需求并确定其要求就越为困难。

对于实现重大技术进步或是开辟新兴市场的项目而言，团队需要在实践中学习新事物、调整任务和改变方向，而传统的风险管理技术鼓励他们"回到计划"。相较于更审慎地使用计划和风险管理尝试应对意外的情形，克里斯托夫·洛赫及其合著者则建议：团队应当依靠"灵活性与学习"的组合。当存在过多未知且无法对风险进行准确预测时，项目目标、正式计划、计划任务和进行中的流程，必须随着新获得的信息、组织对项目及其环境如何互动的更多认知进行相应的调整。正如曼哈顿项目和宇宙神项目所展示的那样（第三章），不可预知的不确定性是可以降低的，它可以采取并行的多项测试，以便在选择备选方案前获取有价值的信息。与一开始时就确定采用某种单一技术的成本相比，重复测试和试验的成本可能要更低，这是因为前者会导致之后会遇到开始时未曾预见到的重大困难，或是在产品推出时已过时了。

　　灵活性和学习，可以帮助管理者们依据不确定程度区分项目的不同类型，并调整他们的管理方法予以应对。正如西尔万·朗夫勒和克里斯托夫·洛赫通过对曼哈顿项目的深入研究所发现的那样，这种适应性流程的需求不仅对于不同类型的项目是显而易见的，对于大型复杂项目亦是如此。有针对性的灵活策略可将大型项目分解成不同的子项目，以响应不同的不确定性需求。明确的结构、流程和风险管理技术须用于处置可预知的不确定性（应急方案和指南）和不可预知的不确定性（并行测试和迭代式学习）。例如，2012年伦敦奥运会项目就针对不同场馆建设的不确定性差异采用了多种合同。合作型风险分担合同用于不确定程度较高的项目（例如由与众不同的扎哈·哈迪德所设计的水上运动中心），而固定总价合同则用于常规的高预见性项目（比如包括标准化、可重复使用构件的临时场馆）。

　　正如我们在宇宙神项目中所见，项目组织的结构反映了它所生产的产品或系统的复杂性。各个项目的产品或成果涉及了许多相互关联的部件、组件、子系统和系统整体，包括有形的人造实体（例如硬件和软件）和无形的服务（例如物流、维护和运营）。多项研究依据日趋增长的复杂性对项目类型进行了区分，其范围从材料、组件和产品组装到更为复杂的平台项目、系统项目和"系统的系统"项目。日益增长的复杂性呼唤形式更为精巧的组织和流程（例如模块化设计策略），用以应对来自多组件集成、子项目界面管理及交互式依存性的挑战（方框6）。

> **方框6 模块化和系统集成**
>
> 为宇宙神项目生产的电子元器件（第三章）常用轮廓分明的黑色金属盒子包装运送，以便组装系统时可以无须打开"黑盒子"。在类似的设计策略启发下，许多建筑、油气、航天及核能发电站领域的复杂项目都是由有着标准化轮廓的模块化部件所组成，以简化建设和集成流程。模块化部件可以在工地现场以外的工厂中以更精确、更廉价的方式生产，通过测试检验后，可以在现场像积木模型套件一样进行组装。例如，由伦佐·皮亚诺设计的伦敦310米高的建筑——"碎片大厦"，就采用了可组装的且事先预装过的模块化部件和钢结构，它们在伦敦桥火车站上方的拥挤工地安装之前，就已经在场外测试过了。
>
> 模块化组件不仅可以像乐高积木那样进行混搭，不确定性较低，还可以通过公平的市场交易予以协调，无须系统集成者的专门介入。但是，在实践中很难实现模块化所需的无缝的企业之间项目协调。通过对复杂项目的研究，斯特凡诺·布鲁索尼和安德烈亚·普伦奇佩发现：具有系统集成能力的企业需要监管各个独立模块的整体设计和开发，适应大量部件之间的互动调整，并加强部件供应商之间的联系。

通过将项目复杂性划分为三种类型，申哈尔和德维尔提出：复杂性会影响任务之间的依存性，并会塑造管理各项目所要求的组织。相对简单的装配式项目是涉及复杂集合的单一组件、服务或产品（例如手机通信网络中的某一无线电基站），它常常由内部的小型产品开发团队予以实施。系统项目常作为某个平台的一部分，包括了多个组件和子系统，并具有共同实现某种具体运作要求的多种功能，例如新型计算机开发、新车型开发或新飞机开发。在具有内部系统集成能力的大型总承包商管理（第三章）中，常常要建立总体项目办公室或项目集群办公室，以协调各个系统项目中由内部职能团队和外部供应商所构成网络的技术尝试。最为复杂的系统集合项目，或是系统的系统项目，包括了大量系统所组成的系统集合，每个系统都服务于其自身的明确目的，且它们通过共同作用来实现共同的目标，例如新机场、城市开发或是全国性手机通信网络。常常需要建立一个大型系统集成者组织，例如某一独立的业主方组织或是交付伙伴联合体，用以处理财务、法律和政治问题，协调项目群中的多个承包商并安排其进度。

　　项目可以根据紧迫性进行分类，这主要取决于有多少时间可用于完成任务，以及何种情况将会在目标未实现时发生。任务的节奏和序列可以通过时序——包括合同和时间轴的日历时间——来予以驱动，从而限制和协调项目中何人在何时做何事。节奏可以通过预先确定的期限和里程碑事件予以驱动，从而保持紧迫感并将焦点放在可用于完成项目的时间上。当应完成某些任务或须在下一阶段之前更快完工时，事先确定的里程碑事件则确定了具体日期，完成产品开发项目中的设计定型即是一例。拉尔斯·林德奎斯特及其合作者发现：在日本，负责引入爱立信第一代移动通信系统的项目团队，被迫接受了极其苛刻的强制性期限要求。在这一"不可能完成的任务"中，该团队之所以显著地缩减了项目交付所需的时间，是因为在他们将顺序开发转变为基于新"喷泉模型"的并行开发。这种开发方式是由清晰的目标（于1994年4月1日完成了全运作系统的交付）、明确的期限和频繁的里程碑事件所驱动的。

通过将项目节奏划分为四种类型，申哈尔和德维尔强调：项目越是紧迫，对于自主权、快速决策和高管参与的需求就越多。诸如多数公共建设项目或组织变革等常规项目，都可以容许一定的工作延迟。与此相反，在大多数行业和营利性组织中，快速竞争性项目必须快速响应市场机遇，建立新的主要业务线，并创造战略优势。进度关键型项目是指那些受限于机遇窗口期的项目（例如千禧年庆典建筑），或者必须在某一特定日期完工的项目（例如体育运动日程表上奥运会或世界杯等重大事件）。无法按时完工会导致项目失败。突击项目的形成是为了尽可能快速地应对自然灾害、突发事件或危机形势等最为紧急的问题。例如2010年成功解救困在700米深地下69天的33名智利矿工。它们比任何其他项目都需要更多的自主权和资源去处理紧急和现场情况，只有进行几乎同步的处置，快速灵活地行动起来，才能拯救生命、保护财产并从混乱形势中恢复秩序。

近年来，多位有影响的学者尝试开发概念性架构模型，以体现项目的权变维度。在《管理未知》（2006）一书中，克里斯托夫·洛赫、阿尔努·德梅耶和迈克尔·皮希提出了管理技术和市场环境中项目的不同方法，其范围从简单的可预测项目到创新性未知的项目。项目管理的权变理论也曾出现在申哈尔和德维尔的论文中，并融入他们的著作《再造项目管理》（2007）中。

项目管理

78

他们主张：适合所有项目的单一的万能结构或流程并不存在。有些项目是简单且可预测的，还有许多项目则是复杂且不确定的，并会受到环境动态性的强烈影响。

在第五章中，我们将考察项目管理在20世纪80年代和90年代是如何进行转型，并在竞争日趋激烈的全球市场中用于管理创新的。 82

# 精益、重量级和颠覆性项目

在20世纪的大多数时间,世界汽车市场都是由少数基于超大批量生产的超大企业所主导的,即美国的福特公司、通用汽车公司和克莱斯勒公司,以及欧洲的大众公司、雷诺公司、菲亚特公司、宝马公司、戴姆勒-奔驰公司及其他几家企业。然而,到20世纪80年代,西方对于全球汽车行业的垄断已面临着威胁。日本汽车制造商本田公司和丰田公司发现了一种开发和生产各种各样新款车型的规模化方式,比它们的西方对手成本更低、速度更快。在一项对1983年至1987年世界汽车行业产品开发项目的研究中,金·克拉克和藤本隆宏发现:一款新型日本汽车从初步设计到用户交付,平均需要170万工时和46个月,而西方生产商则需要300万工时和60个月。日本生产商之所以"精益",是因为每个新产品开发项目实施仅需不到一半的人员和一半左右的时间。

## 精益产品开发

在20世纪80年代,包括日本和西方的所有汽车制造商,都采用某种矩阵的方式来组织它们的产品开发项目（第三章）。来自营销、工程（动力总成、车身底盘和工艺流程）及制造等不同职能单元的专家，都必须进行紧密的项目合作，开发新车型。各家企业都有一系列不同模型、零件和需要共用的工厂。开发新产品时，领导这一工作的分支部门必须与其他分支部门及生产共用部件的零件供应商进行互动。然而在实践中，日本式矩阵型结构与西方的颇为不同。在1990年出版的介绍精益生产思想的著作《改变世界的机器》中，詹姆斯·沃马克、丹尼尔·琼斯、丹尼尔·鲁斯对产品开发的传统西方方法与日本革命性新方法进行了区分。

西方生产者面向"大批量生产"的开发方法，以20世纪80年代的通用汽车公司为代表。在序列开发过程中（第四章），项目会在其生命周期中从一个职能部门"翻墙传递"到下一个职能部门，其工作会随着过程发展依赖不同的、分散的团队执行。参与方必须对规范、性能以及外观进行数以千计的决策，其涉及汽车的目标市场、价格、最偏好特性及物理尺寸等。然后，工程师将会确定各个零件的详细规范要求，以及能从其他通用汽车产品中获得何种零件。竹内弘高和野中郁次郎将这种方法比作接力赛中的接力棒传递。与美国国家航空航天局的"阶段化集群项目规划"（第三章）不同，产品通过高度结构化流程行进：概念开发、可行性试验、产品设计、开发、测试、生产及产品发布。

通用汽车公司会任命一位集群项目经理，领导和协调来自职能部门的项目团队成员承担临时任务。由于项目领导处于公司内的弱势地位，通用汽车公司的集群项目经理缺乏必要的授权，难以保证他的指令得以执行。他们的表现更像是协调者而

84　非管理者,因为他们常会勉力解决冲突,竭力说服成员和职能团队予以合作。当他们敦促工程部及其他部门专注设计决策或加快行动时,他们得到的是口头承诺,而非行动。解决问题所需的沟通常常不足,因为设计过程是序列的且分散的,并不是在团队总部的同一工作地点推进的。设计决策的人员数量在刚开始时很少,随着项目进行到产品发布阶段会增长到顶峰,此时过多的新人员会加入进来解决问题,而这一点在项目开始时就应当予以考虑。

　　精益方法是由本田公司和丰田公司所创造,它可以比它们的西方对手开发出更多品种的系列产品,且更快、失误更少。开发工作被细分,以满足世界各地不同地区市场的需求。一旦产品计划和规范要求确定后,项目团队的专职成员会不间断地进行快速工作,以实现总体目标,必要时也会和职能部门合作。

　　每种新车型开发都会任命一位项目领导者牵头,比如本田公司大型项目领导者或丰田公司的"主管",他具有获取资源并管理开发过程的授权,而非对开发过程仅是进行简单的协调。虽然日本生产者也会采用矩阵型结构,但人员也是从职能部门借调并依据各个项目的生命周期而转入。在"重量级项目经理"(参见"团队结构和领导者")的控制下,他们在一个紧凑组织的团队中工作,团队成员要比西方项目中的人员少得多。通过延续团队成员身份及利用之前项目共事时形成的共同经验,构建起合作式解决问题的方法。设计之初,在成员之间和学科之间的沟通是最多的,此时所有相关的专长都被汇聚在了一起。重

85　量级项目经理的工作是鼓励成员去直面权衡并解决资源上的冲突。在指导性项目愿景的激励下,个体成员签署正式承诺书,如

同团队一样去做每个人都认同的事情。

以富士-施乐和佳能为代表的其他消费品行业的日本企业，也开发出一种适应性"叠加"的方法，在重叠（或并行）阶段开发新产品，通过精益增添开发节奏加速的灵活性。通过叠加法，团队能够吸收新信息并参与到试错式学习导向的循环式适应性过程中，减少他们必须考虑的方案数量，这类似于宇宙神项目中并行性的应用（第三章）。

在过去的二十多年里，精益开发被推广到多个行业，它们往往经历着产品快速更新和产品生命周期缩减，诸如消费电子产品及其他的快节奏环境。它也被单件式生产者所采用，比如航天、建设和电影制作（例如皮克斯动画）。在这些行业中，并行产品开发和合作关系用于产生新想法、驱动绩效，并在项目进行过程中沟通任何必须的变更。

## 数字技术支持的精益开发

到了20世纪90年代，快速、灵活、精益的开发过程逐步和计算机辅助设计（CAD）、计算机辅助制造（CAM）和通信系统等数字技术一起开始使用，以协调涉及新产品设计、生产、集成和测试的各种团队，包括在同一工作地点的团队和分布式团队。

例如，波音777型客机是第一款完全采用电脑设计的商用飞机。它于1988年开始构思，1990年3月确定了这一配备了电传飞行控制计算机的新型远程宽体双引擎的飞机设计。在经历开发和大规模测试阶段后，第一架波音777型客机于1995年6月7日在美国联合航空公司开始投入服务。在波音公司之前的开发项目中，纸质图是在空间上和组织上相对独立的设计和制造

86

团队之间进行交接的。相比之下，在波音777型客机项目中，每一位工程师都可以获取数字信息，紧密互动的团队可以经常在线上对三维设计进行反复沟通。以往需要等纸质图复制后才能进行一致性检查；与此不同，波音777型客机项目工程师能够使用计算机，调阅所有部件并识别当它们匹配在一起时的冲突或"碰撞"（方框7）。

---

### 方框7　波音公司"无纸化设计的飞机"

作为一种设计工具，计算机辅助设计应用于汽车制造、土木工程和建筑领域，但是从未进行过波音公司那样的大范围应用。两个相互关联的计算机系统被用于设计、组装和测试波音777型客机的虚拟模型，包括计算机辅助三维互动应用（CATIA）和基于CATIA的电子化预组装。CATIA是达索公司和IBM公司合作为航天行业开发的。应用这一无纸化系统，工程师能够放大某一部件，并以缩小的方式观察这一部件在由400万个部件构成的飞机整体中是如何匹配的。波音公司位于华盛顿州的埃弗里特工厂作为波音777型客机项目的主要设计场所，配备了2200个连接到IBM主机的计算机终端。最终，项目成员可以利用分布于全球超过17个时区的7000多个工作站。一个专门的私有数据网络穿越太平洋从华盛顿铺设到日本，当地的日本航天工业公司联合体负责20%机身结构的设计。所有的238个项目团队都可以利用计算机数据。每个团队成员包括不超过40名工程师。CAD计划项目为CAM系统提供了

---

机身组件生产所需的数字化数据。该系统提供了波音777型客机项目组件的一个完整的数字化模型,它是飞机开始运作服务后维护人员所必需的。

在波音777型客机项目历程的传记中,卡尔·萨巴格发现,在"激烈竞争的飞机制造世界中,波音公司希望项目管理给予他们的飞机超越空中客车公司和麦道公司的优势"。波音777型客机开发项目,是由波音公司两位最具实力和经验的项目经理领导的。在前任经理菲尔·康杜伊特离任并升任波音公司总裁后,艾伦·马拉利负责执行项目最为紧张的设计和制造阶段,他后来成为福特公司的总裁。波音777型客机数字设计技术之所以得到良好的应用,是因为它嵌入了高度合作性、问题解决导向的项目组织中。在马拉利的领导下,波音公司建立了一种名为"共同工作"的方法,用以激励工程师碰面,交换对双方有用的想法、解决冲突、建立信任,并对他们努力创造的事物形成共同的理解(图8)。波音公司也采用了率先在日本尝试的合作性"设计建设联动"项目团队,因此,航空公司客户和外部供应商可以参与到早期设计决策中。

在过去的二十年里,CAD系统、CAM系统、网络化宽频沟通及"云端"存储等数字技术的利用,与项目管理中精益的、更为协作化的方式是相符的。数字技术从航天部门拓展到建筑等更多的传统部门,用以辅助部件和系统的设计、建设、集成及"虚拟"测试。

举例来说,弗兰克·盖里于1991年从IBM公司购买了CATIA

88

图8 短语"共同工作",作为对于该项目顺利进行贡献最大的管理方式,被用于第一架波音777型客机的命名

航天软件(用于波音777型客机项目),用于设计和建造位于西班牙北部毕尔巴鄂的古根海姆博物馆,包括了画廊空间在内的建筑,用以陈列国际知名的当代艺术家作品。没有计算机的辅助,设计和建造如此复杂的建筑几乎是不可能的。为了捕捉自然光,该建筑被设计成一组曲面的松散组合,通过钢结构来塑造其褶皱的外形,同时适应建筑外表的曲面,覆以玻璃、石灰岩和钛金属镀膜拼贴。钢构件和钛金属构件是事先在工厂中制造并通过高精度切割予以造型,然后再在现场组装起来的。根据开工前详尽可靠的成本估算,项目按时且在不超出预算成本的情况下成功交付。在1997年10月18日博物馆开馆之后,这幢壮观宏伟建筑的收益远远超过其成本。通过将其置于全球艺术和建筑地图之上,它重新激活了一座区域性城市,使其成为一个吸引

89

**86**

全球旅行者前来参观的旅行胜地。

　　古根海姆项目标志着盖里从传统向数字适应性设计实践转型的开端。数字化工具和流程支持合作式项目团队，参与到先锋派、鼓舞人心的建筑的设计和建造中。数字化模型是各项目的唯一信息来源，并用于与客户讨论的"可投影的论据"。在被盖里称为"快速适应"的过程中，数字化模型可用于测试和探索多种可能性，利用快速原型开发技术进行试验（它可以根据3D模型制作实体模型），提出新方向的建议并持续调整，必要时会持续到项目结束阶段。各个独立部件、浮现的问题及变化的项目优先事项能够被高度准确地预见，并及时予以控制和管理。通过将建筑置于包括客户、工程顾问和承包商的合作式流程的核心，盖里认为：当所有建筑和城市都将采用数字化工具进行设计和建造时，数字化工具能够在未来重塑建筑师的"巨匠"角色，就如同波音777型客机项目那样。

## 创新项目

　　开发新产品并将创新想法从构思转变成现实，常被看作一个"漏斗"。从大范围的输入开始，在过程中逐步优化并从中进行选择，造就了一些开发项目。它们或是聚焦于具有稳定客户需求、可以进行渐进式改良的某种产品，或者是为革命性新产品或服务开拓新的高度不确定的市场。

　　在1992年出版的《产品开发革命进行时》一书中，史蒂文·惠尔莱特和金·克拉克根据从渐进式创新到激进式创新连续区间中产品和过程的创新程度，提出了一种开发项目的分类，即存在三种类型的商业产品开发项目。衍生型项目涉及渐进式

90

创新，其范围从成本降低到现有产品和流程的提升。与其他类型项目相比，它们需要更少的开发资源。这是由于能够清楚了解客户要求，在前期阶段就可以确定规格要求。在这一区间另一端的突破性项目，则是基于激进式创新，因为它们引入了全新的流程或是未尝试过的产品，会创造全新的市场和行业。突破性项目需要更多的资源和更大的自主权来决定如何设计全新的产品和流程。位于渐进式创新到激进式创新连续区间中部，平台型项目则为现有客户和已知市场开发新产品和流程（共享标准化、模块化和通用型原件）。

苹果公司提供了一个几乎专注于突破性创新的公司范例。在许多项目中，苹果公司前任首席执行官史蒂夫·乔布斯具有一种天赋，可以创造出多种设计美好的事物，且人们没有意识到对这些事物的需要，但很快会发现离开它们将无法生活。苹果公司转型成为世界上最成功公司之一，始于2001年10月23日发布的iPod音乐播放器。苹果公司改变了人们倾听、制作和购买音乐的方式，并颠覆了音乐产业。尽管苹果公司的设计参考了现有的MP3技术，但是iPod被视作一项突破的原因在于，它可以与iTunes软件协作，允许用户管理他们自己的音乐、图片、视频、文档和其他专属文件。它为其他突破性项目创造了苹果数字化中心，包括苹果手机和iPad平板电脑。乔布斯鼓励开发团队专注于创新想法，而且他对那些谨守计划并为了产品能按时在预算内完成而妥协的人员不太有耐心，这也是众所周知的。正如艾萨克森在他担任苹果公司首席执行官时指出的那样，对于苹果手机、苹果商店和其他项目，乔布斯"会在它们临近完成时按下'暂停'键并决定进行重大变更"。

91

与苹果公司不同，少有公司的项目组合中会有一系列突破性项目。比如，商用飞机制造商会建立平台型项目，开发各种系列化的新产品，比如波音777型到最新的787型客机。每代新产品之间的变化发生在两方面，即满足客户需求的产品和满足这些需求的技术。波音公司会执行衍生型项目，以提供加强式提升和"延伸设计"，这相当于对给定型号产品进行一系列的调整。例如，波音767型客机设计师通过延伸设计满足了航空公司对于更多座位的要求，这使得飞机机长增加了14米（46英尺）。

其他两类则是研发项目及联盟和伙伴合作项目。研发项目将想法转变成新产品、新服务和新流程。它们创造了关于材料、技术和服务的新知识，并将最终融入新的商业开发项目中。因为一个研发项目的过程和成果是高度不确定的，与商业开发项目相比，公司对支持它的资源有着不同的期望。联盟和伙伴合作项目是与多个外部机构一起构成的，可用于任何类型的研发项目，抑或是衍生型、平台型或突破性开发项目。近年来，如施乐、IBM、英特尔、宝洁等多家公司，开始从封闭式创新模式转向开放式创新模式。前者是指研发和产品开发项目很大程度上是在公司内进行，后者则是借助内部和外部创意渠道实现新产品的商业化。

92

## 项目组合管理

组织中适当的冗余被认为是可以促进创新的，它可以通过提供必要的时间和空间以验证不确定的新想法；否则在资源不足的情况下，这些想法可能无法获得支持。创新的花费不菲，而创造太多的冗余也会耗费企业的宝贵资源。项目组合方法提供了一种自上而下的管理创新的战略性方式，并将极为有限的资源分配给有着时序关联的多个产品开发项目组。企业通过对项目组合进行评估并根据其创新程度分为不同类型，确认如何实现项目的分批安排进度，并压缩实施这些项目的工期及其总工期。平台型和突破性项目作为最为创新的项目，则需要更多的资源、余量和冗余，以应对耗时更长、更不确定的开发周期。通过匹配项目类型和识别产品开发策略的不足，项目组合经理能够发现何种新项目应当加入组合中，何时增加以及何时中止其实施。此外，他们能够识别能力和开发技能，这些都是个体成员、团队及项目领导者计划和实施项目组合所必需的。

用于规避严格项目组合评估标准的策略涉及分散组织中各种小型的自发性项目。只要非常有限的资源，这些项目就能悄悄地在现有事业部内部实施，且时常都没有被高管所意识到。一些潜藏中的非正式"未经许可的项目"有时会获得高管的潜在支持，它们是创新创业的重要来源，之后可能被正式接受并纳入主要产品开发活动中。当今，许多高层管理者都有"边缘项目"，以试验新想法、开发新爱好、学习新技能，或者在主流组织限制以外开展"新创业务"。例如，谷歌公司就因为鼓励其雇员开展"边缘项目"作为其日常工作而出名。许多业务，比如推特、克雷格清单广告网站、扁平星球专业服务及高朋团购网站，都是从边缘项目开始的。

## 团队结构与领导者

惠尔莱特和克拉克开发了一个广为人知的项目团队四维分类模型，被用于多个行业的产品开发和创新中。在"职能型团队结构"中，任务从一开始就被分解成多个相对独立的活动，并由职能团队独立实施。项目依次序从某一职能部门向后一职能部门推进，尽管其实施常常不太顺利。当团队成员之间的搭接和互动很少时，职能团队常常会形成其自身的习惯、惯例和观念，且难以和其他团队形成紧密的合作。

在"轻量级团队结构"中，成员们实际上还隶属于其职能领域，但是每支团队会指定一个对外联络经理，作为代表参与项目协调委员会。在矩阵型组织中，该经理之所以被认为是轻量级的，因是为他或她在组织中地位不高，主要资源和权力仍控制在职能经理手中。尽管如此，现在至少能有一位管理者跳脱职能部门的桎梏纵览全局，能让团队成员了解任一跨职能协作的事项，保证相互独立的任务可以及时执行。

在"重量级团队结构"中，从职能团队借调的成员们是专门的人员，与重量级项目领导在同一地点办公。正如本田公司、丰田公司和波音公司的案例所示，项目领导之所以是一位重量级人物，是由于他或她是组织中的高级经理，通常比职能经理拥有更强的专长、更丰富的经验和更高的级别。在同一地点办公与在线数字化沟通之所以更受青睐，是因为可以通过会议碰面的最佳方式直接处理实时出现的问题，而不必等待召开不定期会议，或是采用在线沟通的方式解决跨职能协作问题。核心团队负责分解任务、安排计划项目，并在环境变化时调整工作。正如马拉利在波音777型客机项目所扮演的角色一样，重量级团队需要高超的领导力激发并鼓励团队，守护项目所形成的基本观念。重量级项目经理能够理解客户和市场的需求，用不同职能部门的语言予以表达，协调和集成它们的工作，并识别和解决任何矛盾。这些矛盾是希望不同专长、行为和层级的团队在一起工作时所不可避免的。

在面对着不可预知的环境或机遇时，重量级团队能够发掘新知、重新配置资源并重新分配任务，以尽可能完善的方式完成任务。克拉克和藤本建议：这种结构最适用于平台型项目。20世纪80年代中期，美国的汽车制造商采用职能型团队结构或轻量级团队结构，在数月内雇用了大约1500位全职工程师，而日本的由重量级经理负责的平台型项目同期仅仅雇用了250位全职工程师。

在"自治型团队结构"中，来自各职能部门的人员作为一个集成化团队，在同一地点办公，但是在项目期间，他们也有自己的基地，常设于一幢独立的办公楼中。身为重量级人物的项目领导，对于资源和来自职能部门的人员具有完全控制权，同时也是团队成员个体绩效的唯一评估者。自治型项目有时被视为"老虎团队"，就像"一张白纸"，即：它不必完全遵循既有政策，且几乎能进行任何有利于项目目标实现的变更。在有机型结构的团队中，成员们相互调适并进行非正式互动。美国航天和国防企业洛克希德马丁公司，在冷战期间开创了这一名为"臭鼬工作室"的组织方式。它创造了这种具有跨职能能力的自治型结构，用于开发远离公司主要机构、不受既有规则程序影响的高新技术项目，诸如U2侦察机、SR71黑鸟侦察机以及F117隐身战斗机。

## 平衡行为

服务既有客户或开拓新市场的项目实施涉及极其困难的平衡行为。借用"支流"的隐喻，罗莎贝丝·莫斯·坎特建议：

一个组织要能持续推动项目——"与支流同行",即它投身于发展自身的主流技术及其市场基础之外,还要能开辟新渠道并创建能在未来产生收益的新支流项目。组织需要一定程度的双元性,以了解如何开拓它们的主流业务,同时还要发起突破性项目,探索和开创新的市场机遇。

在公司主流业务中,衍生型项目或平台型项目主要面向现有市场中有着稳定偏好和可预测需求的既有客户,进行渐进式改进和新产品开发。当项目主要依靠成熟技术时,计划和进度在采取行动之前就可以确定下来。公司既要有历史和经验基础,能为未来预测提供数据,为实施之前的详尽计划提供机会;还要有能力将资源分配到不同项目,并对历年活动进行调整。

许多公司在其主流业务市场成功的原因在于,它们会倾听客户的声音,并在投资新产品和改进型产品之前仔细地研究市场趋势。这样实例的存在可能令人惊讶,但是直到20世纪90年代,波音公司在新机型决策之前通常并不会咨询航空公司的建议。它会自行提出新机型的想法,并进行设计和生产,然后等待航空公司的购买。面对来自空中客车公司和麦道公司的激烈竞争、不断变化的航空旅行需求以及其他的不确定性,波音公司亟须一种新方法。波音777型客机项目团队必须与航空公司一起,花费精力确定其对于范围、尺寸、有效载荷和经济性的要求。通过与"八大航空公司联盟"(包括美国联合航空、美国航空、达美航空、英国航空、日本航空、全日空、澳洲航空和国泰航空)有关代表会晤沟通,波音公司设计了777型客机。

当主流业务活动停滞不前或萎缩时,就必须找到新的收入渠道。但是,主流业务部门通常过于缓慢和官僚,难以在快速变

96

化的市场中进行竞争或是应对产品快速的升级换代。而既有资源投入和承诺涉及预算、进度、角色定义和期望等，主要用于维持主流业务项目的开展，难以改变方向。当涉及创造"前所未有"的产品时，通过专门设立的研发部门实施相关项目时常遭遇失败，它们无法满足既有客户对于绩效的要求。正如相机制造商伊士曼柯达公司所发现的那样，这种方式造成了其从胶片向数字化技术转变的致命性延误，不仅标志着该公司开始走向末路，而且也标志着富士通、佳能及其他公司的崛起。

突破性项目则引发了创新的支流。它们想象新的可能、创造全新的物品、颠覆既有的行业。因为它们很少有或是并没有新技术的经验基础，抑或并不存在当下可以倾听的客户，因此很难形成对于用户需求的预测，项目进度计划通常也不会太实际，成本也很可能会超支。在实施项目时，行动必须在计划编制之前就要开展，任务也必须为了应对技术问题和未知事件进行调整。尽管能够最大可能地利用既有知识，但仍需要新的知识去理解知之甚少的技术和未知的客户要求。正如坎特所解释的那样：

> 多方法、灵活性和速度都是创新所必需的。这或是因为新想法来自随机的且通常是高度直觉的洞察力，抑或因为未曾预知的问题的发现。项目团队需要在不受正式计划、董事会审批及其他"官僚性延误"约束的情形下进行工作，因为这些都可能对方向性变革造成阻碍。

由于突破性项目会和主流项目直接争抢资源、关注度及忠诚度，所属母体组织的高管层会因为将过多的控制权下放给

项目管理

自治型团队及其领导者而变得紧张过度。较为常见的风险是，自治型团队会偏离正题，给所属组织造成麻烦。它可能会过于关注单个项目自身的优先级，而非更为广泛的组织需求（第六章）。对既得利益者而言，将突破性项目独立出来意味着较少的威胁，有助于创造新的文化、创业精神和自治性，促进新想法的培育和成形，同时还可以避免既有业务部门的规定以及烦琐官僚程序的过多限制。

正如1981年IBM公司个人电脑开发所示，自治性在发起突破性项目时是必要的。IBM公司建立了一支由比尔·洛领导的自治型团队，有着独立的跨职能结构，代号"象棋项目"。项目团队在佛罗里达州的博卡拉顿，远离公司总部和研发部门。为了实现个人电脑开发的目标，这支名为"叛逆者"的团队具有做任何事情的授权。与此同时，遵循既定内部开发政策进行的IBM主流项目"数据大师"，开发到第四年时就卡了壳，且无法预计完工时间。而从外部供应商购买部件和软件（如操作系统）等打破规则的意愿，使得"象棋项目"团队仅用一年就完成了个人电脑的开发和产品上市。

## 实现突破

正如"象棋项目"一样，最为有效的突破性项目团队与现有组织在结构上是相对独立的，但是在高层管理者的支持下，它紧密地融入了更为广泛的公司结构中。它们与传统单位共享资源，但是在物理空间上和组织上与其分离，以保证新项目过程、价值和方法不会受到官僚程序的挤压。由于如此之高的权力和责任被授予了突破性项目团队，专门的集成机制也必须落实到位，以保障团队与所属组织的紧密联系。高管层需要保有引导项目的能力，同时还需要一位强有力的投资执行人担任重量级经理及核心项目的教练和导师。如果高管团队成员或者其他职能部门负责人关注或需要项目进展的更多信息，这些可以与投资执行人进行沟通。

在发展成熟的行业中，突破是很难实现的，而这些行业往往由少数大型企业所主导，如汽车、飞机、手机和建筑等。比如在20世纪90年代初，汽车行业的创新主要涉及已熟知的技术，其产品需求也是持续增长的。詹姆斯·沃马克及其合著者提出这样一个问题：汽车生产商是否可以通过精益方法应用的"终极考验"来实现突破性创新呢？避免交通拥堵的导航系统、无人自动驾驶汽车、氢燃料汽车与电动汽车开发都是当今社会所需的机动车技术，它们不会造成碳排放水平上升和城市的污染。

克莱顿·克里斯滕森将电动汽车技术视为汽车行业潜在的颠覆性技术，并建议汽车制造商创建一种小型的独立项目组织，将其与主流部门分开，比如通用电气公司为培育和实现新技术商业化而设立的"土星分部"。当少数公司开始电动汽车开发时（比如通用汽车公司和雷诺日产联盟），大多数公司仍专注于改进现有产品或是开发混合动力汽车，比如丰田普锐斯（方框8）。

一家来自行业外的新创公司——自克莱斯勒公司于1925年创建以来在美国成立的第一家车企——通过生产第一款纯电动汽车，挑战了主流制造商。特斯拉汽车公司由马丁·艾伯哈德和马克·塔彭宁共同创立于2003年，并由多次创业的企业家埃隆·马斯克投资。马斯克后来成为特斯拉公司的首席执行官。虽然特斯拉公司的"路行者"作为第一款电动跑车早在

2008年就已发布，但是使得公司成为一家独立的大规模电动汽车生产商的是其2012年发布的特斯拉S型电动汽车。S型电动汽车通过电池组供能，并拥有联通互联网的车载电脑导航、可下载的程序更新及充电站网络的支持。由于可以在夜间接入电源并充电，它被视为"与苹果手机一样的汽车"。在最近的一部自传中，马斯克解释说：现有的汽车生产商之所以不太情愿开发全电动汽车，是因为它们"如此缺乏独创性。它们总是期望在批准和开展某一项目之前，就能够看到它在某处是行得通的"。特斯拉公司必须与世界上所有汽车制造商的核心能力进行竞争，才能达成马斯克的愿望。引发了行业内技术性颠覆的这款汽车， 是通过一支由少数富有经验的工程师组成的自治型项目团队开

## 方框8 颠覆性技术

克莱顿·克里斯滕森建议：倾听客户的声音有助于公司了解何种"维持性技术"是必要的，它可以提升客户长期青睐的主流产品的性能。比如，在20世纪末，汽车行业持续投资于客户所需的产品，即提供具有高性价比的汽油引擎汽车。此时，没有任何汽车生产商受到电动汽车的威胁，且少有公司考虑进入这一不确定的市场。但是有时，"不再倾听客户的声音"是正确的策略。这种情况会出现在企业家投资于诸如电动汽车或自动驾驶汽车这类高风险的"颠覆性技术"时。尽管这种技术可能并不是当前客户所需的，并会导致短期的糟糕绩效，但是它将会开辟一个新的持续成长的高盈利市场。

发的，他们在马斯克的太空探索技术公司的工厂角落拥有自己的办公室，从而能"对他们所做的事情增加一些独立性和神秘感"。在一位"有着自由精神、富有创造性的"的汽车设计师弗兰茨·冯·霍尔茨豪森的领导下，S型车项目团队必须响应马斯克的要求，比如大量的设计变更、先进汽车技术的内部开发及紧迫的产品交付进度计划。

## 敏捷项目管理

另一种融入部分适应性元素的精益方法也正在形成，但是它更专注于实时学习、即兴创作及迭代开发。"敏捷"方法最初是为软件项目所开发，它针对项目管理中传统的标准化瀑布模式提供了一种激进的方法（第四章），并强调要在前期完成初步设计定型和规格确定、锁定范围、明确计划和实施阶段次序以及限制与客户的互动。那些敏捷方法的支持者认为：过于依赖严密的前期计划过程和正式合同的传统，可能会导致各种"下游异常"，诸如针对条件变化的灵活性不够、过多的返工、客户不满意，以及在项目进展过程中对于环境变化实时调整能力不足。以我们在第一章中所见为例，摩托罗拉公司的铱星项目尽管发掘了卫星通话技术的全部潜力，但也仅是发现：在该项目实施时，地面移动电话通信的快速扩张已经极大地削弱对它的需求。

相对稳定的环境适用于前期计划和进度安排，而变化、不确定的环境则需要敏捷方法，从而使得计划及其重构可以贯穿于开发生命周期。敏捷性是一种迭代的渐进式"涌浪"的过程，其设计用以促进灵活性以及对突然变化的技术和市场条件的响应性。敏捷方法要求四个方面：最低程度的文档化，可允许设计定型延迟至最后响应时刻的持续性设计迭代，用户和相关方的频繁互动，以及优化的轻量级项目团队的结构。敏捷方法与第四章中讨论的适应性、实时的"团队化"过程有着许多相同之处。调整会随时进行，以应对突然改变的条件，同时，计划也会随着项目执行过程中获得的客户要求和技术信息而进行修订。越来越多的证据表明，敏捷性有助于实现软件和信息技术项目的成功，且对于高科技和更多传统行业中的项目也是有价值的。

在第六章中，我们采用过去十年中在伦敦实施的若干超大基础设施项目作为例子，以说明21世纪不同的项目组织方式。102

# 伦敦的超大项目生态

伦敦地铁的朱比利延长线项目，是一条有着大空间车站、长约10英里（16千米）的隧道，它建成后可连接有着金丝雀码头市办公楼的伦敦西区和城市南部及东部区域。这个进度优先的项目理应作为一个完整的系统按时启用，从而可运送数以百万的乘客到伦敦千禧巨蛋，参加千禧年庆祝活动。该项目采用了固定总价合同，计划于1997年3月完成，成本为21亿英镑（之前在1989年估算为9亿英镑）。其最初的设计配备了最为先进的无线电行车制动报警信号系统，可以允许列车紧密地运行，且更为快捷、安全。它代表着当时世界高密度城市出行的未来趋势。这条地铁延长线的建设开始于1993年12月，但是隧道建设和信号方面的难题使得项目放弃了新的信号系统，推迟了竣工日期，并造成最终成本的严重超支。某些提交了低价标书的承包商期望，他们能对施工过程中的规格要求变更和意外问题处理提出5亿多英镑的索赔，从而收回成本并获得额外利润。为了解决这些问题，伦敦地铁于1998年从该项目的管理中退出，并由来自美

103

国的柏克德工程公司接手。该项目最终成本达到了35亿英镑，并于1999年5~12月间分三阶段启用。

朱比利地铁线是英国20世纪80年代和90年代及21世纪初的超大项目长名单中的一个，其中还包括英法海底隧道、伦敦千禧巨蛋、苏格兰议会大厦、斯旺威克空中交通管制中心以及其他多个项目，它们都存在超期和超支的问题。在一份关于朱比利地铁线项目的评价报告中，柏克德公司总结道：英国客户和承包商缺乏管理大型基础设施项目的必要能力。

20世纪90年代末，BAA公司（前身为英国机场管理局）作为英国主要机场的所有者和运营者，准备为英国航空公司在伦敦希思罗机场建设五号航站楼，其投资高达43亿英镑（图9）。1989年，

图9　建设中的希思罗机场五号航站楼

104

理查德·罗杰斯赢得了五号航站楼的设计权,航站楼于2002年7月开始建设,2008年3月启用。在20世纪90年代,BAA公司总裁约翰·伊根爵士清楚地了解英国建筑业关于项目交付的不良记录,并注意到:在五号航站楼项目上,任何严重的成本超支都有可能导致公司的破产。BAA公司决定考察英国过去十年中的各个重大建设项目以及在过去十五年里启用的各个国际机场,比如丹佛机场和夏尔·戴高乐机场,探究超大项目为何时常会失败。

答案出奇得简单。客户们假定:未来情况的预测是应当包括在低价投标文件中的,并通过固定总价合同予以明确;固定总价合同能将所有风险转移给承包商,并且不会给环境变化的情形留有空间(参见第三章中美国国家航空航天局对于固定总价合同的看法)。当产生问题时,没有解决问题的合作机制。客户和承包商之间的争议常常诉之公堂,造成了项目的延误。BAA公司曾在20世纪90年代中期采用固定总价合同,造成了从机场到帕丁顿站的希思罗快线项目延误;由此它认识到,项目交付风险不可能全部以合同形式转给建筑公司。如果五号航站楼项目采用传统的方式进行交付,BAA公司估计,项目将有可能超支10亿英镑、延期一年,并有六人会在施工中身亡。在BAA公司看来,在复杂不确定的项目中,当出现问题时,客户最后总会承担风险;由此它断定,五号航站楼项目需要一种激进的新"项目交付模式"(客户和承包商之间的合同和组织关系)。

五号航站楼项目建立了自治型结构,并由一支重量级经理团队领导。他们的经验是从其他行业(例如汽车制造、核能和航空航天)和复杂项目(比如葛兰素史克公司的英国研究设施和中国香港国际机场)中获得的。核心团队通过创造了一种名为

"五号航站楼协议"的新柔性合同"改变了游戏规则",其主要基于两项原则:客户将会承担五号航站楼项目建造中的风险,并会与同一地点办公的集成化集群项目团队协同工作。承包商将会获得成本补偿,并且当其表现超过之前确定的"目标成本"和完工时间时会获得奖金,以激励其创新和绩效改进行为。所有盈利都由团队成员分享。与传统交付模式相比,五号航站楼项目流程灵活兼具适应性,能够应对未预见到的事件,并利用开始时所未曾预料到的创新机会:

> 常规项目逻辑试图事先界定所有要求,项目开始后则不允许更改。然而,灵活性和适应性则是五号航站楼项目的主要目标。因此,常规过程和解决方案不太行得通。它需要灵活性方法,即灵活性解决方案和最终责任型决策。(《五号航站楼交付手册》,1999)

尽管有着混乱的启用(第一章),五号航站楼项目按计划交付,未超出预算。在启用后一年,五号航站楼项目经过乘客们投票,被选为世界最佳航站楼。它彻底地改变了英国超大项目如何交付的过程,并开启了一场行业范围内的对于灵活性、协作性和创新性需求的长期热议。那些在五号航站楼项目中工作过的个人、团队和组织,在继续参与伦敦的其他超大项目时,都会引入许多新的想法和创新实践。这些项目包括投资68亿英镑的2012年伦敦奥运会场馆和基础设施,投资148亿英镑、连接伦敦东西区的城市轨道交通系统"横贯铁路",以及投资42亿英镑、替代建成于维多利亚时期的伦敦地下排水系统的泰晤士潮路隧道方案(方框9)。

## 方框9 进入超大项目的世界

伦敦的横贯铁路项目说明了这些壮举中的某个项目是如何开展实际工作的。该项目旨在建造一条新的铁路——伊丽莎白线。它从西区的雷丁和希思罗出发，穿过21公里长的伦敦市中心地下的双洞隧道，直抵东区的申菲尔德和阿比伍德，它包括了10个新车站和30个更新改造的车站。横贯铁路的很多隧道（图10）要在靠近现有隧道线路处进行开挖和建设。在距离最近处，横贯铁路的一条隧道离地铁北线隧道仅有37厘米（15英寸）。

其中，有一站位于牛津街（欧洲最繁忙的购物街）和查灵克罗斯街的交叉路口下方，一支由建筑工人、电工、工程师和项目经理组成的小型队伍在此进行作业，以完成投资10亿英镑的托特纳姆宫路地铁站改造。该车站和两个售票大厅提供了伊丽莎白线与原有的地铁北线、中央线之间的换乘。250米（825英尺）长的站台和车站位于24米深的地下，其长度与温布利足球场的长度相当。施工作业在中心大楼前面进行，而该办公楼则位于保护区域之中，有着数幢历史保护建筑、商业、商店和餐馆以及其他便利设施。构件和装配式结构必须先运抵现场，挖掘出材料的清理也须尽可能少地减少对伦敦市中心的影响。大量乘客会从原有的托特纳姆宫路地铁站出发，搭乘伦敦地铁北线和中央线，但是他们并不知道在前方的横贯铁路建筑作业围挡后面发生着什么。当完工后，预计每天将有超过20万的乘客在新车站通勤。

107

图10 横贯铁路的盾构机穿越伦敦市中心,利物浦街地铁站地下40米

　　关于伦敦超大项目的简要介绍表明,认识项目的发起及其随时间发展的特定情境是很重要的。它提出了许多项目管理的问题,这些问题是旧有的"孤立项目"成见难以回答的,例如:项目中的个人、团队和组织是如何向过去学习的? 他们如何提升自身的知识并为未来做准备?

## 没有项目是孤岛

　　在过去的二十年中,研究者提供了多种见解、框架和观点,解决组织在项目中是如何共同工作以及项目是如何嵌入组织中的。这一研究最早出现于20世纪90年代初的斯堪的纳维亚半岛,可能是由于这些国家在复杂工程行业有着与之不相称的大量项目导向型企业,比如爱立信公司、ABB公司、萨博公司、斯堪雅公司、挪威国家石油公司及诺基亚公司。这些公司都与当地大学有着紧密的联系。后来，在被称为"项目研究斯堪的纳维亚学派"中，项目管理（第三章）、组织理论（第四章）、创新管理（第五章）及其他学科的文献，被用于深度解析项目在不同情境中是如何演化的问题。

当世界其他地方的学者开始发现许多企业和行业都是项目驱动的，于是起源于斯堪的纳维亚半岛的项目研究领域在20世纪90年代末期开始拓展。这些研究都有着类似的观点：传统的项目管理著作仅仅是狭隘地专注于项目、项目集群和项目组合的管理手册编制，并没有考虑项目是如何影响组织、行业和社会的更广泛发展，以及在这些发展的影响下其自身是如何形成的。马茨·恩瓦尔就清楚地表达了这层含义，正如他所说的，"没有项目是孤岛"：要理解某一项目内部将要发生的事情，就必须了解与之相关的过往、当下和未来的项目，以及其实施运作所涉及的更为广泛的制度情境。

项目是一个临时组织，它在完成任务后就会解散。然而，企业则是一个常设组织，建立以后将会成长、繁盛并会无限期地存续下去。约尔格·赛多及其合著者提出：这种临时性和持续性情境会造成项目导向型组织的两大基本紧张点或困境。

"自治与集成"的困境，存在于各项目的自治性要求与更广泛组织中的项目集成需求之间。在某一特定项目中所从事的专注、快速及自治的工作，可以为每位客户提供新知识和创新（第五章），但是可能与项目母体组织的战略优先事项并无关联。BAA公司认识到这一紧张点，是在五号航站楼项目被确立为一个独立组织，并拥有管理这一复杂集群项目工作所需的自治权和资源的时候，但是这一组织也有着向高管团队直接报告的渠道，以保证项目能被紧密地集成到管辖希思罗机场的企业活动中。

"是行动，还是学习"的困境，存在于满足某一项目即时需求的新知识创造与为提升所属组织的未来项目绩效所采取的学习行动之间。在传统的项目管理文献中，项目通常被视为独特的、不会重复发生的，其实施与过往的项目或未来的项目是相对独立的。"每个项目都是独特的"——这一观念模式激发了组织的信念，即：获得某一项目的学习经验并在后续的项目复制其成功的实践毫无意义。因此，公司在将某一项目的知识转移到后一项目以及更大范围的组织时，时常会苦于组织的失忆（方框10）。

> ## 方框10　独特性项目与重复性项目
>
> 项目涉及一组从独特性任务到重复性任务所构成的任务谱。独特性任务是针对一时的情形，它需要有远见的、灵活的创造行动及实时学习。重复性任务是和现有客户已经实施过多次（如投标、成本控制和风险管理等标准化程序），并会在未来重复执行。人们知道要做什么、如何做并会分享类似的经验和对于特定情形的理解。只有将其置于更广阔的历史情境中，我们才能确实地知道某一项目在整体上是独特的还是重复的。有些项目确实是独特的事业，因为它们代表着母体组织的一个全新体验。然而，其他的多个项目则是重复的，因为它们与之前所实施的项目相差无几。

这两种困境在实践中常常交织在一起，这正如赛多和他的合著者指出的那样，专注的状态意味着团队成员对项目以外的事物不感兴趣；快速的进展意味着人员没有时间反思他们的工作及记住所学习到的教训；自治的状态则意味着项目团队可能正成为一片学习的沃土，迫使别人"重新发明车轮"的同时，也限制了知识向其他项目和公司整体的流动。

现在已经认识到，没有一种组织物种（如灵活机构）能够展现项目中的组织多样性。在《项目社会中的管理和工作》一书中，罗尔夫·伦丁及其合著者提出了项目组织的不同形式，并讨论了它们与工业时代的主流组织有何不同。此处，我们采用最早由乔纳斯·瑟德隆德所提出的简单矩阵图，用以显示不同的临时性和常设性项目导向型组织形式（图11）。通过对单个与多个项目以及单个与多个组织两个维度的区分（比如公司和政

|  | 单个组织 | 多个组织 |
|---|---|---|
| 单个项目 | 单个项目组织 | 项目网络 |
| 多个项目 | 项目导向型组织 | 项目生态 |

图11　项目的组织形式

府部门），这个矩阵图可以帮助我们大致识别出四种类型的项目组织：单个项目组织、项目导向型组织、项目网络及项目生态。在这四类组织中，大多数行业存在着其中的某种或其他的某种组织形式，并涉及不同种类的公司、政府部门、合资企业、政府与公私合作企业及其他机构类型的组织。

## 单个项目组织

单个项目组织通过建立阶段性法人机构或金融机构，以实现明确的目标，并按计划于任务完成时解散。它继承了项目的战略性目标和资金，在任务完成之前并不会被要求产生进一步的收益。尽管如此，在项目实施过程中，传统的资金投入仍是必要的。当完成一艘航空母舰、一部电影、一家医院或一条铁路线路时，单个项目组织将会终止存在。虽然有些组织可能只会存在数周或数月（比如某部主题电影），但是大型公共基础设施和军事项目的组织能存活十年或更长时间的也不鲜见。

单个项目组织鲜少有花时间去形成"组织记忆"、惯例及能力的，而这些则是微软、索尼和谷歌等公司所倚仗的，以实现在变化竞争性环境中的生存、成长和繁盛。在项目过程中所获取和形成的任何知识和学问，在其组织完成任务解散时都将不复存在。此外，也没有时间来培养个人关系和建立信任，而这些都是在公司中人们会花费数年或数十年来予以建立的。但是，对于独立电影制作者这类单个项目组织的极端例子的研究则表明：人们能够发展出"快速信任"，可以弥补在"短暂缘分"型组织中的工作行为。与迪士尼等其他大型工作室不同，一家独立电影公司仅被建立用于一部电影的制作，并会在电影发行后解散。为制作电影而组建的剧组成员之所以能够彼此信赖，协调复杂的独立性任务，是因为他们有着清晰明确的专长和专业职责（比如制作、摄影和舞台设计）。项目的每位成员都知道他们的职责分工，可以像过往一样重复执行专业化任务，并且与新老剧组成员共事时都能做好自己的专业。

为了管理伦敦的大型公共基础设施项目，单个项目组织创造了不同形式，包括公私合作（PPP）、专门组织（SPV）、业主机构及交付伙伴。正如我们在第一章中所见，若干联合体会建立起来并被授予公私合作合同，承担伦敦隧道线路、铁路和医院的设计、建设、融资、运营和维护。作为一个专门组织，铁道线路工程公司（由奥雅纳公司、柏克德工程公司、合乐公司和赛思达公司联合组成）成立于1996年，负责设计和建设高铁一号线，即一条长109公里（65英里）、连接英法海底隧道和伦敦圣潘克拉斯火车站的高速铁路。作为一个完全自治的法人机构，专门组织的相关风险可以相对独立；与新业务单元或新部门相比，它对其投资者或母体组织造成威胁的概率较小。

奥运工程交付局（ODA）设立于2006年。根据议会法案的要求，它是一个英国政府和大伦敦市政府资助和管辖的临时性公共机构。有关法案授予了奥运工程交付局建设奥运会基础设施和场馆的法定权力和职责。雇用了大约220名员工的奥运工程交付局认识到，完全由机构内部人员组建的交付组织不可能拥有足够的资源或按时完成建设，因此它决定任命一位管理整个集群项目的交付伙伴，一个名为"CLM"的私营部门联合体。它在高峰时雇用了超过500名员工，并获得了美国西图公司、奥罗克莱恩公司和梅斯公司三家母公司的支持。CLM联合体之所以被选中，是因为这家联合体的母公司的各种能力都通过以往奥林匹克集群项目和大型基础设施项目的管理得以证明（比如希思罗机场五号航站楼）。奥运工程交付局和CLM联合体在2012年7月27日奥运会开幕以后，大幅度缩减规模，最后也解散了：CLM联合体解散于2013年4月，奥运工程交付局解散于2014年12月。

113

横贯铁路项目本可作为伦敦交通局（TfL）行动规划的一部分来执行的，但是有人担心，如果伦敦交通局更为广泛的需求优先于该项目自身的需求，那么这样一个备受瞩目的项目的进展可能会受到威胁。因此，横贯铁路有限公司被设立为一家独立的企业，以保障其交付人员能够专注于这一有着明确权责和清晰目标的任务。拥有约1200名员工的集成化项目交付团队被建立了起来，它包括业主机构（横贯铁路有限公司）和管理复杂的中段隧道建设的两位交付伙伴。一个是名为"超越"的集群项目合作方，由美国西图公司、AECOM公司和尼科尔斯集团组成的项目联合体；另一个是名为"横贯铁路中段"项目交付合作方，由柏克德公司领导，合乐公司和赛思达公司支持。当项目临近完工时，运营方（伦敦铁路公司）成为集成化项目交付团队中一个非常积极的成员。项目于2019年完工后，业主机构和交付伙伴组织将会解散。

## 项目导向型组织

虽然许多公司依靠项目在竞争激烈和快速变化的市场中创造和开发新产品和服务，但是，它们的主营业务仍是大批量运营作业（第一章）。一个公司或组织之所以被视为"项目导向的"，是因为其大多数的设计、开发和生产活动要满足两方面条件，即：这些活动会以项目的方式开展并服务于客户；这些活动嵌入常设组织中，这些组织在试图保持这类业务的同时，会在每个项目完成时找寻新的工作。在大多数情况下，项目导向型组织的员工有着相对稳定的位置，许多人还会有长期专属合同。

根据明茨伯格的观察（第四章），我们可以区别两类项目导向型组织。有些是用于满足它们内部的项目需求，包括一些大型私营企业（例如石油和天然气行业中的壳牌石油公司和英国石油公司）、政府部门以及美国国防部、美国国家航空航天局和伦敦交通局等各种公有资助机构。与此相比，还有些组织则服务外部客户，它们广泛存在于可以提供一次性单件或小批量的客户定制产品和服务的行业。这些行业包括资本品（比如国防、航空航天、铁路机车车辆、工厂自动化系统、核电站、海上油气平台、造船、软件和电信）、创意产业（比如电影工作室、音乐、电子游戏和电视节目制作）、公共基础设施（比如医院、公路、铁路和学校）、专业服务（比如广告和咨询服务）、建筑工程以及高额定制产品（比如一级方程式赛车、私人飞机和豪华游艇）。

项目导向型组织有时会栖于大型企业和政府机构的部门、业务单元以及附属机构中。作为一家总部设在东京的全球性公司，东芝公司要以多元化企业的方式持续地生存和成长，就要依靠大批量生产运营（例如消费电子产品和家用电器），并需要获得一系列重大的高额资本品项目（比如高铁交通和核电厂）作为保障。负责铁路、公路、供水和其他市政设施网络的政府部门，不仅拥有庞大的组织机构负责运营和提供服务，其内部也设有项目导向型部门，与私营部门承包商一起合作，采购和管理重大项目。比如，伦敦地铁公司（伦敦交通局的附属机构之一）不

项目管理

仅负责运营地铁列车和车站，还负责管理新线路的建设或车站翻新等重大投资项目。

在建筑和专业服务领域中时常可以发现，项目导向型企业的活动完全是建立在任一特定时刻都能管理数十个或成百个项目的基础上的，即便其项目数量没有达到数千个。它们必须平衡各个项目的非连续性要求和公司长期战略性商业目标。例如：作为一家美国大型土木工程、建筑和项目管理公司，柏克德公司曾经担任某些全球最大规模项目的总承包商，这些项目包括胡佛水坝、旧金山湾区快速交通系统、波士顿中央干线/隧道、英法海底隧道、朱比利延长线及横贯铁路。柏克德公司在2016年就雇用了约5.5万人管理其在160个国家的2.5万个项目，它具有充分的能力来应对大型项目的各种需求，包括项目规划、融资、采购、设计、建设及承包商管理。

在项目导向型企业中，各种组织结构则被用于协调嵌入其中的项目，从一端的某个或多个职能团队或部门实施项目的职能型组织，到另一端的项目导向型的专门组织（第三章）。类似奥雅纳公司的组织大多都采用某种矩阵型结构形式，用于整合职能活动和项目活动。虽然单一的项目导向型组织擅长解决问题、推动创新，并能关注每个客户的个性化要求，但是与矩阵型结构相比，它们有时会表现得效率不高。这一情况往往出现在协调关联资源、进行项目母体组织内的跨项目知识分享以及实现组织范围内的效率提升时。项目导向型公司的许多组织单元是由强有力的个人所领导。这些人被戴维·甘恩及其合著者称为"项目巨头"，他们会争取资源，以支持项目的存续及新的创业构想。

当项目类似且呈重复性时，项目导向型组织能发展其智力资源、专长和惯例，从而能在其技术或市场基础上赢得、协调和有效地管理多个项目。当项目任务呈重复性时，具备"项目能力"的组织能以更可靠、更高效的方式执行相关任务。项目能力既包括了项目团队成员所占有的隐性知识（或个人经验），又包括了体现于标准化项目管理程序、流程、工具和导则中的编码化（或显性）知识。比如，当约翰·伊根爵士从之前的捷豹汽车公司首席执行官的岗位离任并加入BAA公司时，他惊奇地发现：每个机场建设项目都被"视作一张白纸"，新组建的团队"倾向于从第一性原则开始进行持续不断的思考"。为了避免管理者将各个项目视作独特的，BAA公司依据导则（基于日本汽车制造商的精益过程）开发相关能力，执行标准化的和可重复的时序型任务、里程碑和阶段关口，并实现了具有成本效益优势、可盈利项目的交付。

正如奥雅纳公司的东滩项目及其所进行的可持续城市设计业务开发尝试所示（第四章），当通过创建"先锋项目"实现突破性创新时，某一公司的项目能力会偶尔重新配置，以跟上快速变化的环境。作为技术和市场在未来将会如何进行演化的标志，先锋项目常常能揭示某一组织项目能力的不足之处，它是在为稳定的客户群和市场实施项目的数年中所形成的。先锋项目的成员会探索潜在的解决方案、参与试错学习，并时常会忽略既有的程序，从而创造新的产品、预期进展、捕捉创新思想，并开发新的项目管理结构、工具和流程。当某一新类型的项目涌现、实施并持续数年或数十年，用以满足已有客户的可预测和明确了解的要求时，先锋项目有时则意味着"项目纪元"的开端。

在培育项目能力的过程中，先锋项目所创造的新知识可以

突破项目的范围继续拓展和重复使用，用以支持公司在新市场
中的增长。比如：对于签署了合同金额最大的参建企业奥罗克
莱恩公司而言，希思罗机场五号航站楼就是一个先锋项目。通
过与BAA公司及其他供应商的紧密合作，奥罗克莱恩公司协助
识别、开发并引入了多项创新流程，用以交付五号航站楼项目。
这些流程包括集成化集群项目团队工作、数字化设计技术、项目
协作软件及场外装配式施工方法。奥罗克莱恩公司在五号航站
楼项目所获得的能力，在此后得到进一步发展、锻炼和提升，这
是由于该公司作为主要承包商和交付伙伴承担了后续的一系列
伦敦和世界其他地方的超大项目，包括圣潘克拉斯火车站扩建、
2012年伦敦奥运会项目和横贯铁路。

## 项目网络

许多项目都涉及与外部参与方某种形式的合作，而最为复
杂的项目则必须协调由承包商和分包商组成的大型网络或临时
性联合体。词语"网络"隐含着这样一层意思，即项目包括了在
某一特定时间段内为共同任务工作的多个组织。它引发了对于
项目中个人和组织成员之间的关系或联系以及互动频率、持续
时间和密集度的关注。

项目网络存在于各种各样的私营部门和公共部门，比如航
空航天、海上油气平台、国防、大学研究、广告、生物技术及工程
建设。它们的范围有小有大，从若干合作伙伴参与的小型项目，
到涉及数十家承包商、数以千计分包商的超大项目，比如五号航
站楼、高铁一号线（HS1）、2012年伦敦奥运会项目及横贯铁路。
它们的工期也长短不一，从制作电视纪录片的短短几日、几周或

几个月，直到某些重大国防系统项目的数十年。例如：联合战斗机开发项目早在1993年就已经开始了，但是至今也没有投入使用。组织在项目网络的生命周期中时常扮演着不同的角色。以大型土木工程项目为例，业主方组织、总承包商或交付伙伴必须在整个工期过程内履职，而其他组织只要参与设计或建设的特定阶段就可以了。

在大型项目网络中，一个或多个组织会负责领导整体工作，协调各方的工作并安排其计划。正如我们在第三章中所见，系统集成的能力（由美国的国防和航空航天企业率先试点的实践）在复杂项目中尤为重要。业主方组织可以发展自身的这一能力，任命一家总承包商，或是与交付伙伴一起合作。比如：2012年伦敦奥运会项目就包括了70多个由总承包商管理的独立项目。其设计和建造任务涉及14幢临时建筑（例如国际广播中心）和永久建筑（例如奥林匹克体育场、自行车馆和水上运动中心）、20公里道路、26座桥梁、13公里隧道及占地80公顷的园区和市政基础设施。通过紧密的合作，业主（ODA）及其交付伙伴（CLM）会协调整个场馆和基础设施工程的设计、建设、集成和交付工作。ODA负责整个项目的进度，并处理与受影响的外部相关方和近邻的关系。而CLM则管理整个集群项目和各主要场馆的总承包商，协调它们之间的界面，将其集成于奥林匹克公园基础设施，并为奥运会举办做准备。

除了这些协调挑战以外，还需要建立项目网络中参与方之间的协作机制。近年来，英国大型基础设施项目的出资方开始尝试在业主与承包商之间建立更为紧密的协作关系。根据BAA公司在五号航站楼项目中所尝试过的方法，越来越多的业主受到启发,不再单一地依靠固定总价合同来实施复杂项目。这一合同会对承包商延误予以惩罚,助长敌对关系,甚至还会造成无法挽回的冲突。正如希思罗机场所示,业主采用了关系合同。它可以与供应商建立长期的协作,平衡好奖惩机制,减少机会主义行为,并对创新和问题解决行为予以奖励。类似的协作形式存在于世界其他地方,比如美国的"集成化集群项目团队"和澳大利亚的"合作联盟"。

以横贯铁路为例,在其不同的目标、时间范围及业主和承包商的优先性之间就存在着一种精心缔造的平衡。业主交付组织专注于长期目标的实现,包括准时、安全地并按预算要求完成项目,处理与外部相关方的关系,并将一条"世界级铁路线"移交给运营方。有鉴于此,各承包商比较紧迫的优先事项都是完成各自的工作和实现利润。为了铁路的建设,横贯铁路与多家企业和联合体签署了60多个主要合同,例如:合同总价达4亿英镑的西部隧道合同被授予由巴姆纳托尔公司、法罗里奥集团和基尔集团组成的联合体(BFK)。合同总价从低至100万英镑的设计服务合同,到总价高达5亿多英镑的隧道和系统合同。业主依靠协作型合同和不同形式的劝说和个人关系,激励承包商(必要时会与承包商的首席执行官直接沟通来施加影响)并使项目保持正常运作至完成。为了解决问题和争议,横贯铁路交付伙伴的成员会在现场与位于同一地点的集成化集群项目团队中的承包商一起工作。

在"全球性项目"中,实现协作是极具挑战的。这些项目从在单一明确地点实施的活动(比如2012年伦敦奥运会),到空间上分散于全球各地的项目(比如波音777型客机项目)。随着公司将其活动逐步外包及国际化,全球项目开始成为理查德·斯科特及其合著者所描述的"全球市场中跨组织协作的节点"。在全球项目中,让各参与方的利益保持一致是非常困难的,这是因为它们面临着制度复杂性、文化多元性以及持续的矛盾冲突。各种组织和文化背景的参与方栖于不同的"思想世界",它时常会造成在同一地点工作的团队之间的摩擦。从美国西图公司的实例可以发现:正如在2012年伦敦奥运会项目期间的成功实践一样,在面对巴拿马运河扩建和现代化升级项目中的跨文化情境时,位于同一地点的集成化集群项目团队工作仍备受挑战。这一项目投资达53.5亿英镑,发起于2006年。在当地客户(巴拿马运河管理局)雇用了美国西图公司后,冲突很快就产生了。关于谁应当领导项目并为成果负责的协商工作,有时会极其紧张,难以解决。这一问题的部分原因在于双方有着相当不同的期望以及制度和文化背景。

## 项目生态

我们所讨论的组织通常是航空航天、广告、软件和咨询等多种行业中的参与者,它们依靠项目来实施它们的大多数生产活动。项目商业网络、地域集群及生态系统等各种名词,都是用于描述这些组织的集合,它们都参与到彼此的以往、当下和未来的项目中。它们可能包括客户、承包商、分包商、咨询顾问、制造商、投资者、大学、资助机构及其他相关方。在项目导向型行业中,组织会建立不同形式的合作伙伴关系,或是与某些项目参与方建立公平的合同关系,同时还会通过竞争赢得新合同并提升自身在其他方面的竞争优势。组织实体之间的关系,通常会随

着一个项目到下一个项目的变化而发生改变。以铁道车辆的供

货商为例,阿尔斯通、庞巴迪、东芝或者西门子,可能是一个城市轨道交通系统项目的总承包商或另一个项目的分包商。在公共部门项目(例如高速公路、铁路和医疗)中,政府部门通常扮演着项目投资者和业主的重要角色,以保障公共机构和私营机构能够共同工作,实现公共政策的目标。

在项目导向型行业中,是可以进行学习和能力开发的,这是因为:在多个项目中合作过的参与方之间所建立的持续关系和信任,会提供共享式学习和过往经验的储备,它们能够在参与方共事时被激活。这种在共事合作时获得的经验被称为"过去的影子",它会决定哪些参与方会被选择参与未来项目的合作。参与方对于将会再次共事的期望和希冀被称为"未来的投影",它们是对当前项目中良好表现和实施的一种激励。例如:BAA公司通过设立五年的"框架协议",与参与希思罗机场及其他机场当前和未来项目的多家供应商构建了建设性的合作关系。将其系列项目中的供应商视为长期合作伙伴,降低了BAA公司的协调成本,并为供应商提供它所需的稳定性,从而使它们能够与时俱进地持续提升能力和改进绩效表现。

赫尔诺特·格拉布赫引入了"项目生态"的概念,来描述地域性项目活动集群中由个人、组织和机构关系所形成的密集型网络,比如:聚集在伦敦苏荷区的广告公司,或是为了规划和建设2012年伦敦奥运会项目而调用的海量人员、公司和机构。项目生态的四个层次,即核心团队、公司、知识社群及个人网络,不仅提供了一个由个体能力、组织能力和制度能力组成的集合,还有项目经验的记忆可被再次激活并用于管理当前的项目和为未来做准备(方框11)。

122

**方框11　项目生态层次**

核心团队层次是指成员个体所承担的专业角色和任务，以及他们如何在项目团队中进行协作。在"累积式生态"中，团队会在持续性项目中保持稳定，以实现绩效的渐进式提升。在"颠覆式生态"中，团队的组成将会调整以吸纳必需的有新想法的人员，从而造就激进变革。

公司层次是指能通过应用以往实践检验的有效实践来提升绩效的项目能力（参见"项目导向型组织"）。当需要创新方案来满足业主方的需求时，新的技术和实践组合可以共同发挥作用。BAA公司的五号航站楼项目即是一例。

知识社群层次是指跨越公司边界的知识。它们是由业主方专业人士、供应商或企业集团所建立的，可以共享非涉密的信息、案例研究及其他经验。

个人网络层次是指超越项目和业务关系的人员关系和联系。当人们被要求去解决具体的问题或提供支持和必要的建议时，这一时常留存于项目背景中的层次会被激活。

在现存的记忆中，一些最为宏大的土木工程项目是伦敦在21世纪初开始实施的，其目标是更新和拓展城市在维多利亚时期建设的日趋老旧的基础设施，实现城市区域整体开发，以及建设新的航空和铁路交通线。它们包括多项备受瞩目的项目，比如高铁一号线、五号航站楼、2012年伦敦奥运会项目、横贯铁路、泰晤士潮路隧道、高铁二号线（投资数十亿英镑，从伦敦经伯明翰到利兹和曼彻斯特的高铁线路）。参与这些项目并在其间流

123

转的个人、团队、承包商和业主所构成网络的拓展，不仅有助于建立伦敦欣欣向荣的超大项目生态，并能在创新项目交付模式领域形成世界声誉。

由于将总部设于伦敦市区及附近，罗杰斯·斯特克·哈伯合伙人公司、奥雅纳工程公司、巴尔弗贝蒂公司、梅斯公司、科斯坦公司、美国西图公司及奥罗克莱恩公司等建筑、咨询、建设、集群项目管理和土木工程公司都彼此邻近。由于它们过于依赖政府基础设施合同，这些公司的高管都与项目出资方、政府官员和政治领导人培养起紧密的关系。它们从一开始就能获知新建议书的信息，处于新任务竞标中的有利位置，通常还会与其当地伙伴中的某个在竞标中进行合作。对于已通过某一超大项目的成功造就了能力和声誉的某些公司来说，它们倾向于以不同的形式在未来再次参与同类项目。以奥罗克莱恩公司为例，它是五号航站楼项目中最大的承包商，也是2012年伦敦奥运会项目的交付伙伴，还被任命为横贯铁路托特纳姆宫路车站的承包商及泰晤士潮路隧道中段施工联合体的成员之一。企业和业主机构的核心团队，通常也会在一个又一个的项目中进行迁移。例如，在完成2012年伦敦奥运会项目的工作后，奥运工程交付局的整个采购团队继续服务于横贯铁路项目。

从高管层到项目经理层和雇员层的很多个体都是"项目牧民"，他们在伦敦超大项目迁徙过程中发现新知识并共享专长。以五号航站楼项目总监安德鲁·沃斯滕霍姆为例，他后来成为横贯铁路的总经理；横贯铁路的项目总监安迪·米切尔后来成为泰晤士潮路隧道项目的总经理；2012年伦敦奥运会项目和横贯铁路的高级项目经理马克·瑟斯顿成为高铁二号线的总经

124

理。通常，他们的专业身份与项目之间的联系，远比与其长期雇主组织之间的联系要更为紧密。多位服务于2012年伦敦奥运工程交付伙伴CLM联合体的管理者必须适应"头戴两顶帽子"的双重身份：他们知道自己最终将加入母公司，但是他们在项目实施时与项目之间的联系更为紧密。在曾经共事过的人员中，他们之间的个人联系和关系会在各个新的超大项目中扩散，从而促进知识、想法与成功实践之间的循环流动。

在伦敦的若干超大项目中，近来开始推动创建一种系统化正式方法的想法来驾驭创新，从而能更为高效地完成项目并创造更好的成果，这类似于第二章伊利运河项目中以非正式的方式所实现的。2013年，横贯铁路项目设立了一个创新计划，鼓励项目中的承包商、供应商和其他相关方去开发、实践和共享新想法、新技术和新经验。一个内部团队负责管理创新计划，并建立了一个数据库，用以记录项目成员提交的所有新想法、建议和方案。2016年10月，横贯铁路和泰晤士潮路隧道项目的总经理们利用他们的个人网络和关系，组建了一个业主方领导的名为"基础设施行业创新平台"的知识社群，并获得了总承包商、政府资助机构和名牌大学的支持。为了避免以往实践过的创新在各个超大项目中再次孤立地开展，该平台（最初是为横贯铁路项目而建立的数据库和协作方法）被建立起来，与伦敦和英国其他地方的超大项目分享新想法、新实践、新技术。

在第七章中，我们将要考察这些新的、正在涌现中的项目组织形式是否能够应对21世纪社会所面对的重大挑战。

125

126

第七章

# 重返未来

项目管理出现于第二次世界大战期间及之后，与此同时，系统方法也被发明出来，用以协调武器和航空航天系统开发及其进度计划安排。20世纪60年代末和70年代，由专业团体正式建立起来的传统的、基于系统的模型，将一致性、标准化的程序和准则引入到了项目管理中，它是基于如下的预期：市场和技术是被充分了解的，且项目能够被充分筹备以满足稳定和可预测的条件。这一模型假设所有的项目都可以通过类似的方式进行管理，这一点被近年来出版的著作论文所质疑，这使得我们重新思考、发明和建构项目管理。在今天，少有项目是可预测且不会发生变化的。在大多数时候，计划必须是现实且灵活的，以满足在开始时难以充分了解的未来，同时计划还必须是可调整的，并对项目实施过程中出现的未曾预料到的、新的和快速变化的条件予以响应。现在已经认识到：由数字化技术支持的项目管理适应性模型，对于21世纪复杂的、创新性的和难以预测的项目来说是必需的。尽管如此，关于项目会受到其计划和实施的环境动态性的影响的想法并不新鲜。美国早期武器系统项目的领导者们——格罗夫斯、施里弗、拉莫、拉伯恩和韦布——都认识到:不确定性、复杂性和紧迫性的程度对于不同类型的项目而言,是存在差异的,每一个项目必须以灵活的、适应性的方式予以管理。直到近来,项目管理似乎忘却了这一根本。

127

## 棘手问题

在21世纪,项目导向型组织的趋势正日益显现,管理者们认识到:创新是竞争性全球市场的规则,而组织也期望对持续性的项目流进行管理。大型组织逐渐被临时性项目组织、小组和团队所渗透,它们突然地出现并随后消失。对于擅长从过去学习、发展项目能力并能与合作伙伴在适应性协作型团队中共事的那些组织来说,它们能更好地为未来做好准备。但是,现有项目管理结构、流程和工具是否足够应付当今社会所面临的艰难挑战呢?譬如日趋老龄化的人口、贫困、恐怖主义、移民和难民危机以及其他。

也许我们的时代最为重大且具有挑战性的"棘手问题",即难以通过明确的方案予以界定的问题,是由快速城市化和气候变化二者的叠加造成的。大批量生产的兴起、汽车和飞机的出现,以及以化石燃料(占2014年全球能源需求的80%左右)所驱动的廉价能源为基础的城市化模式,使我们开始了过去二百年的工业化进程,这从根本上改变了我们的气候系统。目前的预测表明:到21世纪末,诸如二氧化碳和甲烷等温室气体产生的温室效应,将会造成一种不同于工业化之前的气候环境。受到气候系统的不确定性及其社会、政治和经济应对措施的影响,我们未来气候的不确定性意味着：未来的项目组织必须更具创造性、灵活性及快节奏。

城市人口的数量有望从2015年全球人口总量的50%上升到2050年的70%。麦肯锡全球研究所2013年的一项研究估计：2013年至2030年间，57万亿美元将花费在全球基础设施投资上。许多超大基础设施项目正在发起和实施，以便跟上中国、印度等新兴工业化国家中前所未有的加速发展的城市化节奏。在诸如伦敦、柏林、纽约等城市，它们也需要替换日益老旧的建筑楼宇，进行城市更新开发，并更新工业时代建设的分散基础设施。它们需要设计和建设面向未来的、具有生态可持续性的"智慧城市"，通过使用数字传感器和监控设备来控制交通、通信、给排水和其他市政设施，并使得能源供应更具适应性，以满足变化的需求。

在人口高度密集城市区域的超大项目，比冷战时期的系统项目可能更具挑战性。比如，阿波罗项目尽管很复杂且不确定，但它是一个有着几乎无限资源的封闭系统，用于实现明确坚定的目标（在十年后使人类安全地登陆月球），这在很大程度上避免了政治干预以及来自社会、经济和环境方面的其他压力。而如波士顿"大开挖"、2012年伦敦奥运会等超大城市项目则是开放的系统。它们有着可以超越系统的可渗透边界，必须包容存在分歧的、常有利益纠纷和冲突的多个相关方。

我们会将新的或重建后的城市和基础设施设计为具有必要韧性的，以应对气候变化，并在诸如2011年日本福岛核事故等意外事件发生时予以响应。用于实现单一目标的曼哈顿式的整体项目，不太可能用于应对那些有关减缓和适应气候变化的问题，

129 它们是广泛的、分散的且持续演化的。托马斯·休斯建议：各种各样在地理上分散的"生态技术项目"，比如碳捕捉与存储、低成本太阳能电池、洪水风险、潮汐能及生态城市项目，都需要通过低碳和再生能源的驱动而实现后工业化的生态可持续社会的转型。

我们将通过以下问题来结束本书，即：未来应当如何配置项目，以应对在全球市场中创新和竞争所带来的社会挑战和巨大压力。多年以前，阿尔文·托夫勒预测：随着社会向后工业化时代的转型，适应性项目组织通过问题解决团队的自我激励及博学成员之间的横向权责分配，将会挑战并最终取代自上而下的、刻板的科层制。政府部门、公司和个人已经发现很难适应这种新型组织形式，而转型也已持续了较长一段时间，但可能并未达到托夫勒的期望。在本书中，部分实例和案例研究提供了未来项目将是何种面貌的迹象。

## 后工业化的项目

在后工业化的未来，项目成功不再是仅仅评测团队或组织满足进度、预算和专门要求的具体程度。它还取决于运营的成果能否为出资方、客户、运营者和用户创造额外的价值。盖里在毕尔巴鄂设计的古根海姆博物馆项目所实现的，远比按照进度和预算要求建成一幢标志性建筑要多得多。它振兴了一个正日渐羸弱的城市。苹果公司在创造 iPod 和 iTunes 平台上的成功改变了人们倾听音乐的方式，并造就了一家世界上最为成功的公司。许多公司和政府部门发现：明确定义信息技术系统、医院或
130 铁路的运营绩效的标书会创造出更美好、更创新的成果。比如，

针对一定量列车车辆的投标邀请，将会形成一个区间范围的报价，但不大可能激励创新。与之相反，正如我们在阿尔斯通的案例中所见的，对于"车辆可用性"的需求，可能产生各式各样的列出了创新方式的建议书，可以实现一条线路列车在较长时间内的建设、运营、融资和维护。

强有力的出资方和业主组织会在项目开始时，就花时间定义项目目标并选择实施它的最佳方式。对以往项目的系统性学习，有助于标定风险、形成对其响应办法的据实判断，并制定切实可行的工期和投资估算。当面临伦敦希思罗机场五号航站楼建设的不确定性时，BAA公司吸取了以往建设机场项目的教训，并决定创造一个灵活交付模式。它是基于非常柔性的合同，并依靠协作型团队，解决了紧急问题并利用了起初并没有预见到的机会。与此相对的是，2012年伦敦奥运工程交付模式则采用了多种合同，以应对在建设奥林匹克公园中标准化与个性化建筑组合中的多种不确定性。

在前期定义阶段，出资方或母体组织将会提出一种令人信服的愿景，说明项目是如何满足既有客户需求或创造新的市场机遇的。运营者和用户将会更多地参与到前期阶段，从而保障他们的要求、关注点及优先事项在最终成果的设计中得到充分的满足。以波音公司为例，它仔细倾听了八家主要航空公司的需求和优先级，从而确定它们的要求并调整了777型客机的设计。但是，埃隆·马斯克也非常清楚，有时不倾听现有客户的声音也很重要。比如，直到最近，汽车制造商还不太愿意开发电动汽车和无人驾驶技术，因为它们认为客户对此没有购买的需求。131当20世纪20年代以来的行业内第一家新创公司，成功开发出来全电动的特斯拉汽车时，这一突破才出现。正如我们所见，在快速变化的市场中竞争的企业，比如苹果、微软和谷歌，都有着平衡的项目组合，以了解如何保住现有的市场以及何时开拓新市场。

组织需要动态灵活的团队，有能力在项目规划和实施阶段解决问题、实现创新及适应环境变化。项目领导者要善于建立协作型团队并克服矛盾和创造性紧张点，这些通常都是有着不同的想法、文化价值观、个性和竞争优先级的多样化队伍开始共同工作时出现的。奥雅纳公司的东滩项目团队和北京水立方项目团队成员都曾必须学习如何在多学科、多元文化的团队中共同工作，他们或是在同一地点办公，或是分布于多个大洲。这些团队会涌现和解散，以响应高要求客户的变化需求，以及工作进展中意想不到的问题。精益和敏捷过程可以拓展到其他行业，这些行业中的项目团队在快速变化、创新性的市场竞争中，必须能够同时开发出多个备选方案和并行工作，并实时地适应与客户和出资方高管频繁互动的反馈。

在以往，超大项目有时会在某个基础设施系统（比如伦敦朱比利线中先进的信号系统技术）的设计中融入新技术，但是项目一旦开始后，很少会去尝试新想法、新实践和新技术。实施过程中的创新被视为与进度延误和成本超支相关的一个不必要的负向风险。相反，未来的出资方和业主方必须拥抱创新，作为设计出更好成果和提升超大项目完成效率的一个正向机会。他们需要通过利用现有的知识和采取可靠的技术来改进绩效，这些知识和技术在其他地方都已得到过检验。但是，他们也需要认识132 到：尝试新技术和新实践的不确定性是可以最小化的，这可以通过在引入之前对相关备选方案进行尝试性的开发、测试、演练和学习来实现。例如,在横贯铁路中,为了创造、分享、实施新的和已有的技术、想法及实践而设立的创新计划,正被应用到在伦敦及其他地方的超大项目中。

　　未来的系统集成者需要能够设计和集成日趋复杂和相互依存的基础设施系统。以高层建筑和核电站建设为代表的许多复杂项目,将通过场外工厂生产的更廉价、更精准的标准组件的灵活组合来实现模块化,并在运到现场后实现更安全高效的组装。包括组件、子系统和系统在内的项目各部分将会被设计作为一个集成化整体进行工作,以实现可持续低碳的高效运营绩效目标的要求。奥雅纳公司就做到了这些,它阐述了一个生态可持续或智慧城市的社会和技术组件及系统(比如给排水、能源、交通、治理、文化、教育、通信和住房)在整个系统开始运作以后彼此之间是如何互动的。在系统建设过程中,集成者将会更多与系统内部和外部相关方进行合作。在伦敦的许多超大项目中,业主方组织提供了与政府部门、地方当局、市政设施、商业、社区及其他相关方所有外部关系的单一联络处,同时交付伙伴则须专注于相互关联活动所构成的集群项目的内部管理,它是由承包商和分包商组成的大型网络所实施的。

　　在数字技术的支持下,未来的项目将会与信息数据共生,以协调产品系统的设计、建设、移交和运营,并对环境中的任何变化予以实时响应。在同一地点工作和分布于不同地点的虚拟团队,都拥有同一个数字模型,从而可以可视化复杂产品的最终设计,提前发现部件之间的冲突和碰撞,测试虚拟原型,并识别出装配和建设之前允许设计变更的最后时刻。通过创建一个可以准确显示建筑的供电系统、供暖系统和制冷系统等组件位置的数据库，数字技术的用途可以拓展到资产运营维护。随着设计师、建造方和用户之间的传统边界日益模糊，弗兰克·盖里也在使用自己的数字化项目软件来控制在这一协作过程中的建设成本。在未来，项目会使用头戴式"增强现实"技术，它可以将电脑生成图像置于现实世界影像之上而对其进行补充。在配备智能眼镜以后，设计师能够从不同的有利位置监控产品，将三维影像覆于其上，并重新调整虚拟组件的位置。以全球性建筑和工程公司 AECOM 为例，它采用微软公司生产的 HoloLens 头戴式设备，帮助设计师在复杂几何外形建筑的数字化展示附近进行走动审查。

对于在项目中工作的个人而言，后工业化的未来将会带来新的挑战和机遇。许多组织将充溢着暂时性团队及流动性更强的个体。与以往相比，同事之间的关系不会持久、更为短暂。人员需要在每个临时性工作中建立短暂紧密的关系，并学习承受更加持久关系的消逝。他们必须适应频繁地在一个又一个的项目中被重新分配和流动。随着每个新的变化，个人必须重新自我定位。每个变化都带来了新的学习需求，并会抑制个体的适应性，从而造成社会和心理的紧张点。但是，其他人则会在这种临时的、快速变化的世界中蓬勃成长。尽管职业生涯曾被定义为对于某个或多个常设组织的忠诚度，但越来越多的人将会在他们的职业生涯中在一个又一个项目之间愉快地迁徙。正如托夫勒所预测的那样，项目对于那些喜欢在更具挑战性和创造性的环境中工作的个人更具吸引力，这些人"热衷解决问题"并被鼓励进行创新。他们需要开始思考他们的工作、日常活动，甚至于将个人的雄心抱负作为项目予以管理。

# 索 引

（条目后的数字为原书页码，
见本书边码）

## A

adaptive project 适应性项目 7, 18, 61, 69, 78, 86, 90, 106, 127, 130, 132

adhocracy 灵活机构 9, 70—72, 111

administrative adhocracy 行政灵活机构 71—72

agile project management 敏捷项目管理 101—102, 132

airline customers 航空公司乘客 77, 96—97, 131

Allen, Thomas J. 托马斯·J. 艾伦 70

alliance and partnership project 联盟及伙伴合作项目 92

Alstom Transport 阿尔斯通交通公司 9

ambidexterity 互惠性（互补性）96

Apollo Programme 阿波罗项目 54—57, 60, 72

  Boeing Company 波音公司 56

  contractors 承包商 54

  cost of moon landing 登月的成本 54

  contracts 合同 56

  incentive contracts 激励性合同 56

  Kennedy, John F. 约翰·F. 肯尼迪 54

  matrix organization 矩阵型组织 55

  Mueller, George 乔治·米勒 55

  NASA Project Development Plan 美国国家航空航天局项目开发计划 55

  Phillips, Samuel C. 塞缪尔·C. 菲利普斯 55

  system integration 系统集成 54
  参见 Webb, James E.

Apple 苹果公司 7, 130

  digital hub 数字化中心 7, 91—92

  Jobs, Steve 史蒂夫·乔布斯 91—92

  portfolio 项目组合 7

ARPANET 美国高级研究项目局 61

array (system of systems) project 系统集合项目 79—80

Arup 奥雅纳公司 62—66, 116, 132, 133

  Arup, Ove 奥韦·奥雅纳 11, 62

  Beijing 2008 Olympics Water Cube 2008 年北京奥运会水立方游泳馆 74

  Blair, Tony 托尼·布莱尔 65

  computer aided design 计算机辅助设计 62

  Integrated Resource Model 集成化资源模型 66

  matrix organization 矩阵型组织 65

  Sydney Opera House 悉尼歌剧院 62, 66

  Total Design philosophy 总体设计哲学 62
  参见 Dongtan eco-city project

assembly project 装配式项目 79

Association for Project Management (APM) 项目管理协会 57

Athens Olympic Games 2004 2004

年雅典奥运会 17

Atlas project 宇宙神项目 13, 39, 44—54, 55, 57, 60, 61

  AVCO manufacturing Corporation AVCO 制造公司 50

  Change Control Board 变更控制委员会 51

  Consolidated Vultee Aircraft Corporation (Convair) 康韦尔公司 47, 51—52

  contractors 承包商 47—50

  digital computer 数字化电脑 50

  Eisenhower, Dwight D. 德怀特·D. 艾森豪威尔 45

  Glenn L. Martin Company 格伦·L. 马丁公司 47, 52

  matrix organization 矩阵型组织 51—52

  Minuteman "民兵"导弹 45, 55

  prime contractor 总承包商 46

  project officer 项目办公室人员 47, 49, 50

  project manager 项目经理 47, 50

  Ramo-Wooldridge 拉莫-伍尔德里奇公司 45—50, 55

  special project office 特别项目办公室 45

  systems engineering 系统工程 46—49

  systems integrator 系统集成者 46—51

  Teapot Committee 茶壶委员会 45—46

  Titan "泰坦"导弹 45, 47, 49

  Western Development Division 西部研发部 45—46, 48

Wooldridge, Dean 迪安·伍尔德里奇 45

  参见 Ramo, Simon; Schreiver, Bernard

atomic bomb 原子弹 13, 40

autonomy versus integration dilemma 自治与集成的困境 109

autonomous team structure 自治团队结构 95—96, 105

## B

BAA (formerly British Airports) BAA 公司（前身为英国机场管理局）104, 109, 119, 122, 131

baseline plan 基准计划 58

Bechtel 柏克德公司 103—104, 114, 116

Bennis, Warren 沃伦·本尼斯 67

Bernstein, Peter 彼得·伯恩斯坦 19

blitz project 突击项目 82

BMW 宝马公司 15

Boeing 波音公司 56, 92

Boeing 767 波音 767 型客机 92

Boeing 777 project 波音 777 型客机项目 14, 86—89, 95, 131

  Conduit, Phil 菲尔·康杜伊特 87

  Gang of Eight airlines 八大航空公司联盟 97

  Mulally, Alan 艾伦·马拉利 87, 95

  Working Together 共同工作 87, 89

bootlegging projects 未经许可的项目 93

Boston Big Dig 波士顿"大开挖" 35, 129

Boston Central Artery/Tunnel 波士

项目管理

顿中央干线 / 隧道 35—37, 60, 129

Brassey, Thomas 托马斯·布拉西 11

breakthrough project 突破性项目 91—93,
97—99

    autonomy 自治性 98—99

    car industry 汽车行业 99—101

Brunel, Isambard Kingdom 伊桑巴
德·金德姆·布鲁内尔 10

Brusoni, Stefano 斯特凡诺·布鲁索
尼 80

bureaucracy 科层制 10, 12, 14, 130

budget 预算 58

Burns, T. 伯恩斯 67


## C

Capital Hospitals 首都医院 16

car industry 汽车行业 83—86, 99—101

Castells, Manuel 曼纽尔·卡斯泰尔
14

CH2M 美国西图公司 113—114, 121

Challenge disaster "挑战者"号事故
59

Champion 第一领导 19, 34, 84

Chandler Margaret K. 玛格丽特·K.
钱德勒 60

Change Control Board 变更控制委员
会 51

Christensen, Clayton 克莱顿·克里
斯滕森 100—101

chronological time 时序 81

cities 城市群 60, 129

civil engineering 土木工程 10, 19—20,
33, 38

Clark, Kim 金·克拉克 83, 91, 94—95

client 业主 11, 63, 65, 113—114, 119—121,
123, 125

climate change 气候变化 128—130

Clinton, De Witt 德维特·克林顿
22—23, 25—26, 31, 34

closed system 封闭的系统 60, 129

Coca-Cola 可口可乐公司 15

Cold War 冷战 39, 60

collaboration 合作 6, 28, 71, 74, 85, 87,
105, 119—120

co-location 同一地点 47, 65, 70, 74—75,
94—95, 121, 133—134

Columbia accident "哥伦比亚"号事
故 59

complexity 复杂性 79—81

compression strategy 紧缩策略 72—73

concurrency 并行性 50

concurrent development 并行开发
39, 50, 68—69, 81, 132

configuration management 配置管理
51

context 情境 18, 108—109

contingency plans 应急计划 54, 56, 58,
76, 78

contingency theory 权变理论 67, 75,
82

contract variation 合同变更 28

contractor 承包商 12, 20, 27, 41, 47—50,
103, 105, 115, 119—120, 124—125

contracts 合同 3, 27—29, 56—57, 76, 78—79,
103, 105—106, 119—120

cooperation 协作 69, 119—120, 132

    Alliancing 合作联盟 120

Integrated Program Team 集成化集群项目团队 120

coordination 协调 6, 50, 68—69, 73
参见 interdependency

cost 成本 3—4, 35—37, 55, 58, 104—105

creativity 创新性 6, 37, 132

cross-functional team 跨职能团队 69, 71, 94

Crossrail project 横贯铁路项目 106—107, 114, 124

  client delivery organization 业主交付组织 120

  contracts 合同 120

Crossrail innovation programme 横贯铁路创新计划 125—126

Crossrail Limited 横贯铁路有限公司 114

## D

Datamaster project 数据大师项目 98

Defoe, Daniel 丹尼尔·笛福 2

DeMeyer, Arnoud 阿尔努·德梅耶 82

derivative project 衍生型项目 91, 96—97

design 设计 10, 86—90

  design freeze 设计定型 50, 101

  preliminary 初步 49

  progressive design freeze 逐步式设计定型 51

  design specification 设计规范 50, 69

design-build team 设计建设联动团队 88

Digital Project software 数字化项目软件 134

digital technology 数字化技术 9, 14, 74—75, 86—90, 133—134

  augmented reality 增强现实 134

  computer-aided design (CAD) 计算机辅助设计 86, 88

  computer-aided manufacture (CAM) 计算机辅助制造 86, 88

  Computer-Aided Three Dimensional Interactive Application (CATIA) 计算机辅助三维互动应用 88—89

  digital communication 数字化沟通 94—95

  digital computer 数字化电脑 50

  digital information 数字化信息 14, 87

  digital model 数字化模型 90

dispersed team 分布式团队 74—75

disruptive technology 颠覆性技术 100—101

doing versus learning dilemma 行动与学习困境 109—110

Dongtan eco-city project 东滩生态城项目 63—66, 71, 76, 117, 132

Dvir, Dov 多夫·德维尔 17, 77, 81—82

## E

eco-city project 生态城项目 63—66

ecological environment 生态环境 60

eco-technological projects 生态技术项目 130

Edmondson, Amy 埃米·埃德蒙森 73—74

Egan, Sir John 约翰·伊根爵士 104,

117

Eisenhardt, Kathleen 凯瑟琳 · 艾森哈特 72

electric car 电动汽车 100—101

engineering 工程 10, 37

Engwall, Matts 马茨 · 恩瓦尔 109

environment 环境 18

  balance stability and innovation 平衡稳定性与创新 56

  fast-changing 快速变化的 7, 13, 15, 56, 81—82, 117

  predictable 可预测的 7—8, 56, 117

  stable 稳定的 7, 12, 56

  turbulent 动荡的 7

epistemic community 知识社群 123, 125

Ericsson 爱立信公司 3, 81

Erie Canal 伊利运河 19—33

  Big Ditch 大渠 23

  budget 预算 25

  Canal Bill 运河预算议案 24

  Canal Commissioners 运河委员会委员 23—25, 27, 31

  Canal Fund 运河基金 25

  Canal Law《运河法》25

  cement 水泥 30—31

  Commissioners' 1817 report 委员们的 1817 年报告 25—26

  competitive tendering 竞争性招标 27

  construction 施工 24—30

  contractors 承包商 27—29

  cost 成本 23—25, 32

  Deep Cut "大深挖" 29—30

  design 设计 25—27

  Dibble Crane 起重挖掘机 29—30

  Erie School of Engineering 伊利工程学院 32—33

  federal funding 联邦资金 24

  finance 融资 21, 25

  Geddes, James 詹姆斯 · 格迪斯 22, 25—26, 33

  innovation 创新 29—30

  opening 启用 31—33

  Roberts, Nathan 内森 · 罗伯茨 26—27, 33

  route 路线 24—26

  survey 调查 22, 26

  Wedding of the Waters "水流的婚礼" 31

  Western Inland Lock Navigation Company 西部内陆船闸航运公司 21, 23—24

  White, Canvass 坎瓦斯 · 怀特 26, 30—33

  Wright, Benjamin 本杰明 · 赖特 23, 25—26, 33

  参见 Clinton, De Witt

event-based time 基于事件的时序 81

experiential strategy 体验策略 73

# F

fast competitive project 快速竞争性项目 81

fast-paced conditions 快节奏条件 65, 73, 81—82

fixed-capital formation 固定资产投资完成 16

fixed-price contract 固定总价合同 7, 56, 103—104

flexible contract 柔性合同 56, 105

flexible project 灵活项目 5, 7, 13—15, 55—56, 61, 73—74, 78, 86, 98, 102, 106, 127, 132

flexible team 灵活团队 73—74, 132

Flyvbjerg, Bent 傅以斌 16, 34—36

Ford, Henry 亨利·福特 12

foreseen uncertainty 可预知的不确定性 56, 76

forecasts 预测 35, 39

fountain model 喷泉模型 81

fourth constraint 第四项限定 4

framework agreements 框架协议 122

front end 前期 33—34, 36—37, 131

Fujimoto, Takahiro 藤本隆宏 83, 95

functional organization 职能型组织 43, 52, 68, 84, 94, 116

functional team structure 职能型团队结构 94

funding 资金支持 20—21, 24—25, 58

## G

Galbraith, Jay 杰伊·加尔布雷斯 69—70

Gann, David 戴维·甘恩

Gehry, Frank 弗兰克·盖里 11, 89—90, 130, 134

global projects 全球项目 120—121

Google 谷歌公司 94

government 政府 9, 15, 130

approval 审批 23, 46

funding 资金支持 22—23

politicians 政治家 20, 23

publicly funded projects 公共资助项目 60

Grabher, Gernot 赫尔诺特·格拉布赫 122

Great Fire of London 伦敦大火 10

Gropius, Walter 瓦尔特·格罗皮乌斯 62

Groves, Leslie 莱斯利·格罗夫斯 41—42, 44, 47

Guggenheim Museum in Bilbao 毕尔巴鄂的古根海姆博物馆 89—90, 130

## H

Hall, Peter 彼得·霍尔 5

Hawley, Jesse 杰西·霍利 21—22

Heatherwick, Thomas 托马斯·赫斯维克 11

heavyweight project manager 重量级项目经理 85, 94—95

heavyweight team structure 重量级团队的结构 94—95, 105

Heimer, Carol 卡罗尔·海默 75

Hiding Hand principle "隐藏的手"规则 37

High-Speed 1 project 高铁一号线项目 113

Hirschman, Albert O. 艾伯特·O.赫希曼 37

Hough, George 乔治·霍夫 17

项目管理

**136**

Hughes, Thomas P. 托马斯·P. 休斯 13, 60—61, 129

# I

IBM Personal Computer IBM 个人电脑 98—99

incentive contract 激励性合同 56, 106

independent film production 独立电影制作 112—113

industrial revolution 工业革命 10, 12

Infrastructure Industry Innovation Platform 基础设施行业创新平台 125

innovation 创新 6—7, 11, 14—15, 29—30, 37—38, 56, 61—62, 75, 90—92, 97—99, 132

innovation balancing act 创新平衡行动 96—99

innovation in complex projects 复杂项目中的创新 56, 61

innovation projects 创新项目 90—92

institution of civil engineers 英国土木工程师学会 10

integration 集成：

    integration mechanisms 集成机制 69, 99

    liaison position 联络岗位 69

    linking pins 连环别针 69

    matrix 矩阵型结构 69—70

intellectual property 知识产权 30

intercontinental ballistic missile（ICBM）洲际弹道导弹 13, 39, 44—54, 57

interdependency 依存性 68—69, 73

International Project Management Association（IPMA）国际项目管理协会 57

International Space Station 国际空间站 1, 58

invitation to tender 招标邀请 3

iron triangle 铁三角 3

Iridium project 铱星项目 7, 102

# J

Jones, Daniel 丹尼尔·琼斯 84

Jubilee Line Extension project 朱比利延长线项目 103—104, 132

# K

Kanter, Rosabeth Moss 罗莎贝丝·莫斯·坎特 96, 98

Kodak, Eastman 伊士曼·柯达 97

# L

Laing O'Rourke（LOR）奥罗克莱恩公司 113, 117—118, 124

Lawrence, Paul 保罗·劳伦斯 69

lean development 精益开发 83, 85—86

learning 学习 17—18, 25, 32, 78, 98, 109—110, 122

Lenfle, Sylvain 西尔万·朗夫勒 61, 78

Lessard, Donald R. 唐纳德·R. 莱萨德 35

lightweight team structure 轻量级团队的结构 94, 102

Lindkvist, Lars 拉尔斯·林德奎斯特 81

索引

Loch, Christoph 克里斯托夫·洛赫 61, 78, 82

Lockheed Martin 洛克希德马丁公司 96

London Heathrow Airport 伦敦希思罗机场

  Heathrow Express project 希思罗快线项目 105

  Terminal 2 project 二号航站楼项目 8—9

  Terminal 5 project (T5) 五号航站楼项目 8, 72, 104—106, 109, 118—119, 131

  T5 Agreement "五号航站楼协议" 105—106

  T5 Delivery Handbook《五号航站楼交付手册》106

London 2012 Olympic and Paralympic Games 2012 年伦敦奥运会和残奥会 4, 78—79, 129, 131

  CLM Delivery Partner CLM 交付伙伴 113, 119, 125

  Olympic Delivery Authority (ODA) 奥运工程交付局 113, 119, 125

  ODA contracts ODA 合同 78—79

London Underground 伦敦地铁 9, 115

London's megaproject ecology 伦敦的超大项目生态 124—126

Lorsch, Jay 杰伊·洛尔施 69

Lundin, Rolf 罗尔夫·伦丁 15—16, 111

# M

McNamara, Robert 罗伯特·麦克纳马拉 57, 60

mainstream project 主流项目 96—97

managing projects 项目管理 6

Manhattan Project 曼哈顿项目 13, 39—44, 46—47, 61

  bomb design 原子弹设计 43

  budget 预算 40

  Einstein, Albert 艾伯特·爱因斯坦 40

  Los Alamos Scientific Laboratory 洛斯阿拉莫斯科学实验室 43

  Manhattan Engineering District 曼哈顿工程区 41

  Oppenheimer, Robert J. 罗伯特·J. 奥本海默 43, 47

  outcome 成果 44

  parallel development 并行开发 42, 44

  plutonium production 钚的生产 40—42

  Roosevelt, Franklin D. 富兰克林·D. 罗斯福 40—41

  uranium production 铀的生产 40—42

  参见 Groves, Leslie

market uncertainty 市场不确定性 77, 91, 97

mass production 大批量生产 7, 12, 15, 67, 128

master builder 巨匠 10—11, 90

matrix organization 矩阵型组织 51—52, 55, 83, 85, 94, 116

mechanistic organization 机械型组织 67, 73, 76

megaproject 超大项目 16, 34—37, 104, 107, 124, 129, 132

Miller, Roger 罗杰·米勒 35

Mintzberg, Henry 亨利·明茨伯格 70—72, 114

modularity 模块化 80, 133

Morris, Peter 彼得·莫里斯 17, 33

Motorola 摩托罗拉公司 7, 102

multidisciplinary team 多学科团队 13, 63

multiple approaches 多方法 98

Musk, Elon 埃隆·马斯克 100—101, 131—132

mutual adjustment 相互调适 69, 73

## N

National Aeronautics and Space Administration (NASA) 美国国家航空航天局 54—57, 59, 60, 72

Phased Program Planning 阶段化集群项目规划 84

zone of uncertainty 不确定性地带 56, 69

National Health Service (NHS) 英国国家医疗系统 16

newstream project 新支流项目 96—97

Nike 耐克公司 15

Nonaka, Ikujiro 野中郁次郎 84

novelty 创新性 31, 77, 91, 93

## O

organic-adaptive 有机适应性 67

organic organization 有机型组织 67

organization theory 组织理论 67—72

open innovation 开放式创新 92

opening projects 项目启用 8, 31—33

open system 开放的系统 60, 129

operating adhocracy 运营性灵活机构 71

operational readiness 运营就绪 8

operations 运营 7—9, 13, 15, 33

optimism bias 乐观偏差 34, 59

organizational breakdown structure (OBS) 组织分解结构 58

organizational memory 组织记忆 112

outcomes 成果 8, 130—131

outputs 产出 8

## P

pace 节奏 81—82

Panama Canal project 巴拿马运河项目 121

parallel development 并行开发 39, 47, 61, 78, 132

performance 绩效 17—18, 34—37

permanent adhocracy 常设性灵活机构 71

personal network 个人网络 123, 125

Peters, Tom 汤姆·彼得斯 14

Piano, Renzo 伦佐·皮亚诺 62, 80

Pich, Michael 迈克尔·皮希 82

plan 计划 5—6

Platform project 平台型项目 91—93, 95—97

Polaris Programme 北极星项目 51—52,

57, 61

pooled interdependency 集合式依存性 68

portfolio 项目组合 7, 93

Posner, Barry Z. 巴里·Z. 波斯纳 5

post-industrial society 后工业化社会 10, 14, 17

   people 人员 134—135

   post-industrial organization 后工业化组织 9, 130

   post-industrial projects 后工业化项目 130—135

Prencipe, Andrea 安德烈亚·普伦奇佩 80

prime contractor 总承包商 46, 79

Private Finance Initiative (PFI) 私人融资倡议 9, 16

procurement 采购 15

product development 产品开发:

   General Motors 通用汽车公司 84—85

   Honda 本田公司 85

   Japanese approach 日本的方法 85—86, 117

   lean development 精益开发 83, 85—86, 95

   overlay approach 叠加的方法 86

   product development funnel 产品开发"漏斗" 90

   Toyota 丰田公司 85

   Western approach 西方的方法 84—85

product life cycle 产品生命周期 15

product platform 产品平台 15

Program Evaluation Review Technique

(PERT) 项目计划评审技术 52—55

programme 集群项目 7, 119

project baron 项目巨头 116

project capabilities 项目能力 116—118, 122—123, 128

Project Chess 象棋项目 98—99

project definition 项目定义 2

project goal 项目目标 3, 5—6

project-based firm 项目导向型公司 114

project-based industry 项目导向型行业 9, 17, 121

project-based organization 项目导向型组织 9, 111, 114—118

project delivery model 项目交付模式 105—106, 124

project ecology 项目生态 111, 121—126

   core team 核心团队 123

   cumulative ecology 累积式生态 123

   disruptive ecology 颠覆式生态 123

   four layers 四个层次 122—123

project life cycle 项目生命周期 3, 35—36, 58

project management 项目管理 11, 13, 37, 39, 46, 57—61

Project Management Body of Knowledge (PMBoK) 项目管理知识体系 57—58, 66

Project Management Institute (PMI) 项目管理协会 57—58, 66, 69

project manager 项目经理 3, 39, 47

project network 项目网络 14, 111, 118—121

project nomad 项目牧民 124—125

project organization 项目组织 2—3, 13, 46, 52, 79

project phases 项目阶段 3, 33

project proposal 项目建议书 3, 21

psychological safety 心理安全 74

Public-Private Partnership (PPP) 公私合作 15—16, 20, 113

## R

Raborn, William F. 威廉·F. 拉伯恩 51, 127

railways 铁路 12—13

Ramo, Simon 西蒙·拉莫 45, 47, 50, 59

Randolph, Alan 艾伦·伦道夫 5

reciprocal interdependency 交互式依存性 68—69

regular project 常规项目 81

Renault 雷诺公司 15

repetitive tasks 重复性任务 7—8, 110, 116

Research & Development (R&D) projects 研发项目 70, 92, 97—98

risk management 风险管理 6, 58, 76—78

Rogers, Richard 理查德·罗杰斯 62, 104

Roos, Daniel 丹尼尔·鲁斯 84

Royal Institute of British Architects 英国皇家建筑师学会 11

## S

Sabbagh, Karl 卡尔·萨巴格 87

Sayles, Leonard R. 伦纳德·R. 塞尔斯 60

Scandinavian School of Project Studies 项目研究的斯堪的纳维亚学派 108

schedule 进度安排 6, 50—51, 55

Schriever, Bernard 伯纳德·施里弗 45—46, 50, 70

Scott, Richard W. 理查德·W. 斯科特 120—121

Scranton, Philip 菲利普·斯克兰顿 12

sequential development 序列式开发 68

sequential interdependency 序列式依存性 68

serial development 串行开发 50

services 服务 8—9

Shard 碎片大厦 80

Shaw, Ronald E. 罗纳德·E. 肖 30

Shenhar, Aaron J. 亚伦·J. 申哈尔 17, 77, 81—82

*shusa* 主管 85

side projects 支流项目 93—94

single-project organization 单个项目组织 111, 112—114

skunkwork project "臭鼬工作室"项目 96

smart city 智慧城市 129, 133

Söderlund, Jonas 乔纳斯·瑟德隆德 111

soft opening 柔性启用 8

software development 软件开发 75

Space Shuttle 航天飞机 58—59

Special Projects Office 特别项目办公

室 45, 51

special purpose vehicle (SPV) 专用组织 113

specification 规格 2, 7, 10, 26, 28, 49, 84

sponsor 出资方 33—34, 99, 131—132

stable team 稳定的团队 73

stakeholders 相关方 23, 34, 46, 129, 133

Stalker, G. M. 斯托克 67

Stinchcombe, Arthur 阿瑟·斯廷科姆 75

strategic misinterpretation 策略性虚报 34

success 成功 4, 8, 34, 130—131

sustaining technology 维持性技术 101

Sydney Opera House 悉尼歌剧院 4—5, 62—63, 66

Sydow, Jörg 约尔格·赛多 109

systems approach 系统方法 13, 51, 60

systems engineering 系统工程 39, 46—51

system integrator 系统集成者 46, 133

system integration 系统集成 47—51, 54, 80, 119

system project 系统项目 79

systems project management 系统项目管理 55, 60—61

counter culture and opposition 反主流文化与反对 60

predictable and controlled phases 可预测和受控的阶段 66

single best way of organizing 单一最优的组织方式 66

standardized and fixed model 标准化的和确定的模型 66

T

Tabrizi, Behnam 贝南·塔布里兹 72

Takeuchi, Hirotaka 竹内弘高 84

targeted flexibility 有针对的灵活性 78

Taylor, Frederick W. 弗雷德里克·W.泰勒 12

team 团队 3, 5—6, 10, 72—75

teaming 团队化 74, 102

team structures 团队结构 94—96

technological gatekeeper 技术守门人 70

technological uncertainty 技术不确定性 56, 61, 77, 132

Telford, Thomas 托马斯·特尔福德 10, 26

temporary adhocracy 临时性灵活机构 71

temporary organization 临时组织 2, 10, 12, 14, 67—68, 109

Tesla Motors 特斯拉汽车公司 100—101

Thames Tideway Tunnel Project 泰晤士潮路隧道项目 125

Thompson, James 詹姆斯·汤普森 68—69

time 进度 6, 50, 81

time-critical project 进度关键型项目 81—82, 103

time, cost, and quality trade-off 进度、成本和质量之间的权衡 3—4

Toffler, Alvin 阿尔文·托夫勒 9—10, 14, 70, 130, 135

Toshiba 东芝公司 115

transition 过渡 8—9

项目管理

trials 测试 8

trust 信任 70

   shadow of the past 过去的影子 122

   shadow of the future 未来的投影 122

   swift trust 快速信任 112

## U

uncertainty 不确定性 5, 19, 37, 56, 58, 61, 63, 73—78, 97—99, 102, 127, 132

unforeseen uncertainty 不可预知的不确定性 56, 73, 76, 78, 102

uniqueness 独特性 7, 13, 110, 117

unit production 单件式生产 68, 115

urban development 城市开发 60, 129

   urban problems 城市问题 60

   urban renewal 城市更新 60

   参见 climate change

urgency 紧迫性 81, 127

   参见 pace; time

user requirements 用户需求 77, 97, 131

Utzon, Jørn, 约恩·乌松 62

## V

vanguard project 先锋项目 117—118

virtual team 虚拟团队 75

## W

waterfall model 瀑布模型 68

Waterman, Robert H. 罗伯特·H. 沃特曼 14

Webb, James E. 詹姆斯·E. 韦布 54, 56

Weber, Max 马克斯·韦伯 12

Wheelwright, Steven 史蒂文·惠尔莱特 91, 94

wicked problems 棘手问题 128—130

Womack, James 詹姆斯·沃马克 84, 99

Woodward, J. 伍德沃德 68

Work Breakdown Structure (WBS) 工作分解结构 33, 58

World Bank 世界银行 16

Wren, Sir Christopher 克里斯托弗·雷恩爵士 10

索引

# 译后记

2021年，我与本书作者安德鲁·戴维斯教授相识刚好十年。还记得第一次联络他，是询问能否前往他当时任职的英国帝国理工学院商学院进行中英重大项目管理的合作研究。尽管那次访问未能成行，但是此后一直与他保持了学术联系，不时会研读他新发表的大作，此后还曾数次在国际会议期间进行过简短的交流。本书的翻译源起于2018年底首次在亚太地区举办的国际重大工程论坛，他作为这一系列国际会议的发起者和特邀嘉宾参与了此次盛会。其间，我和他聊起了他2017年新近出版的这本牛津通识读本。他很兴奋，告诉我这是受他的老同事撰写了牛津通识读本《创新》（2010）的启发而开始的，而且撰写这一看似薄薄的小册子颇不轻松。实际上，与同类项目管理著作不同，这本书从创新管理的视角重新对西方项目管理发展历程进行了全景式解读，从曼哈顿项目到日本公司的精益产品开发方法，再到伦敦超大项目生态，读来颇有令人有耳目一新的感觉。我相信，阅读此书能帮助读者了解项目管理这一学科的根基，以及时至今日根本的系列行动和变化。2021年美国项目管理协会最新发布的《项目管理知识体系指南》(第六版),作为与以往版本大为不同的颠覆之作,其很多理念和观点与此书颇有共通之处。

这里且容许我再将本书作者作一简短的介绍。戴维斯教授现任职于萨塞克斯大学科学政策研究组,担任R. M.菲利普斯·弗里曼讲席教授,主持创新与项目管理方向的教研工作。根据美国宾夕法尼亚大学2018年的评估,他所任职的机构在全球科技政策智库排名中位列全英第一、全球第三。戴维斯教授曾先后任教于荷兰阿姆斯特丹大学、英国帝国理工学院及伦敦大学学院,拥有丰富的国际经历;在著名科学期刊《自然》及创新管理领域内的重要期刊《科研政策》《麻省理工学院斯隆管理评论》《加利福尼亚管理评论》等发表论文五十多篇,并在剑桥大学出版专著和论文集两部,同时兼任工程管理和项目创新领域内的重要期刊《IEEE工程管理通信》副主编,曾荣获IBM教员奖。作为发起人之一,他还曾为伦敦希思罗机场扩建、悉尼地铁、大巴黎快线等项目提供咨询建议。

最后,由衷地感谢陈志强教授和陈凡、徐启雄及王夏晗的审校,他们都对完善译稿提出了很多好的建议。此外,本译作还得到了国家自然科学基金项目(71971157)的支持。

2021年10月于同济园

Andrew Davies

# PROJECTS

A Very Short Introduction

*For my mum, Ann,*
*and*
*daughters, Abi and Hannah*

# Contents

Preface  i

List of illustrations  iii

1 Introduction  1

2 America's venture into the unknown  19

3 From Manhattan to the Moon  39

4 Arup's adhocracy and projects in theory  62

5 Lean, heavy, and disruptive projects  83

6 London's megaproject ecology  103

7 Back to the future  127

Further reading  137

# Preface

Like many things we do at work and in our daily lives, making this book was a project. It started with an idea. There are some excellent books on project management, but too often they provide 'how-to' guidebooks and simple recipes of best practice tools, techniques, and procedures. Each project is treated as a lonely endeavour that can be managed in isolation from the environment within which it is planned and executed. I had recently joined The Bartlett Faculty at University College London (UCL) as Professor of the Management of Projects and wanted to introduce a wider audience to the new thinking about how projects are organized. This theoretically informed approach—sometimes called project studies—seeks to understand how projects adapt to complex, uncertain, and rapidly changing conditions and examines projects in their rich and varied organizational, institutional, and historical contexts. I turned my idea into a proposal, submitted it to a potential sponsor (Oxford University Press), and after some revisions received a contract to produce a book that met the sponsor's specifications. Like many projects, this one was delayed (I missed several deadlines), but was produced within budget (it was a fixed price). In the long term, the success of my project is uncertain: it depends on whether the outcome produces lasting benefits and value for the customer—you the reader.

The outcome is my responsibility, but like most projects this one involved a team of collaborators. I thank Mark Dodgson, David Gann, and David Musson for encouraging me to develop *A Very Short Introduction* to projects and Jenny Nugee and her colleagues at OUP for being so patient and supportive during the execution of my writing project, even when I missed another deadline. My thanks go to managers I have collaborated with in project-based organizations and high-profile projects and to colleagues and students at UCL and elsewhere who continue to make this such a rewarding and stimulating topic which has become the centre of my professional life. I thank those colleagues who provided detailed comments and valuable suggestions for how to improve the book, including Mark Dodgson, Tim Brady, Sam MacAulay, Jonas Söderlund, and Sylvain Lenfle, and those with whom I have co-authored articles and worked most closely with in recent years, particularly Andrea Prencipe, Jennifer Whyte, Nuno Gil, Niels Noorderhaven, Lars Frederiksen, Jens Roehrich, Eugenia Cacciatori, Stephan Manning, Ilze Kivleniece, and Paul Nightingale. I thank colleagues at UCL Donna Cage, Brian Collins, Juliano Denicol, Andrew Edkins, Jim Meikle, Stefano Miraglia, Beth Morgan, Peter Morris, Alex Murray, Natalya Sergeeva, Hedley Smyth, and Vedran Zerjav for clarifying issues and helping with specific questions. Thanks to Mark Thurston, Tim DeBarro, John Pelton, and Sam MacAulay for the creative work and fun we had developing an innovation programme for London's Crossrail project. My gratitude goes to Hans Jörg Gemünden and Carla Messikomer for leading, supporting, and enthusing members of the project studies community. I especially acknowledge Peter Morris, Ray Levitt, Bent Flyvbjerg, and Aaron Shenhar—scholars with a deep appreciation of theory and managerial practice who have had a profound influence on my thinking about projects.

# List of illustrations

1 The challenge of managing project trade-offs has always been with us **4**
www.CartoonStock.com.

2 Innovative Dibble cranes **30**
New York Public Library.

3 The finished Deep Cut of the Erie Canal **32**
New York Public Library.

4 Western Development Division and Ramo-Wooldridge organization **48**
Adapted from T. P. Hughes, *Rescuing Prometheus* (New York: Pantheon Books, 1998).

5 Functional, project, and matrix organizations **53**

6 The Sydney Opera House **63**
State Archives NSW.

7 Dongtan East Village **64**
Courtesy of Arup.

8 Working Together **89**
© The Boeing Company.

9 Heathrow Terminal 5 during construction **104**
© LHR Airports Limited see photolibrary.heathrow.com.

10 Crossrail's tunnelling machine **108**
Anthony Devlin/PA Archive/PA Images.

11 Forms of project organizing **111**

# Chapter 1
# Introduction

We depend on projects to transform the natural environment and create the human-built world. We have participated in projects since people first lived and worked in the villages, towns, and cities of the earliest agrarian societies. Projects were established to coordinate work undertaken by temporary groups of people involved in one-off tasks ranging from small informal activities such as hunting and building shelter, to very large and elaborate endeavours such as military campaigns, foreign expeditions (each new voyage overseas was a project), and the construction of buildings, roads, ports, and entire cities. The world's great ancient projects—the pyramids of Egypt, irrigation schemes in Iraq, the temples, aqueducts, roads, and bridges of Imperial Rome, the Great Wall of China, and Gothic cathedrals, for example—were massive in scale, involved enormous numbers of people, and often took years, decades, or even longer to complete.

Today projects are literally everywhere. Complex, one-off endeavours using advanced technology such as the $100 billion International Space Station, Avatar (the first film to go on wide release shot entirely in 3D), and Shanghai's 500 km per hour magnetic levitation train are more obvious examples of projects. The products we use in our daily lives, such as cars, cameras, smartphones, and pharmaceuticals drugs, all start out as projects before being produced in high volume. Many things we do to create change in organizations, think up new ideas and implement them (e.g. an entrepreneurial start-up for customized 3D printing), or respond to emergencies (e.g. humanitarian aid provided by NGOs in a war-torn region of the world) are projects. While they may differ in purpose, scale, and scope, and span many industries, each project is established to bring together people with diverse knowledge to complete a temporary assignment, solve a complex problem, or turn a novel idea into reality.

## What is a project?

The word 'project' in the modern sense only came into common use during the 20th century. Before that, it had several different meanings. The *Oxford English Dictionary* finds the word being used in the 2nd century. In classical Latin, the verb *prōiect* means to throw forth or cast away. It was in the 15th century that the word was used to refer to the act of conceiving an idea, proposing a plan, putting something into action, or venturing into the unknown. Daniel Defoe used the word in the title of his book *An Essay Upon Projects* (1697) to describe a 'projecting age' when ventures in foreign expansion and trade, and innovative improvements in science, art, and manufacturing, were being proposed and executed through projects, in pursuit of profits, and 'adventured on the risk of success'.

This *Very Short Introduction* defines a project as a combination of people and other resources brought together in a temporary organization and process to achieve a specified goal. What distinguishes projects from all other organizational activities—such as manufacturing and services—is that a project is finite in duration, lasting from hours, days, or weeks to years and in some cases decades. Unlike manufacturing or service firms, which are presumed to be permanent, a project organization is temporary and disposable by design. Each project brings together people and resources needed to accomplish a goal and disappears when the work is completed. When firms like Bombardier, Siemens, and

2

Toshiba set out to win contracts for a fleet of high-speed intercity trains, for example, they create a project organization to coordinate work undertaken by their own staff and a network of subcontractors. The organization has a planned life of only a few years and dissolves after accomplishing the job.

Projects range in size from small teams to large international joint ventures and temporary coalitions of public and private organizations. Each one of them has a life cycle with a beginning and an end. Each undertakes a sequence of distinct, but often overlapping, phases or activities to conceive and promote the idea, prepare a proposal and develop a plan, and undertake and complete the work. For example, when Ericsson, the Swedish mobile communications producer, sets out to win a contract from a global mobile network operator (e.g. Vodafone or T-Mobile) it establishes a team with diverse expertise (e.g. technology, services, and sales) borrowed from various units of the firm. The team works to gather information and anticipate the operator's requirements for next-generation mobile systems even before the operator requests bids. When the operator issues a formal invitation to tender, the pre-bid team is disbanded. Many of its members return to their units and a new team is assembled to write the actual proposal. Once the proposal is submitted, the proposal-writing team is dissolved and a new team is established to execute the project. Some individuals move along with the project joining each successive team, but others with specialized expertise are brought in to work on only one or two phases.

A clearly defined project goal and progress toward the goal has traditionally been measured by the three constraints of cost, time, and quality—the so-called 'iron triangle' of project management. The job of the project manager is to complete the project on time, within budget, and according to the desired quality and performance specifications. Trade-offs between time, cost, and quality are often made to meet a project's goal (Figure 1). For example, although

3

" We had to cut corners ! "

**1. The challenge of managing project trade-offs has always been with us.**

the time available to construct the venues for the London 2012 Olympics Games was fixed—it was an 'immoveable deadline'—cost and quality could be manipulated to achieve the desired outcome. Too often, however, trade-offs are made without taking into account their impact on customer satisfaction—the 'fourth constraint'—and longer-term strategic objectives.

We now recognize that project success is multidimensional and varies over time. Other dimensions include whether the project develops the knowledge and skills of people, teams, and organizations involved and whether it contributes to an organization's commercial success, profitability, and market share. Projects considered unsuccessful in the short term (measured in cost, time, and quality) may provide new knowledge about technologies, products, services, and customer requirements that open up future business opportunities. As the Sydney Opera House illustrates, great projects considered short-term failures by the triple constraints model can be successful in the longer term if the outcome creates additional benefits and a lasting legacy for owners, users, communities, and even entire countries (Box 1).

4

## Box 1  Sydney Opera House

The Sydney Opera House project was originally estimated in 1957 to cost just over $7 million (Australian dollars: AUD) and scheduled to be completed by January 1963. The building was eventually opened in October 1973 (over ten years later than originally planned) at a cost of $102 million (AUD)—a staggering 1,400 per cent over budget. During planning and construction, the project faced a great deal of opposition and criticism. By the time it opened, it was said that the building could not function as a major opera house because the original design had to be changed so many times to accommodate new requirements, cost increases, and delays. Measured against time, cost, and quality objectives, the project would be considered an abject failure, setting a possible world record for poor performance. Yet today the Sydney Opera House—with its roof structure resembling luminous sails—is admired as one of the world's most distinctive buildings. In *Great Planning Disasters* (1980), Peter Hall stated that 'It *is* Sydney' and 'put the city on some sort of mental map of great world cities' (p. 138).

Project managers are responsible for establishing a well-defined plan and then managing the plan until the project is completed. They define the project goal, establish checkpoints, schedules, time estimates, and resource requirements. They manage, motivate, and empower individual members of a project, facilitate communication and build agreements that vitalize teams, and encourage innovation, risk taking, and creativity. Alan Randolph and Barry Z. Posner identify ten simple principles to help managers plan and manage projects (see Table 1). When projects are complex, unpredictable, and changing, plans have to be flexible and projects adjusted to situations that cannot be foreseen at the outset. Managers of uncertain projects have to iteratively plan/manage, plan/manage until they accomplish the goal.

# Table 1 Principles for planning and managing projects

## Planning projects

| | |
|---|---|
| 1. Set a clear project goal | Start at the finish and work backward. Setting a project goal involves the sponsor, project manager, the project team, and the users of the project. |
| 2. Determine project objectives | Establish detailed objectives to help members of the project understand how their contributions relate to the overall goal. |
| 3. Establish an action plan and time estimates | Create an action plan to detail what is going to be done and how you will monitor your progress towards project completion. |
| 4. Draw a picture of the project schedule | Draw a picture or a schedule of the project to visualize project activities, relationships among activities, and time estimates. |

## Managing projects

| | |
|---|---|
| 5. Direct people individually and as a project team | Develop a strong team of collaborators, encouraging them to learn from experience, and to expose and solve problems. |
| 6. Reinforce team commitment | Encourage people to join a project where they feel a sense of ownership and are committed to its success. |
| 7. Keep everyone connected | Overcome barriers to communication, keep people informed on a regular basis, listen and use information brought to them by team members. |
| 8. Build agreements that vitalize team members | Projects require the coordination of tasks and integration of different units and people. Conflict can be a force for imagination and creativity. |
| 9. Empower yourself and others on the project | Project managers need power arising as much from individual competence as from formal authority. Managers of high-performing projects share power. |
| 10. Encourage innovation, risk taking, and creativity | Plan for innovation. Sharing ideas and creativity requires support and communication. Innovation is reinforced by goals, budgets, and deadlines. |

Projects

6

The need to adjust to changes in the environment explains why a project can achieve its goal, but still result in failure. For example, Motorola's $5 billion Iridium project was a fixed-price contract (a price set at the start that remains unchanged through to completion) to build a constellation of satellites providing voice and data communications for satellite phones. It could be considered a success because it was completed on time, within budget, and satisfied the technical specification, but was a failure in commercial terms. While the project was under way, Motorola's management team failed to see that rapidly expanding terrestrial mobile phone networks which we now all depend on would completely undermine Iridium's satellite-based business model.

A project can be complete in itself such as the creation of a new consumer product, building, or urban metro system. It can form part of a continuing programme of interrelated projects using shared resources and coordinated to achieve a common objective such as the nationwide rollout of a mobile communication system. A portfolio can be established to allocate resources to a set of projects that are planned, mapped, and sequenced to achieve an organization's long-term strategic objectives such as Apple's digital hub of products and online iTune services (Chapter 5).

## Projects and operations

A distinction is made between projects and operations. Projects perform novel, non-repetitive, one-off tasks and produce unique, one-off, or customized outcomes for individual customers, such as a building, change programme, or new airport. Operations undertake ongoing, repetitive tasks and produce standardized products and services in high volume for mass markets, such as cars, computers, and fast-food meals. Projects are a flexible and adaptable way of organizing, dealing with individual client requirements, and promoting innovation when conditions are turbulent and fast-changing, whereas operations are designed to perform standardized routines in a stable and predictable

7

environment. We will discover, however, that projects vary in complexity, pace, and uncertainty (Chapter 4) and perform tasks ranging from unique to repetitive (Chapter 6).

A distinction is also made between the outputs and outcomes of projects. Outputs are the tangible and intangible things a project creates such as a building, IT system, or organizational process. Outcomes are the results or benefits created for the sponsor, customer, and user when the project becomes operational, such as improved performance, enhancements to existing products, and the creation of new markets.

There is a transition between project and operations when outputs (e.g. a new fleet of trams) are handed over and translated into operational outcomes (e.g. a functioning urban tram system). As the project moves to completion, components and subsystems have to be integrated, tested, and end users have to learn how to operate the outputs (hardware, software, and services) before the project becomes operational.

Many complex projects fail because of unsuccessful transitions. A timely and seamless operational transition is more likely if there is a strong sponsor presiding over the project and the operator is embedded at an early stage, articulating its requirements and deeply involved in all preparations for opening. Take for example the chaotic opening of Terminal 5 at London Heathrow Airport in March 2008 when many flights were cancelled and baggage was delayed and misplaced over a period of twelve days. Learning from this misguided attempt to open a complete terminal in one go, the airport operator decided to prepare for the 'soft opening' of Terminal 2—the next major construction project at Heathrow. A dedicated 'operational readiness' team was embedded in the project organization two years prior to the official opening on 4 June 2014. A successful handover was achieved by opening the terminal in stages including 180 trials with 14,000 volunteers,

1,700 training sessions, a digital 'mock-up terminal' to assess
check-in software, a test with a live flight, and staged process to
move each airline into the live terminal building.

Some projects extend into the provision of operational services and
can last many years. For example, Alstom Transport (a division of
French-based Alstom) was awarded a £429 million Private Finance
Initiative contract (see Box 3) in 1995 to renew the fleet of trains
on the London Underground's Northern Line. Rather than specify
the exact size of the fleet, the London Underground requested an
outcome: it required that 96 trains be available for service each
day over a period of twenty years. To achieve this target, Alstom
produced 106 trains and established a dedicated maintenance
organization to service them. Demand for projects that include
the provision of services has encouraged many project-based
firms—IBM, Alstom, and Rolls-Royce—to change their entire
business models so that they can both design and integrate
systems *and* provide services to operate and maintain them.

All organizations engage in projects to a greater or lesser degree,
but the activities of some organizations and industries are almost
entirely based on projects, such as Airbus's aeroplane business,
IBM's information technology solutions, and Zaha Hadid's
architectural practice. For project-based organizations, each new
customer order constitutes a new project, whereas high-volume
producers like Sony, Samsung, and Starbucks, and large government
agencies, rely on projects alongside their operations to implement
strategies, develop new products, create organizational change,
build new assets and systems, and deal with one-off problems or
opportunities.

## A brief history of projects

Alvin Toffler introduced the word 'adhocracy', popularized in *Future
Shock* (1970) and *The Third Wave* (1980), to describe a new species
of post-industrial organization: temporary, ad hoc, and adaptive

project groups and teams. Toffler argued that the invention of agriculture associated with the first wave was brought to an end by a second wave initiated by the British industrial revolution in the late 18th century and subsequent rise of mass production in the United States and Germany. A third wave, initiated in the mid-20th century, is based on the radically new principles of post-industrial information society. Toffler believed that temporary project structures and access to information made possible by the invention of the computer would overwhelm the previous social arrangement and counter the standardization of tasks, bureaucracy, hierarchy, and other second-wave values and interests.

Many construction projects of the agrarian age were accomplished by the 'master builder'. Combining the roles, knowledge, and practical experience of architect, engineer, and craftsman, the master builder was responsible for generating new ideas and turning them into reality, designing the building, and employing craftsmen to construct it. Sir Christopher Wren, for example, was appointed as chief architect after the Great Fire of London in 1666 to survey the damaged area, plan the new city, design the buildings including St Paul's Cathedral, and manage construction.

This bond between design and construction was broken around the time of the industrial revolution when engineering and architecture evolved into specialized scientific and elite professions, largely segregated from the rest of the building trade. With the establishment of elite professional civil engineering bodies in France in the late 17th and 18th century, engineers assumed responsibility for the design, specifications, and procurement of bridges, roads, and other government projects and for defining the tasks performed by contractors during their execution. Professional civil engineers appeared later in the UK. After the Institution of Civil Engineers was founded in 1818, the engineers that designed the roads, canals, and railways—Thomas Telford and Isambard Kingdom Brunel, for example—became organizationally and contractually separate from those that built them. Thomas Brassey's general contracting firm, for instance, constructed much of Britain's railway network. After the foundation of the Royal Institute of British Architects in 1834, architecture was established as a profession and architects were prohibited from engaging in profit-making contracting. The designer of the building subsequently became disconnected from engineering and the daily practice of construction. In recent years, architects, civil engineers, and product designers—such as Frank Gehry, Ove Arup, and Thomas Heatherwick—have attempted to re-establish the role of master builder to preside over projects in a collaborative process linking design closely with construction (Box 2).

Until the mid-20th century, the most widely practised and advanced form of project management was found in construction. Yet projects were ignored as a form of organization by industrial

## Box 2 Project maker and master builder

Thomas Heatherwick's London design studio is a 'project maker'. It experiments with new materials, develops new ideas, and produces innovations ranging in scale from products (e.g. a new fuel-efficient London bus) to the design of iconic buildings (e.g. the UK Pavilion at the 2010 World Expo in Shanghai) and shape of future cities. As Heatherwick emphasizes, generating new ideas and making them happen means that each project 'is an intense mixture of certainty and doubt, breakthroughs and dead ends, tension and hilarity, frustration and progress'. The studio works as a collection of overlapping projects; each one is formed around a client's problem and led by an experienced member of the studio. Influenced by the historical figure of the master builder, Heatherwick believes the separate roles of the architect, craftsman, engineer, and designer should be combined in a collaborative team so that the design of a product or building is closely connected to the process of turning it into reality.

society's scholars and practitioners. Instead they focused on understanding how improvements in operations—stretching back to the railways and the birth of the modern corporation—gave rise to the large, hierarchical, and permanent organization. Max Weber, the German sociologist and the era's leading theoretical proponent, argued that there was one best way of organizing large groups of people. Rules about the breakdown of work, top–down authority, and large-scale bureaucratic structures were designed to perfect standardized operating procedures and improve performance in a stable environment. Frederick W. Taylor's scientific management and Henry Ford's Model T assembly line put some of these ideas into practice. Mass production became the key to the growth and competitive survival of corporations such as Ford, Standard Oil, Carnegie Steel, and Coca-Cola. Volume producers integrated backwards into sources of raw materials and component manufacturing and forwards by buying distributors and controlling channels to mass markets.

Management theory and practice had little or nothing to say about projects where an entirely different organizational logic prevailed. In a fascinating essay on projects in economic history, Philip Scranton notes that the railways were held up as a model that other organizations should emulate, but the question of how they 'could be operated at a profit overshadowed issues of how they could be built in the first place'. This is surprising because the British and American industrial revolutions could not have occurred without large-scale endeavours organized through projects: the construction of canals, railways, telegraph, and telephone networks carrying large volumes of raw materials, people, information, and goods; the factories, plants, and machinery of mass production; the energy, lighting, water, sewer, and other utility systems; and the built environment of rapidly urbanizing societies. Almost everything was contracted out to multiple independent parties working jointly on a shared activity in a temporary organization that disappeared on completion of its task. Projects created something one-off and unique, whereas running the completed outcome was a continuing operation.

The key historical turning point was during and after the Second World War when management scholars and professional managers began to recognize the importance of projects in the defence and aerospace industries (Chapter 3). The challenges involved in developing America's technologically advanced weapons systems—particularly the Manhattan Project that produced the atomic bomb and the Atlas and Polaris ballistic missiles—called for a radically new and more sophisticated way of managing complex projects. The 'systems approach' created for these projects encouraged managers to focus on understanding the whole system, including the interfaces and interconnections among components. New forms of project organizations, processes, and tools were established to bring together, schedule, and coordinate scientists, engineers, and managers working in multidisciplinary project teams.

The systems approach to project management spread in the 1960s and 1970s to many other industries in the United States and elsewhere in the world. In his book *Rescuing Prometheus* (1998) on post-war American technological projects, Thomas Hughes suggested that the systems approach to project management is as significant as:

> the spread of scientific management in the early twentieth century under the aegis of Frederick W. Taylor and his followers. Taylorites, however, applied scientific management techniques to ongoing manufacturing operations rather than projects.

By the 1980s, many organizations that had previously focused on improving their operations were finding it difficult to adapt to an increasingly turbulent, uncertain, and fast-changing environment. Some began to search for more flexible ways of dealing with ceaseless change, rather than seeking to control it. As Toffler wrote in *The Adaptive Corporation* (1985), the adhocracy emerged because:

> A 'one-time' or temporary problem, however, requires a 'one-time' or temporary organization to resolve it. It is obviously inefficient to build a full, permanent structure to deal with a problem that will not be there after a fixed interval of time. The result is a necessary proliferation of modular, temporary, or self-destruct units—task forces, problem-solving teams, *ad hoc* committees, and other groups assembled for a special and temporary purpose.

In their book *In Search of Excellence* (1982), Tom Peters and Robert H. Waterman expected the adhocracy to spread to new industries and environments that were becoming more uncertain, complex, and demanding of innovation, even penetrating the largest and most successful bureaucratic organizations of the 20th century, such as IBM and General Electric. In the expanding middle ground between firms and markets of the post-industrial information society, Manuel Castells emphasized that the unit of production '*becomes the business project enacted by network*, rather than individual companies or formal groupings of companies' (original emphasis).

The adoption of the project form accelerated in the 1990s when the diffusion of personal computers, the Internet, world wide web, the smart phone, social media, and other digital technologies began to reshape all forms of work. Boeing, for example, chose a 'paperless' approach using computers to design, test, manufacture, and integrate the 777 aeroplane project (Chapter 5). Digital technologies are now widely used to support activities undertaken during the entire project life cycle and often continue into the operation and maintenance of an asset. In our Internet-enabled world, digital information can be shared in real time by participants with access to a smart phone or laptop computer working collaboratively in almost every type of project.

In the 21st century, projects are the vehicle for sustaining an organization's existing activities, but they play an even more fundamental role as the engine of innovation—from idea to commercialization—in a globally competitive market. The world's most competitive firms use projects to develop new technologies, design innovative products, processes, and services, introduce organizational change, launch internal corporate ventures, and implement business strategies. As product life cycles become shorter, firms have to accelerate the development of new and diverse products and services before existing offerings become obsolete, particularly in fast-paced and highly competitive consumer markets. Large firms are increasingly honeycombed into projects in a move to create flexible, problem-solving structures focused on innovation. Some mass producers are outsourcing the volume manufacturing parts of their vertically integrated operations and focusing on being 'project orchestrators' of a network of external manufacturers and suppliers involved in new product development. BMW and Renault treat each new product platform, the basis for the next family of vehicles, as a project. Nike no longer makes running shoes; it manages footwear projects. Coca-Cola outsources bottling and marketing of drinks and is now run more like a collection of projects.

Changes in government procurement policy, privatization, and the opening up of state sectors to competition have resulted in a great proliferation in the number and types of public projects such as university research, highways maintenance, schools, housing, hospitals, airports, concert halls, urban railway systems, water waste, flood defence, and sustainable energy projects. These changes have created new opportunities for public and private organizations, often working in partnership, to take on the risks and responsibilities of projects in the public sector, subject to social obligations, resource conservation, and environmental protection (Box 3).

In a recent book, Rolf Lundin and his co-authors describe a trend, beginning in the 1960s, when the share of operations in

**Box 3  Public–private partnerships**

In the 1990s, the UK pioneered new forms of contracts for public projects. The Private Finance Initiative (PFI) requires that the private sector design, build, finance, and operate projects and receive payments spread over many years or decades. In contrast to PFI where the private sector finances projects and assumes much of the risk, the Public–Private Partnership (PPP) finances public projects partly from the private sector, while government shares or underwrites some of the risk. In 2013, for example, the UK's National Health Service had over 130 PFI/PPP projects worth £12 billion. The largest PFI hospital project was awarded to Capital Hospitals, a private consortium. Under the £1.1 billion contract, Capital Hospitals is responsible for designing, building, redeveloping, and maintaining two new London hospitals until 2048 on the sites of St Bartholomew's and Royal London hospitals.

organizations began to decline and the proportion of projects started to increase rapidly. World Bank data on fixed capital formation (expenditure on construction works, machinery, and equipment) in 2015 provides a rough indicator of a class of economic activity undertaken mostly as projects: 23 per cent of the world's $114 trillion expenditure on gross domestic product is fixed capital formation and in some newly industrializing countries the figure exceeds 30 per cent—31 per cent in India and 46 per cent in China. Much of this investment is delivered by 'megaprojects': large-scale, complex, and high-risk scientific, engineering, or infrastructure projects that cost $1 billion (established at 2003 prices) or more. With spending on global megaprojects at $6 to $9 trillion annually, Bent Flyvbjerg believes this is 'the biggest investment boom in human history'.

The growth of project organizing is likely to be even more pervasive than these figures suggest. It is spreading beyond new product development and traditional project-based industries that always produced one-off and customized products and services (e.g. defence, aerospace, construction, consultancy, software, media, and entertainment) to almost every corner of post-industrial society. Consumer goods suppliers, government organizations, universities, schools, non-governmental organizations, 'pop-up' fashion or retail shops, volunteer groups, charities, and many other organizations now depend on projects to create innovation, break away from established patterns, solve complex problems, and explore entrepreneurial opportunities.

## Project performance

Organizations in the 21st century continue to improve their standardized operations through lean production, business process re-engineering, quality management, six sigma, and other management innovations. They have not been so successful with projects. Despite the growth in the number and the opportunities to improve performance by learning from experience, projects often fail to achieve their cost, time, quality, and longer-term objectives.

Several influential studies provide an indication of the poor performance of projects since the late 1950s. In a review of the publicly available reports on project overruns published between 1959 and 1986, Morris and Hough found that around 3,500 projects in a variety of industries from around the world experienced overruns of between 40 and 200 per cent. Shenhar and Dvir's data on over 600 projects in private, public, and non-profit sectors in various countries found that 85 per cent of projects failed to meet their original time and cost objectives: with an average overrun of 70 per cent in time and 60 per cent in cost. Poor performance does not just affect the stakeholders directly involved in a project. The prosperity of cities and even countries can be affected by the failure of a single project. The cost overruns and debt resulting from the 2004 Olympic Games in Athens, for example, were so large they severely weakened the Greek economy.

As we will discover in the rest of this *Very Short Introduction*, what is common to most of these poorly performing projects is that they failed to adapt to the environment. Project sponsors, executives, and managers have to define the purpose and appreciate the conditions—the complexity, uncertainty, and time available to complete the task—at the start and adapt to unforeseen situations as the project progresses. Projects have a past to learn from and a future to create. Too often they are treated in isolation from previous projects and the wider historical and organizational context within which they are conceived and executed.

In Chapter 2, we will find that large-scale engineering endeavours were delivered, often very successfully, long before the formal tools, language, and discipline of project management were available.

# Chapter 2

# America's venture into the unknown

America's most ambitious and largest engineering project of the early 19th century faced challenges that managers of today's megaprojects would recognize. When the project was conceived, however, there were no professional civil engineers or managers in the United States with the knowledge required to organize such a large and complex endeavour. The project created knowledge where no such capability existed before and where many unknown conditions would have to be faced and overcome. It became its own school of engineering and a training ground for project managers. It was the key to America's industrial future. The project was the Erie Canal.

The goal of the project was to create the world's largest inland waterway connecting New York with Lake Erie. For many years the project was considered wildly unrealistic. In 1809 President Thomas Jefferson considered the construction of the canal through America's internal wilderness as 'little short of madness'. Peter Bernstein writes that the idea of a massive artificial inland waterway binding the east to the western frontier of the nation 'appeared as fantastic as sending a rocket to the Moon'. The project had to overcome the enormous physical challenges such as traversing rivers, dense forest, malarial swamps, valleys, and rock escarpments. It had many champions, but was fiercely contested right up to and many years after funds for its construction were approved in 1817. Despite these obstacles, the project was completed on time, close to the original cost estimate, and opened for service on 26 October 1825.

The Erie Canal created a channel for an increasing flow of raw materials, grain, and produce to the Hudson River at Albany in the east and almost unlimited supplies of goods and people to travel to the Niagara River at Buffalo in the west. The 363-mile (584-kilometre) inland waterway was over thirteen times longer than America's largest canal. The canal was 4 feet deep (1.2 metres) and 40 feet wide (12.2 metres) with 83 locks made of stone so that boats could rise and fall a total of 675 feet (206 metres) along its entire course over 18 aqueducts. It inspired the construction of a 3,300-mile network of canals—America's first mass transportation infrastructure.

The project was funded, designed, and managed by government and succeeded where private canal ventures had tried and failed. A group of elected New York politicians defined the goals of the project, set the political stage, secured funding, and oversaw the canal's design and construction. They appointed surveyors with no civil engineering experience—but with a willingness to learn and a talent for innovation—to identify the route, develop the design, estimate the costs, solve technological problems, and plan and inspect the work. In what today we might call a public–private partnership, the project was managed by a temporary public body and undertaken by private contractors selected by competitive tender to build short stretches of canal under the direction of state-employed engineers.

## Conception and promotion

The idea of an interior route for a canal between the Hudson River and Lake Erie taking advantage of the Mohawk River gap—the only water-level route through the Appalachian Mountains—was conceived by New York politicians and wealthy speculators long before construction began in 1817. If the canal could be built, it would unlock the immense natural resources of America's west and bring them through New York City on freight-laden barges at a fraction of the costs incurred over land routes. One of the earliest proposals to improve inland navigation along this route was put forward by Sir Henry Moore, governor of New York, in 1768. But like many subsequent proposals it failed to gather the political support required to develop the idea.

The Western Inland Lock Navigation Company was formed in 1792 to make improvements on the Mohawk River. Although the Western Company lacked the engineering expertise needed to navigate larger natural obstacles along the river, the work undertaken indicated that an inland waterway through the Appalachian Mountains might be possible. Many of the leading engineers and politicians later involved in the Erie Canal project worked for the Western Company. The company was short of private finance and badly managed, but it provided an important lesson for those who went on to create the Erie Canal: a project this large would have to be managed and financed by government.

The first concrete proposal for the Erie Canal can be traced to fourteen essays written in 1807 and 1808 by Jesse Hawley, a New York grain merchant. Hawley explored different designs, technological options, and routes for the canal. He considered possible sources of funding and suggested that the canal be built with federal money rather than private finance, which he dismissed as inadequate, monopolistic, and self-interested. Based on his readings about the dimensions, complexity, construction time, and the cost of major European canals, he predicted that the canal would cost $5 million to build. Completed in 1681, the Canal du Midi connecting the Atlantic Ocean and the Mediterranean Sea across south-western France demonstrated that it was possible to build a canal on a massive scale—although the Erie Canal was more than twice as long as the French one. A few months later, after reading about France's Canal du Midi and Scotland's Clyde canals, Hawley's revised figure of $6 million accounted for the additional costs of his favoured design concept—an inclined plane design with twenty-six locks falling from the elevation of Lake Erie to Mohawk. Hawley's estimates about the costs and benefits of the canal proved to be incredibly accurate. The project which started a decade later was publicly funded, based on roughly the same cost estimate, and followed a route similar to the one he suggested.

Those promoting the canal were concerned that New York's ascendancy as a commercial centre was under threat. The journey west was difficult through the great physical barrier of the Appalachian Mountains and easier routes were available further south. Baltimore, Philadelphia, and other cities were growing rapidly because they were connected by turnpike from Pittsburgh to Philadelphia and the national road to Baltimore. The burgeoning trade route from the Mississippi and Ohio rivers to the Gulf of Mexico threatened to hand commercial supremacy to New Orleans. The Erie Canal's supporters were convinced that an inland waterway was required to establish New York as America's main gateway to western markets.

In the first legislative step toward the building of the canal, federal government provided the modest budget of $600 to conduct a survey of the most direct route for the canal between the Hudson River and Lake Erie. The survey was undertaken in 1808 by James Geddes—a young and inexperienced surveyor who went on to be chief engineer on the western section of the Erie Canal. His 1809 report anticipated the future layout and design of the Erie Canal, including a series of locks and a great embankment to scale the forested ridge at what became Lockport.

Inspired by Hawley's essays, De Witt Clinton first began supporting the Erie Canal project in 1810. During his long political career, Clinton served as United States senator, mayor, and governor of

New York. He threw his political weight behind the project and risked his career in turning it from a dream into a reality. Clinton was named as a member of the Canal Commission of New York State in April 1810. So important was his role in the project that some would call it Clinton's 'Big Ditch'.

Clinton and the other commissioners championed the Erie Canal in a highly uncertain and contested political environment. Politicians representing southern states and cities actively resisted a scheme that would increase the commercial strength of New York. Many of those who would eventually benefit most—New York politicians and residents along the route—actively opposed the canal until it opened for service. The commissioners had to negotiate with many stakeholders along the canal's route and convince those who were openly hostile to the construction of the canal, including powerful politicians, residents, and the New York press. The commissioners built momentum behind the project by attracting popular support for a scheme few thought could be built. In 1815 and 1816, Clinton organized mass public demonstrations for canal supporters in New York City and a populist campaign—collecting thousands of signatures—to support a memorandum to the legislature demanding that the project be approved.

The commissioners' efforts to gain approval and funding for the project depended on detailed surveys of the route and an estimation of the construction costs. In the summer of 1811, the commissioners appointed Benjamin Wright—a surveyor with some experience of canal construction gained while working for the Western Company, who was later appointed chief engineer for the middle section of the canal. In 1816 Wright and Geddes conducted in-depth surveys of alternative routes to Lake Erie and considered various design concepts to prepare for construction the following year. On the basis of these surveys, the commission raised the total cost of building the canal from $5 million to $6 million.

The commissioners were empowered to seek financial support from Congress as part of a programme of infrastructure investment in national road and canal projects. Federal funding was preferred because other private canal ventures, such as the Western Inland Navigation Company, had ended in failure. But the federal government was reluctant to fund a massive public project that represented New York's interests, particularly in a period of economic instability, rising public expenditures, and trade restrictions imposed during the Anglo-American War. Despite attracting political allies and support in Congress, the Erie Canal was unable to secure federal funding when, in 1816, President James Madison used his constitutional right to veto the bill. After this option was closed, the commissioners were forced to seek funding from the New York state government. The state legislature asked the commissioners to come up with recommendations on how to raise the $6 million needed to build the canal. This was a huge amount of money at the time, equivalent to almost a third of all the banking and insurance capital in New York state.

The commissioners' report published in February 1817, complete with maps and profiles, recommended a canal following a northern route that was 353 miles long with seventy-seven locks (slightly shorter and with fewer locks than the eventual outcome). They rejected the inclined plane design and used the same dimensions and shape as the 27-mile (44-kilometre) long Middlesex Canal connecting the Merrimack River with Boston. Apart from this, there were no other American examples to prepare for such a massive and complex endeavour. Based on a construction estimate of $13,800 per mile, they reduced the total estimated costs of construction from $6 million to just under $5 million, primarily to make the expenditure more agreeable to the New York legislature.

Construction of the Erie Canal was finally approved on 15 April 1817 when a Canal Bill was passed by the New York state government. A new group of five commissioners including Clinton were responsible for overseeing the construction of the canal, which was largely financed by selling state government bonds to the public and financial markets abroad, particularly British investors. As significant as the project's technological achievements, this innovation—the Canal Fund—in public finance was widely adopted to fund other canal projects. Efforts to attract extra funding continued while construction was under way. By 1824 the state government and commissioners had sold nearly $7.5 million in canal bonds.

## Design and construction

After gaining government approval and securing funding, those championing the canal now had to decide how to achieve the objectives of the Canal Law of 1817. As governor of New York and president of the commission, a position he held until 1824, Clinton was the project's main sponsor responsible for attracting support and overcoming political obstacles encountered during the execution of the project. Two acting commissioners were appointed to manage the day-to-day activities of the project: Samuel Young as the commission's secretary and Myron Holley as the commission's treasurer. Benjamin Wright and James Geddes became chief engineers responsible for the design and construction of the canal. With no formal training as engineers and little or no knowledge of canal construction, they had to learn as they went along.

The commissioners' 1817 report, which synthesized the previous surveys and design considerations, became the construction blueprint for the Erie Canal. The 363-mile canal was built between 1817 and 1825 in three sections with engineers and contractors assigned to each. The middle section extended about 94 miles (151 kilometres) from the Mohawk to Seneca rivers. Work began with a ground-breaking ceremony on 4 July 1817. Facing fewer natural obstacles, construction of this relatively flat section was finished in October 1820. The experience and new techniques devised to build this section proved valuable when the project moved on to the far more difficult western and eastern sections which began in parallel in 1819. The 110-mile (177-kilometre) eastern section along the Mohawk River was finished in the autumn of 1823. When the 160-mile (257-kilometre) western section to Lake Erie was finished in 1825 the entire canal was integrated as a complete system and ready for operation.

Wright and Geddes assembled a group of inexperienced young men to undertake detailed surveys of each section of the canal, notably John Jervis, Nathan Roberts, and Canvass White, who would go on to become America's leading engineers and canal builders. They had to establish design specifications for each section, estimate the costs of construction, and plan the schedule of work. The original plans, design, and route layout had to be adjusted to address difficulties encountered when the project was under way. At Clinton's request, but using his own money, White visited Britain in 1817 to study canals, tunnels, underwater cements, and aqueducts. After visiting Thomas Telford's Pontcysyllte Aqueduct built on iron arches a hundred feet above the River Dee in North Wales, White understood how bold and innovative engineering design could overcome the most difficult natural obstacles. When he rejoined the project in 1818, he was more knowledgeable about canal engineering than almost anyone in the United States and contributed greatly to the design and construction of locks, dams, and bridges on all parts of the Erie Canal.

Whereas simple excavation was the main work on the middle section, tackling the eastern and western sections called for far more advanced engineering solutions. On the eastern section, the lower Mohawk Valley required twenty-seven locks over 30 miles (50 kilometres) to climb over a series of natural rapids including the Cohoes and Little Falls. On the western section, an 802-foot (244-metre) stone aqueduct carried the canal over the Genesee River at Rochester. An even more imposing natural obstacle had to be overcome on the far western end of the canal. The commissioners invited several engineers to submit plans to scale the ridge of solid rock on the Niagara Escarpment. They chose the design proposed by Nathan Roberts: two flights of five locks—one flight for the eastern route and one for the western route—to climb the 66-foot (20-metre) limestone ridge at the new town of Lockport. Constructed in four years, this landmark structure was the most remarkable feat of engineering on the entire Erie Canal.

The commissioners met in June 1817 to design the project organization and contractual approach used to employ and manage the canal builders. They decided to let out construction work to multiple private contractors. Each of the three sections of the project was broken down into smaller, more manageable components—a practice widely used on today's large engineering projects. A contractor was employed to build a stretch of canal—as short as a quarter of a mile (about 400 metres) and no longer than 3 miles—under the supervision of canal engineers employed by the state. Contracting out work in small stretches had been used on a small scale on the Middlesex Canal, but the Erie Canal promoted and perfected the practice. Each contractor was effectively responsible for building a miniature canal largely in isolation from canals constructed by other contractors on either side. Building the canal in short stretches meant that the risks of employing contractors with little or no experience in canal construction were limited by the size of each contract. It was a risk the commissioners believed worth taking in a state with limited resources and no experience in public construction projects.

The use of competitive tendering—now widely used on government projects—was considered novel in a period when canal labourers were traditionally employed directly by the state. Contractors were compensated for the risks incurred and received extra payments for overruns due to changes in the scope of work (such as the decision to use stone rather than wood in the aqueducts) or additional work required to deal with unexpected problems (such as the great flood of 1817). They were not supposed to receive payment until the work was completed and inspected by an engineer. Few had the financial resources to pay for the tools, provisions, and horses required to undertake the work. So the commissioners offered contractors monthly advances of up to $2,000, with a final payment made on completion of the work, less advances. Safeguards were put in place to suspend in-progress payments and enforce strict compliance when a contractor was found to be corrupt or covering up mistakes. A contractor who failed to start the work, complete it on time, or meet the required specifications had to repay the advance with interest. Some less reputable contractors sought to earn extra profits by making questionable claims for extra work that were often hard to reject. In most cases, however, the relationship between the commissioners and contractors was less formal and often more collaborative. The difficulty of settling contractors' accounts upon completion of their work was eventually solved by ensuring that any changes in the scope of work were openly and frankly discussed, documented, and settled as formal written contract variations.

Competitive tendering helped keep the project on schedule, but the cost of constructing some of the more challenging parts of the canal exceeded the original estimates. Completed on time in 1820, the middle section cost about $1 million and was only about 10 per cent over budget. The more difficult Genesee aqueduct was finished in September 1823, eleven months behind schedule and $83,000 over the original cost estimates. By 1821, however, the commissioners were able to reduce the overall cost of canal construction because of the large number of contractors bidding for work at reduced prices. While some contractors failed, others successfully developed and honed their skills and capabilities as they completed one contract after another. For example, John Richardson, the canal's first signed contractor, went on to become one of the largest contractors on the entire project.

There was one exception to this policy of employing private
contractors. The excavation work on the 'Deep Cut'—through
3 miles of solid limestone and another 4 miles through a mixture
of rock and earth extending south-west from the brow of the ridge
at Lockport—was originally let out to private contractors in four
stretches. This was the most difficult part of the western section.
Work began in 1821 but proceeded slowly. By September 1823 the
commissioners decided that the task was beyond the capabilities
of private contractors and would have to be undertaken as a public
works project. Thousands of employees were hired by the state to
blast and cut their way through the rock under the direct control
of canal engineers.

To make a profit from contracts awarded to the lowest bidder,
contractors had to develop numerous innovations—new processes,
tools, and materials—to complete the project efficiently and deal
with unexpected problems that might delay it or push it over
budget. Many innovations were developed by workers with the
least training and experience, but who were willing to conduct
repeated experiments until they got it right. Several new tools
were developed soon after work began on the middle section.
Contractors responded to the extraordinary flooding of 1817,
which made work much harder than expected, by creating a new
canal excavation technique. Operated by three people and a team
of horses or oxen, the 'plough and scraper' was used to sever and
remove small roots. Developed in 1818, the 'tree-felling' machine
operated by one person was used to clear larger areas of forest.
For trees cut down in the traditional way, by axe or saw, a 'stump
puller' operated by seven men and horses was developed to
remove residual stumps and roots.

Constructing a canal through the difficult terrain and mountainous
obstacles on the western section required even more significant
innovation. A new device called the 'Dibble Crane' was developed
when it became impractical and inefficient to continue removing
large volumes of excavated material from the Deep Cut by small

**2. Innovative Dibble cranes used to excavate the Lockport Deep Cut section of the Erie Canal.**

wheelbarrows. This massive wood-framed crane used a large bucket raised and lowered by rope and pulley to excavate the material as quickly as it accumulated (Figure 2).

Ronald E. Shaw writes that the discovery of waterproof cement was 'one of the epochal achievements of the building of the Erie Canal' because it gave birth to the American cement industry. Canvass White is often credited with discovering a quicklime cement that hardened under water after conducting repeated experiments with varieties of local limestone. Abundantly available and easily prepared, this waterproof lime was used to construct the entire Erie Canal, reducing costs and eliminating the dependence on imported European cement. White took out patents on his original innovation in 1820 and on an improvement in 1821. Initially the Erie commissioners regarded the discovery as their intellectual property and encouraged contractors to supply the cement without payment of royalties. But White was eventually successful in winning the suit and defending attempts to purchase his patent rights.

## Opening and outcome

When the canal opened, the whole nation celebrated America's mastery over nature—a symbol of progress that united political leaders, militia, traders, industrialists, and the general public. Clinton was voted out of office in 1822 and removed from the Canal Board of Commissioners in 1824. But he benefited from the great excitement and increasing popular support for the canal as it approached completion. He was re-elected as governor of New York in time to preside over the grand opening ceremony in Manhattan when he poured a keg of water from Lake Erie into the Atlantic Ocean to mark the 'Wedding of the Waters' on 4 November 1825.

The Erie Canal was the longest canal in the world, built with the least experience, and provided benefits that exceeded the most optimistic predictions (Figure 3). It must be considered a success in the terms we now use to evaluate project performance. It was completed on schedule on 26 October 1825, at a cost of $7.1 million that was surprisingly close to the original estimates, and without experiencing a significant failure or delay during construction. The accuracy of the original estimates is extraordinary given the novelty of the task and uncertainties involved in traversing dramatic and abrupt changes in elevation, manoeuvring the towering Niagara escarpment, and clearing and digging through large areas of forest. Most of the designs worked precisely as planned and many innovations were successfully deployed to keep the project on track and within budget. The state's debt was paid off in less than a decade.

The Erie Canal project did much more than construct a 363-mile ditch connecting western territories to New York. It propelled

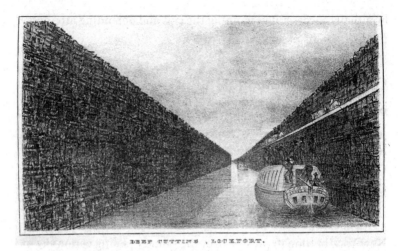

3. The finished Deep Cut of the Erie Canal, 1825.

the rise of America as an industrial nation. The volume of east–west trade more than doubled in the first year of the canal's operation. The costs of transporting goods from Buffalo to New York City dropped from $100 to less than $10 per ton. The flow of revenues quickly exceeded the canal's operating costs. By 1833, the tolls charged on the canal repaid the cost of building the canal. The economic growth generated by the canal exceeded the aspirations of those involved in promoting it, accelerating western migration, stimulating urban development along the banks of the canal, and opening up new markets for the flow of goods and people to the Midwest and large volumes of grain and raw materials to New York and Europe. Benefiting from America's first east–west trade link, New York quickly became the Empire State and commercial centre of a new global power.

The Erie Canal project was a learning experience for engineers who went on to design and build America's canals and railways in the 19th century. With no engineering training available in the United States, building the canal became the so-called 'Erie

School of Engineering' with Wright and Geddes as its deans.
Wright developed a reputation for building canals and railways
in Canada, Cuba, and the United States and received the
posthumous honour of 'Father of Engineering' awarded in 1969
by the American Society of Civil Engineers mainly for his work
on the Erie Canal. Geddes went on to design canals in Ohio,
Pennsylvania, and Canada. Some of the most notable graduates of
the Erie School became the greatest American civil engineers of
the 19th century. Canvass White left the Erie Canal before its
completion to become chief engineer of Pennsylvania's Union
Canal. John Jervis and Nathan Roberts went from canals to
design America's railways.

## Implications for the management of projects

The Erie Canal raises fundamental issues about the management
of large, complex, and uncertain projects. A project starts with
an idea, vision, or proposal. If the idea is taken forward, a project
sponsor defines the goal, explores alternative designs, estimates
the costs and benefits, secures funding, identifies the uncertainties
facing the project and how they can be overcome, and plans
a schedule of work with demanding but achievable targets.
After securing funding and gaining approval, an organization
has to coordinate and schedule work undertaken by multiple
contractors. In large projects, the work is divided up into
manageable chunks (which we now call the 'work breakdown
structure') and undertaken in phases that are completed
sequentially, but can overlap or occur simultaneously. A project
ends and an operational activity begins when the newly
constructed facility is used to provide a service.

The Erie Canal illustrates what Peter Morris has emphasized: a
project is more likely to be successful if the sponsor (owner and
operator of the asset) spends time at the beginning—in the 'front
end'—defining the goals, understanding the benefits and risks, and

shaping the strategic approach. The sponsor has to engage with multiple stakeholders (e.g. politicians, users, contractors, local businesses, and the public) whose interests, expectations, and concerns may be impacted positively or negatively by the performance and outcome of a project. The difficult task of setting a goal should involve a dialogue between the sponsor, project manager, and end users to clarify what they want from the project.

Although we should not underestimate the vital role played by De Witt Clinton, the success of the Erie Canal, like most engineering projects, is attributable to the judgement and insights brought into play by the leadership group rather than any single individual. The project had many champions: visionary thinkers who first proposed the idea; commissioners who shaped the project, secured funding, and gained approval in the face of strong political opposition; acting commissioners who managed and pushed the project through to completion; and engineers and contractors who were able to overcome the huge technological challenges facing the project.

The Erie Canal is an example of a large-scale engineering endeavour which we would now call a 'megaproject' (Chapter 6). In their efforts to gain approval and secure funding, sponsors frequently underestimate the costs, risks, and completion times and overstate the benefits of a megaproject. Bent Flyvbjerg and his colleagues have shown that the tendency to underestimate the costs—'optimism bias'—can be avoided in the planning stage by learning from other comparable projects. Although no canal project in the world was as large and complex as the Erie Canal, studies of other canals and detailed surveys of the route did help to obtain a realistic estimation of the costs and risks involved. The final cost was deliberately underestimated—this is what Flyvbjerg calls 'strategic misrepresentation'—to make the project more attractive as an investment to the New York legislature.

Ultimately the project was delivered on time and almost within budget. Perhaps more importantly, the benefits far exceeded the most wildly optimistic expectations of Hawley, Clinton, and other promoters.

Despite the opportunities to learn from large-scale endeavours undertaken over the two centuries that have passed since the Erie Canal, most of today's megaprojects are late, over budget, and fail to meet their original goals. In a study of sixty large engineering projects around the world, Miller and Lessard found that 40 per cent of the projects were inefficient in terms of cost, time, and technical performance, over 18 per cent had extensive cost overruns, and nearly 27 per cent had long schedule overruns. In a study of 258 railway, fixed-link, and road megaprojects, Flyvbjerg and his co-authors found that cost overruns of 40 per cent are common and overruns of 80 per cent are not uncommon. In an article published in 2014, Flyvbjerg found that nine out of ten megaprojects have cost overruns of up to 50 per cent. Table 2 provides a list of megaprojects with huge cost overruns, but let's consider one in more detail.

The Boston Central Artery/Tunnel (CA/T) was America's largest and most expensive civil engineering project at the time of its construction. Boston's 'Big Dig' was originally scheduled to open in 1998 at an estimated cost of $2.6 billion. The project involved a 7.5-mile (12-kilometre) new highway system with tunnels and bridges to improve the flow of traffic through the Boston region with links to Logan International Airport. Design and construction was managed by the state-owned Massachusetts Turnpike Authority, and a joint venture between Bechtel and Parsons Brinckerhoff coordinated the multiple contractors involved in the project. These organizations confronted many technical, geological, political, and environmental problems that had not been accounted for at the outset and called for modifications and creative ways to resolve them as the project

**Table 2  Large-scale projects have a calamitous history of cost overrun (adapted from Flyvbjerg 2014)**

| Project | Cost Overrun (%) |
| --- | --- |
| Suez Canal, Egypt | 1,900 |
| Scottish Parliament Building, Scotland | 1,600 |
| Sydney Opera House, Australia | 1,400 |
| Montreal Summer Olympics, Canada | 1,300 |
| Concorde Supersonic Aeroplane, UK, France | 1,100 |
| Troy and Greenfield Railroad, USA | 900 |
| Excalibur Smart Projectile, USA, Sweden | 650 |
| Canadian Firearms Registry, Canada | 590 |
| Lake Placid Winter Olympics, USA | 560 |
| Medicare transaction system, USA | 560 |
| Bank of Norway headquarters, Norway | 440 |
| Furka Base Tunnel, Switzerland | 300 |
| Verrazano Narrow Bridge, USA | 280 |
| Boston's Big Dig Artery/Tunnel project USA | 220 |
| Denver International Airport, USA | 200 |

*Projects*

Source: Table 2 in B. Flyvbjerg, Project Management Institute Inc., *Project Management Journal: What You Should Know About Mega Projects, and Why: An Overview, 2014.* 45(2): 6–19. Copyright and all rights reserved. Material from this publication has been reproduced with the permission of PMI.

progressed. CA/T was finally completed eight years behind schedule in December 2007 and cost about $15 billion: after adjustments are made for inflation this is a cost overrun of about 220 per cent.

Inadequate front-end planning, strategic misrepresentation, optimistic behaviour, and escalating commitment to a failing cause are some of the reasons why megaprojects perform so badly. But megaprojects also fail because the organizations involved are unable to adapt plans and innovate when conditions change unexpectedly and new opportunities arise during their execution. Albert Hirschman introduced the principle of the 'Hiding Hand' to explain how innovative resources are brought into play to deal with uncertainties not foreseen when planning large-scale projects, particularly those with long gestation periods, when unexpected problems arise much later and require more serious efforts to resolve them. Challenging projects are undertaken, Hirschman argued, because we misjudge 'the nature of the task, by presenting it to ourselves as more routine, simple and undemanding of genuine creativity than it will turn out to be'. It is better not to know the real costs involved. An invisible hand hides the difficulties from us and helps get projects started.

We now know that the Hiding Hand principle is overly optimistic about the downstream innovative capacity of megaprojects to solve problems overlooked by upstream planners. Yet it does at least help us to recognize the potential for applying innovation at every point in the life cycle to complete megaprojects more efficiently, as the Erie Canal case illustrated. Innovation in the front-end stage is enhanced by learning from other contexts and how similar projects elsewhere in the world are designed, financed, and organized. Since megaprojects are rarely executed and completed as originally planned, the parties involved have to find ways of resolving problems and innovating as they go along.

The Erie Canal marked the beginning of long and close association between engineering and project management. The rapidly industrializing countries in Europe and North America depended on large technological systems—canals, railways, and telegraphs—that could not be designed and constructed without well-developed engineering and project management capabilities working in unison. Already established as a profession in France and the UK when the Erie Canal project started, civil engineering would acquire a similar status in the United States as a formally recognized discipline and soon be widely taught in American universities. Project management would have to wait until the 1960s before it would receive similar attention and recognition.

# Chapter 3
# From Manhattan to the Moon

The Panama Canal, Henry Ford's River Rouge automobile production plant, the Hoover Dam, Tennessee Valley Authority complex, and Empire State Building are some of the great early 20th-century projects that would shape America's future. Like the Erie Canal, these projects accomplished their goals long before project management was established as a formal discipline. The real breakthrough in the management and organization of large, complex projects, however, can be traced back to the Second World War Manhattan Project, which developed the atom bomb, and the early post-war Atlas Project, which produced the intercontinental ballistic missile. With few precedents to guide them, new structures, processes, and tools had to be created to coordinate, schedule, and integrate the vast networks of people, resources, and organizations involved in these projects. To accelerate progress, multiple systems were developed in 'parallel' and phases of research, design, testing, and production were undertaken simultaneously—or 'concurrently'—rather than sequentially. Scientists now collaborated closely with engineers and managers in interdisciplinary teams. Dedicated organizations with 'project managers' and 'systems engineers' were created for each project. As the Soviet threat intensified during the Cold War of the 1950s and 1960s, increasingly complex and technologically advanced systems had to be designed and produced at rapid pace. Originating in the Atlas and subsequent missile projects before migrating to the Apollo space programme, a new 'systems approach' was established to manage the immense proliferation of technological projects.

## Manhattan Project

The goal of the Manhattan Project was to produce the atomic bomb and bring the Second World War to a successful completion more quickly than was possible by conventional warfare. By the summer of 1945 when its mission was accomplished, the original $6,000 authorized in February 1940 to initiate research on fission chain reaction had increased to an expenditure of $2.2 billion. The project was unprecedented in its concentration of human and physical resources dedicated to the production of a single product and comparable in size to the American automobile industry. At its peak, this geographically dispersed government-led project employed about 130,000 scientists, engineers, managers, and workers to achieve an urgent goal in the utmost secrecy under the command of President Franklin D. Roosevelt and a few senior Cabinet officers.

In 1939, Albert Einstein wrote a letter urging President Roosevelt to support the development of 'extremely powerful bombs', fearing that the United States might fall behind Germany in the race to develop the military potential of atomic energy—the idea that immense quantities of energy would be released if fissionable materials (either uranium-235 or the recently discovered plutonium-239) could be developed to cause a nuclear reaction. A great release of energy occurs when fissionable materials break down (fission) more quickly than they can escape from an assembly. In response, Roosevelt established an advisory committee to oversee a programme of research to produce a fuel source of fissionable material for a nuclear explosion.

The Manhattan Project was formally established in June 1942 when it became clear that a vast array of laboratories, production plants, and reactors would have to be constructed at multiple locations to produce the bomb. Most of the early research was undertaken by Columbia University in the Manhattan District of New York where the army established the 'Manhattan Engineering District'. As a result, the project became known as the Manhattan Project even though it was geographically dispersed at sites across the country with plants in the states of Tennessee, Washington, and New Mexico and university research laboratories in Columbia, Chicago, Virginia, and Berkeley.

In September 1942, General Leslie Groves—an experienced engineer who had recently overseen the construction of the Pentagon, the largest building in the world at the time—was appointed to lead the project. The United States Army Corps of Engineers with its vast experience in large-scale construction projects was responsible for materials procurement, engineering design, and construction of the plants and facilities. Stone & Webster had already been appointed in spring 1941 as principal contractor for the project, bringing its knowledge of engineering, consulting, finance, and large-scale construction. On 28 December 1942 President Roosevelt approved a budget of over $2 billion to build full-scale processing plants to supply large quantities of uranium and plutonium explosives and design the bomb. Formal contracts were made with large industrial corporations such as Eastman Kodak, Du Pont Company, General Electric, and Westinghouse to design, construct, and operate the laboratories, plants, reactors, and processing equipment of the nuclear-production system.

With ample funds available, completing the project in less than three years was more important than saving money. At such an early stage, it was not possible to foresee which technology would eventually prevail. The military's preference for a production line of atomic bombs was not feasible. Given the limited supply of fissionable material, only one or two bombs would be built. To have a chance of completing the project as quickly as possible,

Groves and his advisory committee decided that two bomb designs (uranium and plutonium) and three processes to produce fissile material should be pursued in parallel. As Groves put it: 'The whole endeavour was founded on possibilities rather than probabilities.' There was no certainty which bomb design would work or which fissionable explosive material would be required for each bomb.

Initially two processes for uranium-235 isotope separation—electromagnetic and gaseous diffusion—were installed at Oak Ridge, Tennessee. The 70-square-mile (180-square-kilometre) Oak Ridge complex was carefully selected because of the availability of electric power, water supply, and railway connections, and the remoteness of the location helped maintain secrecy. After making insufficient progress with these processes, Groves decided that a third process—thermal diffusion—should be investigated and it was this process that was eventually selected for the preliminary separation of uranium.

The only process available to produce plutonium was a reactor pile of uranium and graphite blocks. Plutonium research was undertaken at the Metallurgical Laboratory of the University of Chicago. In order to set production schedules and determine plant capacity, Groves needed to know how much plutonium would be required for each bomb. But in autumn 1942, he discovered that the Chicago scientists had no accurate idea of the quantities of plutonium needed and compared his position to 'a caterer who is told that he must be prepared to serve anywhere between ten and a thousand guests'. With such limited scientific and technical data, Groves decided to press ahead 'at full speed' with plutonium production despite the possibility of failure. In December 1942 Du Pont Company was contracted to design, construct, and operate plutonium production piles and separation plants. In February 1943, Groves acquired another large and remote site at the Hanford Engineer Works, near Pasco, Washington, to build three large-scale production piles, or reactors, and four plants for separating plutonium. Du Pont faced the challenge of freezing the engineering designs and proceeding with construction (involving 42,000 people during the peak period) using experimental and incomplete data supplied by the Chicago Lab.

While waiting for fissionable uranium and plutonium material, parallel efforts were under way to design the atomic bomb. In 1942, the physicist Robert J. Oppenheimer was appointed as head of the Los Alamos Scientific Laboratory to lead the research and development (R&D) team of scientists responsible for combining fissionable material to achieve a nuclear explosion and designing bombs that could be dropped from a plane and detonated in the air above the target. A seminar organized by Oppenheimer in July 1942 identified as many as five different bomb designs. The various design solutions were explored in parallel before two designs were selected: the 'gun design' for the uranium bomb, the 'implosion design' for the plutonium bomb. To preserve the open communication and traditional independence of scientists, Los Alamos initially adopted a functional department structure organized by academic disciplines. By the spring of 1944, however, the project was in crisis when tests showed that the plutonium gun assembly bomb design failed to work. Finding that the development of the more complex implosion bomb design was proceeding too slowly, Oppenheimer decided to create a dedicated project organization focused on the end product to improve communication, facilitate cross-functional integration, and instil a greater sense of urgency.

Small quantities of the uranium and plutonium material eventually arrived from Oak Ridge and Hanford respectively, the implosion design was frozen in February 1945, and by the summer of that year the two bombs were assembled. With insufficient material available for testing, the uranium bomb utilizing the gun method, known as 'Little Boy', was shipped directly to operations in the Pacific region. There was enough plutonium available to test the 'Fat Man' plutonium bomb named after Winston Churchill and for another bomb to be used against Japan. A field test was undertaken because there was less confidence in the performance of the plutonium bomb and reliability of the implosion method. The world's first atomic bomb was exploded in a test facility near Albuquerque in New Mexico on 16 July 1945.

The project achieved its primary goal of producing the atomic bomb and bringing the war to an end as early as possible. The uranium bomb was dropped on Hiroshima on 6 August 1945. It killed 70,000 people on impact and another 70,000 died by the end of 1945. The plutonium bomb was dropped on Nagasaki on 9 August 1945. It killed 40,000 people and the death toll reached 70,000 by January 1946. The Japanese offer to surrender was announced on 10 August.

According to General Groves, the project was 'successful'—despite the catastrophic consequences—because it had a clearly defined mission (even though how the goal would be accomplished was entirely unclear at the outset), the work was divided up into specific tasks, and authority was delegated to the right level of responsibility. The Manhattan Project set a precedent for parallel development on post-war missile projects by developing two bomb designs and several processes of fissile production simultaneously. It benefited from extensive trial-and-error learning from parallel trials of alternative technologies and designs, progressively resolving uncertainties and taking advantage of unexpected developments while the project was under way.

## Atlas Project

After the Second World War, the United States and Soviet Union entered into an arms race to develop increasingly powerful weapons systems. America started Intercontinental Ballistic Missile (ICBM) research after hearing reports about missile projects in the Soviet Union and the explosion of a fusion device in 1953. An ICBM missile consisted of a rocket engine, a giant cylinder of fuel, a nose cone carrying a nuclear warhead, and a guidance and control system. It was designed to follow a ballistic (a gravity-shaped trajectory) flight of about 5,000 miles (8,000 kilometres) at a velocity of over 10,000 miles per hour and deliver a nuclear warhead within 5,000 feet (1,500 metres) of its target.

In 1953, the Air Force established an advisory task force—known as the 'Teapot Committee'—of elite scientists and engineers to oversee ICBM research. It included Simon Ramo and Dean Wooldridge, the founders of the systems engineering firm Ramo-Wooldridge Corporation that would play a major role in the Atlas Project. The committee recommended that missiles should be developed 'to the maximum extent that technology would allow' and made the formal recommendation to President Dwight D. Eisenhower in February 1954 to launch an ICBM programme on a 'crash basis'. Placed at the top of the nation's military priorities, ICBM development was undertaken by the Air Force with few limitations on funding.

America's ICBM programme depended on advances in engineering and project management that were even more tightly connected and focused on solving the 'systems problems' than any previous endeavour. The ICBM programme produced three missiles: Atlas, Titan, and Minuteman. In 1957, during its most intensive design phase, the entire programme involved 18,000 scientists, engineers, and technical experts, 70,000 people in 22 industries, 17 principal contractors, and 200 subcontractors. The first Atlas and Titan test missiles were launched in 1958 and proved feasible for a 5,000-mile flight. Initiated in 1958 and deployed in 1962, the Minuteman missile eventually superseded the Atlas/Titan missiles.

In July 1954, the Air Force established the Western Development Division—located in a vacant church in Ingelwood, near Los Angeles—as a 'special project office' under the leadership of Brigadier General Bernard Schriever (promoted to General soon after his appointment) to develop the ICBM missiles. Schriever is considered to be the father of project management because the 'systems approach' that he created for Atlas—with the help of Simon Ramo and other advisers—was widely adopted to manage many other military, aerospace, and civil projects.

Schriever spent a considerable amount of his time managing key stakeholders 'outside the system' and working across organizational boundaries to secure funding, gain access to senior decision makers, and ensure his managerial initiatives were not handicapped by a slow-moving bureaucratic approval process. But the most pressing task initially facing Schriever was to decide what organization could provide the Air Force with the technical and systems engineering expertise required to coordinate the efforts of numerous participants from industry, government, and universities involved in the Atlas Project. The Teapot Committee recommended the creation of a 'Manhattan-like' project organization, but Schriever rejected this advice because neither the Air Force nor scientists had the technical capability required to manage ICBMs, which were considered even more complex than the atomic bomb.

The Air Force could have resorted to the traditional practice honed during the Second World War of appointing a single airframe manufacturer as 'prime contractor' to design and coordinate the subcontractors involved in the development of the ICBMs. But Schriever was not convinced that any airframe manufacturer had the breadth of capabilities in systems engineering and physical sciences required to develop a broad base of technology extending beyond airframe manufacture and assembly to electronics and computing. After considering various alternatives, Schriever and his advisers decided that a radically new type of organization was required to assist the Western Development Division. Ramo-Wooldridge was assigned to act as 'systems integrator', providing the Air Force with the systems engineering and technical advice required to manage the project.

The configuration of the missile system shaped the organization of the project (Figure 4). A parallel structure was created to facilitate the close interaction between Air Force project officers and Ramo-Wooldridge project managers. Each subsystem of the Atlas missile, such as propulsion and guidance, was assigned its own project officer and project manager. As Simon Ramo described it, all the parties were 'locked into a single integrated project and a single integrated design of the ICBM missile and system'. The physical layout of the building reflected the close cooperation between the two interdisciplinary groups. Ramo and Schriever, as well as their deputies, met frequently and were 'co-located' in adjacent offices in Ramo-Wooldridge buildings.

Ramo-Wooldridge worked alongside the Air Force and together they decided upon the 'associated contractors', coordinated their activities, and monitored their performance. Consolidated Vultee Aircraft Corporation (Convair), which had already been developing a long-range missile called Atlas, was contracted for the final assembly of the airframe. However, Convair's missile had not yet been flight tested and was years away from production. Schriever discussed the challenge of developing such unproven ICBM technology with General Groves and Oppenheimer and decided to adopt the practice used on the Manhattan Project of developing systems in parallel. The Glenn L. Martin Company was contracted in October 1955 for the final assembly of a backup system, the Titan missile, using alternative airframe technology. Each major subsystem of the Atlas and Titan missiles—the airframe, guidance, propulsion, nose cone, and computer—was also developed simultaneously by associated contractors to stimulate the search for alternative technical solutions and assure that the failure of one contractor could not delay the project (Table 3).

As the systems integrator on the Atlas Project, Ramo-Wooldridge's staff of a hundred or so civilian engineers and scientists were able to see interconnections among parts of the whole system. Guided by a common vision, they were responsible for optimization of the

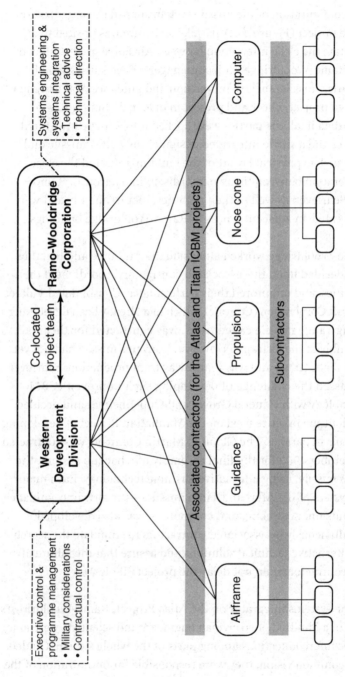

Projects

Executive control &
programme management
• Military considerations
• Contractual control

Systems engineering &
systems integration
• Technical advice
• Technical direction

Western
Development
Division

Ramo-Wooldridge
Corporation

Co-located
project team

Associated contractors (for the Atlas and Titan ICBM projects)

Airframe

Guidance

Propulsion

Nose cone

Computer

Subcontractors

4. Western Development Division and Ramo-Wooldridge organization.

48

**Table 3  Associated contractors for the Atlas and Titan ICBM projects**

| Subsystem | Atlas | Titan |
|---|---|---|
| Airframe | Convair | Martin |
| Guidance | | |
| *Radio-inertial* | General Electric | Bell Telephone |
| *All-inertial* | A.C. Spark Plug | American Bosch and MIT |
| Propulsion | North American | Aerojet General |
| Nose cone | General Electric | AVCO |
| Computer | Burroughs | Remington Rand |

Source: T. P. Hughes, *Rescuing Prometheus* (New York: Pantheon Books, 1998).

entire system, which involved making trade-offs among its component parts that could reduce the reliability, range, or accuracy of each missile. Developing a lighter warhead, for example, involved a trade-off that reduced the propulsion, or thrust, requirement of the ICBM. Ramo-Wooldridge's systems engineers prepared background studies, produced preliminary designs, and defined specifications for the performance of each subsystem and the interfaces between them. Designs were considered 'preliminary' until they were finalized, incorporated in working drawings, and used to produce prototypes of missile components and systems. If specifications for components or subsystems changed during the project, Ramo-Wooldridge engineers modified the affected parts in the missile system to achieve a compatible match. After that, they controlled the test and operational environment within which the missile was put to work.

After specifications were defined and produced as working drawings, Ramo-Wooldridge's systems engineers assumed responsibility for the technical direction of the Atlas Project, working closely with Schriever's project officers to select the contractors and monitor their performance. Contractor selection was a drawn-out process lasting almost three months. It involved ranking potential firms for their technical and management capabilities, inviting the highly ranked firms to bid, evaluating their proposals, and selecting the preferred contractor. General Electric, for example, was selected as the nose cone contractor for the Atlas missile and AVCO Manufacturing Corporation for the Titan missile. Schriever and Ramo held what were known as 'Black Saturday' meetings with their project officers and project managers in a control room with an early digital computer displaying real-time information supplied by contractors to deal with cost overruns, delays to scheduled milestones, and failures to meet performance standards during tests.

Schriever believed that the traditional 'serial' approach to develop subsystems in sequential phases would be too slow to win the ICBM race with the Soviet Union. In serial development, research led to design, which led to prototype development, testing, and production of the weapon, which led to maintenance and training methods to use it. To accelerate development, each activity had to be undertaken in overlapping phases. The term 'concurrency' was coined by Schriever to explain the process and justify why it was needed. Under concurrency, the design and test facilities started before the details of the test programme were finalized. Work on the assembly and launch facilities at Cape Canaveral, Florida, for example, started before the missile's size, shape, performance, and operational specifications had been determined. Years later Schriever qualified that concurrency is a prerequisite for large systems projects when 'time is of the essence' because of the attendant risk of costly duplication and massive coordination failure.

Coordinating the concurrent development and testing of components and subsystems was one of the most difficult tasks facing the Atlas Project. Systematic planning and scheduling was required because subsystem and interface designs could not be frozen until preliminary specifications were defined for related parts of the system. Specifications could not be finalized until extensive research and testing had been completed on individual subsystems and the interactions between them. Ramo-Wooldridge's systems engineers developed procedures for progressively freezing the design to reduce the 'ripple' effect of corrective and costly design alterations. Configuration management procedures were created to ensure that any proposed design changes were reviewed and signed off by a Change Control Board and communicated to all affected parties.

Convair's role in the Atlas Project illustrates how contractors shifted from dedicated project organizations to a new type of matrix structure. In 1954, Convair created the Astronautics division to undertake work for the Atlas Project. The number of staff working on the project increased from 300 in 1953 to 9,000 in 1958 and to 32,500 in 1962. During most of the 1950s, Convair ran Atlas as a single-project organization, but soon experienced priority problems and conflicts of authority in its functional departments when it began to develop different versions of Atlas and initiate new subsystem projects, such as the Azusa tracking system. The Astronautics division addressed this problem by creating a matrix organization with a director for each programme working with project and functional managers to schedule tasks and resolve priority issues. By 1963, every one of Astronautics major new programmes was organized as a matrix to sustain and manage the growing number of projects (Box 4).

Pioneered by Schriever, Ramo, and others, the systems approach created for the Atlas Project helped achieve the programme's goal—to win the race with the Soviet Union to develop the first operational ICBM missile. A similar story could be told about the Navy's Polaris Programme under the leadership of Admiral William F. Raborn. The Navy established a Special Projects Office (SPO) to develop and integrate Polaris fleet ballistic missiles for use on board submarines. Unlike Atlas, however, systems integration on the Polaris Programme was undertaken in-house

## Box 4 Functional, project, and matrix organizations

Traditional 'functional organizations' proved unable to cope with the growth in ICBM projects. Communication across separate engineering, manufacturing, sales, and other functional departments was simply too long and cumbersome to provide effective managerial coordination of many large, complex projects.

Contractors like Convair and Martin Company originally established 'project organizations' bringing together people from manufacturing, engineering, research, sales, finance, and other functional departments into groups focused on a single project. A project manager controlled and integrated all of the functional resources required to achieve each project's goal. However, the growth in ICBM work in the late 1950s called for a further organizational innovation.

In the new two-dimensional 'matrix organization', each employee was attached to a functional department and assigned to one or more projects that could not be accomplished by a single department. Members of projects now reported to a functional and a project manager. When their task was accomplished, they returned to their functional home. The matrix structure was designed to accelerate the flow of information, allocate resources more efficiently across multiple projects, and discourage people in functional 'silos' from looking at problems from their own narrow perspective.

Figure 5 provides a simplified illustration of the three structures used to organize projects.

by the Navy's SPO. Polaris also created its own notable project management innovations, such as the Program Evaluation and Review Technique (PERT) network planning tool, run on computers from 1957, to display and provide time estimates for a sequence of planned activities and their anticipated completion dates.

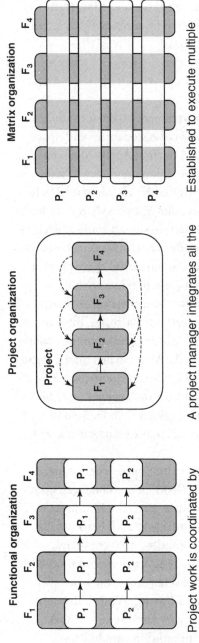

**Functional organization**

Project work is coordinated by functional managers and completed sequentially as it passes from one function/department to another

**Project organization**

A project manager integrates all the functions and work is undertaken sequentially and concurrently in a dedicated, standalone structure (e.g. Convair and Martin Company in the 1950s)

**Matrix organization**

Established to execute multiple projects. Each project is coordinated by a functional and a project manager (e.g. Convair Aeronautics in the 1960s)

Key:

$F_1$ – $F_4$    Functional departments (e.g. R&D, engineering, manufacturing, and operations) or disciplines (e.g. scientific and engineering expertise)

$P_1$ – $P_4$    Projects established within an organization

→    Sequential development of project work in stages

⤎----    Feedback from later to earlier stages in concurrent development

5. **Functional, project, and matrix organizations.**

53

However, PERT contributed surprisingly little to the success of the Polaris programme. It was primarily used to allow technical development to take place unhindered by excessive interference from outside politicians and officials.

## Apollo Moon landing

The influence of the systems approach benefited enormously from the establishment of the National Aeronautics and Space Administration (NASA) in 1958 and the first Apollo Moon landing on 20 July 1969. In 1961, the Soviet Union announced that it was winning 'the space race' with the United States when it launched Yuri Gagarin into space. President John F. Kennedy responded in May that year by stating that 'this nation should commit itself to achieving the goal, before this decade is out, of landing a man on the Moon and returning him safely to the Earth'. Starting with almost no knowledge of how people function in a weightless state, NASA designed and built a system incorporating many new technologies—rockets, spacecraft, test facilities, life-support systems, and a computer-controlled tracking and communications network—that would place men on the Moon in less than a decade. The final cost of over $20 billion for the Moon landing was close to the original estimate of $13 billion plus a contingency of $7 billion. Captured visually with television broadcasts, Apollo sold the benefits of the system mode of project management to the world.

James E. Webb, Head of NASA's entire Space Programme, believed that the first Apollo Moon landing mission faced even more profound managerial challenges than the Manhattan Project. NASA had to coordinate 300,000 staff working for 20,000 contractors and 200 universities in 80 countries. The Apollo programme was led by NASA in collaboration with the space-system divisions of several large contractors—such as General Electric, Lockheed, and Boeing. While subsystem development work was undertaken by contractors, NASA had to retain sufficient systems integration capabilities in-house to know more about the whole endeavour than any individual contractor.

Project management ideas and practices pioneered on Atlas, Polaris, and other missile projects were transferred to the Apollo programme when staff working on these projects joined NASA. In September 1963, George Mueller, formerly of Thompson-Ramo-Wooldridge (TRW), became head of NASA's Office of Managed Space Flight. Mueller joined the programme after the key design choices had already been made. But he soon discovered that the chances of achieving a Moon landing before 1970 were no more than one in ten. Mueller created a matrix structure to improve communications and surveillance of the programme: work divided into functions (programme control, systems engineering, flight operations, test, reliability, and quality) was undertaken in the three centres working on manned missions (Huntsville, Houston, and Canaveral). He abandoned the long-drawn-out process of having numerous flight tests and different vehicle configurations and decided instead to have all components developed and ready for 'all-up testing' using the full Apollo flight configuration.

Recognizing that NASA had little capability in planning and managing large programmes, at Schriever's suggestion, Mueller recruited Brigadier General Samuel C. Phillips from his position as director of the Minuteman missile project to become the Apollo Program Director. Phillips and Mueller had to maintain the flexibility required to tackle unforeseen problems, while introducing disciplined systems-based management (e.g. configuration management, change control board, PERT, and systems engineering) to accelerate the programme schedule, control costs, and achieve the 1969 deadline of landing a man on the Moon. Introduced in January 1965, NASA's Program Development Plan, which identified how the programme's schedule and phases would be managed and organized, became one of the main tools of systems-based project management.

In *Space Age Management* (1969), Webb wrote that NASA's Moon landing was successful because the organization created to manage the project was flexible and adaptive with the 'capacity to adjust to and to move forward in an unpredictable and sometimes turbulent environment'. NASA recognized that many of the predictions about Apollo's technology and operating environment would turn out to be wrong and that it had to 'make the most careful analysis of all known factors at the start of a project and still be prepared to adjust when actual conditions turn out to be different from those foreseen'. Webb suggested that 70 or 80 per cent of tasks undertaken by NASA could be known and prepared for in advance with some degree of certainty, but the remaining 20 to 30 per cent represented a zone of uncertainty that had to be addressed by adaptation and innovation when the project was under way. A balance has to be struck, Webb concluded, between 'orderliness and stability' for the known and predictable part of a large, complex project and 'procedures that will foster innovation' for the fluid and uncertain part.

Given the technological uncertainties involved, NASA could not afford to rely entirely on fixed-price contracts favoured by the Department of Defense. Fixed-price contracts specified the task to be performed for a definite quantity of money. They focused attention on the start of a project, when the specifications were defined and the contract was agreed upon, and the conclusion, when the technology was accepted or rejected. But they ignored the need for adaptation to unforeseen contingencies while projects were under way. NASA acknowledged that fixed-price contracts worked well when conditions were known and predictable, but preferred to use incentive contracts for the development of novel technologies, with bonuses for efforts to improve on the original specifications and address unexpected problems and opportunities. For example, Boeing Company had an incentive contract to produce five spacecraft to photograph the Moon on five missions including incentives on cost, schedule, and spacecraft performance in orbit.

This flexible contract encouraged parties to adjust tasks and alter schedules when conditions changed and new information became available (see Chapter 4).

## Project management's lost roots

By the end of the 1950s, the new systems ideas and practices circulated informally and began to take hold when individuals involved in the ICBM and Polaris programmes moved on to occupy leading positions on other projects. The foundations of a new discipline called 'project management' were laid when engineers, managers, and academics formally articulated and codified the new approach. Articles began to appear in management journals and when the first project management textbooks appeared in the 1960s they were based on the systems approach. When Robert McNamara became Secretary of Defense in 1960 he reorganized military procurement and established systems-based project and programme management.

Systems-based project management spread quickly in the 1970s to the European space programmes and other industries and government agencies throughout the world. The influence of project management led to the foundation of professional associations in the United States and Europe—the International Project Management Association (IPMA) in 1967, the Project Management Institute (PMI) in 1969, and Association for Project Management (APM) in 1972. Proponents of project management (Box 5) emphasized its practical nature and the need for people trained in project management to implement standardized guidelines, processes, and bodies of knowledge that are universally applicable to all projects, programmes, and portfolios, such as the PMI's Project Management Body of Knowledge (PMBoK).

Despite the achievements of the Atlas and Apollo projects, systems project management experienced difficulties during and after the 1970s when many government-funded military and space projects

## Box 5 Standardizing project management

The PMI's *A Guide to the Project Management Body of Knowledge (PMBoK® Guide)* (2013) defines phases of the project life cycle and the processes required to identify client and stakeholder requirements, and ensure that the project is completed on time, within budget, and according to requirements.

A project starts with a plan based on a scope statement including: a work breakdown structure (WBS) defining the packages of work, an organizational breakdown structure (OBS), network schedule diagrams, a budget, and resources. A 'baseline plan' determines how the project will be executed in some detail and provides a fixed target against which the performance of the project team will be assessed. A risk management plan assumes that the uncertainties facing a project can be identified up front and establishes a contingency plan for dealing with them.

Once the project is executed, performance is measured against the baseline plan. Changes to the plan should be kept to a minimum or seen as an exception that needs to be corrected. Execution should conform to the baseline plan for the project to be a success, even though key assumptions in the plan may be rendered invalid when circumstances change.

suffered from severe time and cost overruns and poorly performing outcomes. Projects were often approved and funded without an adequate consideration of technological alternatives that available funds might make possible and without providing well-reasoned objectives based on a realistic estimation of the cost, timing, and performance of each individual project. Some were initiated—such as the Space Shuttle and International Space Station—with too many unknowns to allow accurate forecasts of costs, time to completion, performance, risk to human life, market demand, and usefulness.

NASA's Space Shuttle programme was first proposed in 1969 when the country was still excited by the Moon landing and the possibility of landing a crew on Mars in the 1980s. After its initial expensive proposal received little support, NASA sought to gain government approval by developing a more cost-effective space-adapted aeroplane based on a reusable system and off-the-shelf components. The Shuttle was a recoverable system that was designed to launch a manned space vehicle that would return to Earth and be used on repeated flights. The government decided to concentrate all of its resources on the Shuttle, eliminating alternative technologies such as non-recoverable launch vehicles. As Simon Ramo explains, optimism bias (Chapter 2) shaped efforts to gain approval and funding for the Shuttle:

> NASA based all estimates of cost, time, and performance on the most optimistic of possibilities. Because of this extreme optimism, the Shuttle program and its difficulties started at almost the same time. With the technical problems badly underestimated and the time allowed to complete the necessary steps far too short, the Shuttle's progress quickly slipped behind schedule.

It is highly unlikely the project would have been funded had the original estimates and forecasts on the Shuttle been realistic. Under pressure to minimize costs, NASA had abandoned its original plan to build a small test vehicle to ensure all the technology was proven before embarking on a full-scale vehicle. The Shuttle ran into significant cost overruns and Shuttle flights were cancelled following the Challenger disaster in January 1986 which killed all seven astronauts. Attempts were made to understand the causes of the accident and the Shuttle programme resumed in September 1988. After the Columbia accident in February 2003, which also tragically killed all seven crew members, NASA's Shuttle fleet was grounded until July 2005 and completed its final mission in 2011.

By the late 1960s, there was a widespread belief that the systems approach developed on the Atlas and Apollo projects could be applied to rebuild America's rapidly decaying and congested cities. But it failed to fulfil its promise and proved unable to cope with the immense social, political, and environmental problems of large urban areas. Many believed that America's urban renewal and construction projects were even more complex and messy than putting a man on the Moon. In their fascinating study of the Apollo programme, Leonard R. Sayles and Margaret K. Chandler pointed out that compared with America's urban projects, 'NASA had a simple life. NASA was a closed loop—it set its own schedule, designed its own hardware, and used the gear it designed. It was both sponsor and user. Space was no one's territory.' In contrast to this 'closed system', projects in densely populated urban areas are 'open systems'. During the design of the Boston Central Artery/Tunnel (Chapter 2), for example, many different voices and stakeholders in the city—federal, state, and local governments and local-interest groups with poverty, ethnic, and environmental concerns—all had a say in shaping a project which was years late and hugely over budget.

The aerospace-generated systems approach used to manage large projects became increasingly discredited from the late 1960s because of its failure to address America's urban problems, its association with the failing military campaign during the Vietnam War, and its contribution to the escalating arms race of the Cold War. Civil rights, anti-Vietnam War, environmental, and nuclear disarmament activists blamed the threat to liberal values, damage to local communities, and destruction of the natural environment on their government's amoral use of military and large-scale technology. Many managers, engineers, and scientists involved in America's publicly funded projects came to distrust the highly rational, planned, and coordinated system of analysis and management developed by McNamara for the purpose of military destruction. Thomas Hughes suggests that the 1960s may be a watershed decade in the history of project management when projects like the ARPANET—which built the computer communications system used by the Internet—began to express the counterculture values of the age. The creators of the ARPANET project preferred a flat management structure and its members were collaborative, meritocratic, and reached decisions by consensus (see Chapter 4 on the adhocracy). They rejected the hierarchy, bureaucracy, and control by experts used on pre-1960s projects like Atlas and Polaris.

The systems model of project management assumes that uncertainties facing a project can be identified at the outset and contingency plans put in place to deal with them should they arise while the project is under way. While this approach may work well on routine and simple projects, it ignores the need for adaptability in truly novel and complex projects. In defence, aerospace, and urban construction projects, for example, a planned and clear sequence of action is not always possible because of their extended duration, too many technological unknowns, and the constantly changing conditions, constraints, and pressures. As most large, complex projects contain both predictable and uncertain elements, a balance has to be found between frozen and flexible project planning, and between orderly routines and innovation during project execution. Sylvain Lenfle and Christoph Loch have recently called for project management to return to its 'lost roots' in the adaptive approach pioneered on the Manhattan, Atlas, and Polaris projects, rather than the orderly, rational systems approach with which they became associated.

In Chapter 4, we consider how the spread of the adaptive project structures in the 1960s and 1970s encouraged management scholars to develop new ways of thinking about organizations.

# Chapter 4
# Arup's adhocracy and projects in theory

Ove Arup was one of the leading structural engineers of the 20th century. He worked closely on projects with some the world's greatest architects such as Berthold Lubetkin, Renzo Piano, and Richard Rogers. Influenced by Le Corbusier's celebration of engineering and Walter Gropius' belief in the fusion of art and technology, Arup's vision of a 'Total Design' practice called for architects and engineers to work closely together from the start of a project. His firm, Ove Arup and Partners, established in 1946, embodied this design philosophy.

The Sydney Opera House, the firm's breakthrough project, established a new model of architect and engineer collaborating in project teams to innovate and solve challenging problems. With its dramatic roof, the Sydney Opera House was an engineering project of unprecedented complexity. Based on some evocative sketches, the original design was created by the Danish architect Jørn Utzon, without engineering consultation (Figure 6). Arup forged a close partnership with Utzon to find a way of turning his idea into reality. Arup's engineers made pioneering use of computers to model the roof structure and design a building made of large, prefabricated concrete shells.

Although Ove Arup died in 1988, his collaborative problem-solving approach is evident in Arup's current projects. Today Arup is a

6. An early sketch of the Sydney Opera House, 1956–7.

global professional service organization headquartered in London employing nearly 13,000 staff in about 90 offices in 37 countries. Specialists in engineering, architecture, design, planning, project management, economics, and other disciplines work on as many as 10,000 projects at any particular time. Each project addresses a client's requirement for a system, building, infrastructure, or an entire city. Clients change their minds, building requirements alter, regulations change, and political circumstances are often in flux. All of these constantly changing situations, uncertainties, and overlapping activities have to be addressed by multidisciplinary groups of experts within and outside Arup.

From the Sydney Opera House to Centre Pompidou in Paris and the UK's Channel Tunnel Rail Link, Arup has been involved in challenging projects which have opened up new markets for the firm. One of Arup's more recent high-profile projects was a pioneering urban design completed in 2008 for a Chinese 'eco-city', called Dongtan, situated on Chongming Island near Shanghai. With a proposed population of 500,000 by 2050, Dongtan aimed to be the world's first purpose-built ecologically sustainable city and as close to zero-carbon as possible, with efficient water, renewable energy and recycling systems, and city vehicles that produce no carbon or particulate emissions (Figure 7). Arup's Dongtan contract with the Shanghai Industrial Investment Corporation was followed by a deal signed in London in the

7. Arup's eco-city vision of Dongtan East Village and East Lake.

presence of Hu Jintao, China's president, and Tony Blair, Britain's prime minister, for the two companies to cooperate on future eco-city projects.

Bringing together people with expertise in architecture, urban design, project management, environmental consulting, and economics, a small team of highly motivated and experienced individuals, including Roger Wood, Alejandro Gutierrez, Shanfeng Dong, and others, was formed to lead the Dongtan project and develop the masterplan design. Arup's co-located Dongtan project team was based in the client's Shanghai head office. The project grew into a large multidisciplinary and multicultural organization of around 150 staff at peak, including people born in twenty different countries and located in twelve offices around the world. It was eventually established as part of a separate new business unit, Integrated Urbanism, led by Peter Head. The new unit comprised thirty specialist teams, each consisting of three or four people borrowed from Arup's disciplines, to deal with the cross-cutting social, economic, environmental, and physical components of an eco-city.

Using Arup's matrix approach, the specialist teams (for example, water, waste, logistics, and the new discipline of cultural planning) collaborated with others in multidisciplinary groups to enable quick resolution to design matters. This approach stimulated innovation, but it also brought its own creative tensions as the Dongtan team was under intense pressure to deliver the design quickly to meet the changing priorities and needs of a demanding client. With few precedents to learn from, a radically new sustainable urban design and process for managing a fast-paced project had to be created almost from scratch. As one of Arup's senior designers noted in an interview, 'we did what normally takes four years in one year'. Arup had to address the poorly understood preferences of future residents, businesses, government bodies, and other stakeholders and achieve challenging targets for sustainable performance. A new digital modelling tool, the Integrated Resource Model, was created to identify the numerous interdependencies among multiple technological and organizational components of an integrated urban system.

Although Dongtan was called a 'City of Dreams' by *The Economist* and ultimately never built as a zero-carbon development, the project did provide Arup with an experience base in eco-city design and a credible reputation in this growing market. Members of the Dongtan team were redeployed to win and execute a number of eco-city design projects. The knowledge gained during this significant but unrealized project was codified and new digital planning and project management processes were developed and applied on subsequent projects in China and around the world.

In the late 1960s, when Arup was designing the Sydney Opera House and other firms were discovering adaptable ways of organizing project work, the founders of PMI, APM, and other professional bodies formulated and promoted guidelines, processes, and bodies of knowledge that have become standard in the discipline of project management (Chapter 3). Perhaps inspired by industrial society's view that there is a single best way of organizing, they developed an optimized, fixed, and simple model to execute projects as planned in predictable and carefully controlled phases. This approach assumes that project management can be decoupled from changes in the environment. It works well when technologies and markets are reasonably well understood and plans can be established to deal with known and predictable conditions when the project is under way. As the Arup case illustrates, however, a standardized approach is less well equipped for uncertain, changing, and complex projects.

In the rest of this chapter, we discuss some of the theoretical insights and perspectives introduced by organizational scholars to help us think about projects as a flexible and adaptive structure in a dynamically changing environment.

## Organization theory and the adhocracy

While projects became widely used in the defence industries in the 1950s, it was not until the mid-1960s that researchers first noticed this new species of temporary and adaptive organization. About the same time, an influential group of scholars began to challenge the prevailing view that there is one best way of organizing suitable for all environments. In what became known as 'contingency theory', they argued that the design of a successful organization—including a project-based one—reflects the complexity, uncertainty, and rate of change in the technology and market environment.

Traditional industrial organizations have 'mechanistic' structures to perform standardized operations (e.g. mass produced consumer goods and services) and solve routine problems in a relatively stable environment with a greater reliance on predictable tasks broken down into functional specialisms. Individuals occupy sharply defined slots in a division of labour and fit into a vertical hierarchy, with communication running from the boss at the top down to the lowliest worker. In a departure from this rigidity and permanence, Tom Burns and G. M. Stalker argued that organizations adapted to unstable and changing environments have 'organic' structures. This fluid form of organization depends on people communicating horizontally—or 'sideways'—with colleagues as peers working on novel and complex problems that require the continuous adjustment and redefinition of tasks.

Warren Bennis coined the term 'organic-adaptive' to describe the growth in ad hoc project groups combining diverse functional specialists—such as finance, engineering, and marketing—in temporary, problem-solving organizations, which he believed were better equipped to survive in an increasingly turbulent environment. Whereas the mechanistic organizations are designed to survive and grow indefinitely, a project is a temporary organization: it terminates at a specified end state or when a goal has been accomplished. Diversely skilled people who are often unfamiliar with each other's skills are brought together to work on interdependent tasks to achieve a specific goal in a defined period of time. Joan Woodward suggested that organizations drawn to organic structures include those that frequently change their products and 'unit producers' of unique, one-off, or heavily customized products in projects for clients in industries as diverse as aerospace, defence, shipbuilding, music recording, and film making.

James Thompson introduced some of the concepts we use to understand how organizations coordinate interdependent tasks in projects. In 'pooled interdependency', work is broken down into simple tasks performed separately by a functional department with little or no input from others. Standardized rules and procedures are required to ensure that tasks performed in isolation by one functional department provide a discrete contribution without impairing the activities of another department.

In 'sequential interdependency', there is a direct serial relationship between project tasks: the outputs produced in one phase of a project (information, materials, and components) become inputs necessary for the performance of the next phase. Tasks performed sequentially are planned and scheduled in carefully defined phases to achieve a defined project goal. As we saw in Chapter 3, this occurs in serial development when a functional group (e.g. engineering) in a project finishes its task before handing the finished job to the next group (e.g. manufacturing). In the traditional 'waterfall model' of project management, sequential phases of a project are separated from each other by strict exit and entry criteria. Downstream phases cannot start until earlier ones have fulfilled certain conditions.

In 'reciprocal interdependency', each task is penetrated by the other and tasks must be reciprocally adjusted to match changes to other tasks. This is illustrated by the concurrent development of weapons systems in dedicated project organizations (Chapter 3). Design specifications were an input for the production of a missile (technical specifications) and the production of a missile system was an input for the design (the performance requirements of assembly, testing, and launching facilities). Dealing with reciprocal interdependencies requires back-and-forth communication and coordination by the 'mutual adjustment' of tasks as new information becomes available about the project's goal, technology, and market environment.

Projects can be prioritized according to the degree of task interdependency and the coordination required to deal with them. Many projects have pooled, some have pooled and sequential, and the most complex and uncertain have pooled, sequential, and reciprocal interdependencies. In a stable and predictable environment, projects can be defined, planned, and scheduled in advance (using processes identified by the PMI) to deal with pooled and sequential interdependencies. In unstable and rapidly changing conditions—NASA's zone of uncertainty (Chapter 3)—coordination by mutual adjustment is required to address unforeseen interactions, respond to feedback from experience, and adapt in real time to changes in circumstances and goals.

Paul Lawrence and Jay Lorsch help us understand that members of multiple parties in a project organization have to be combined, or 'integrated', to reach agreement on how to respond to the demands of the environment. When projects are complex and interdependent, various liaison positions, or 'linking pins', are needed to coordinate work laterally and obtain cooperation within and between project teams and functional units. As an integrator, a project manager acts in a liaison, persuasion, and negotiation capacity, resolving conflicts that arise when people with specialized knowledge and different interests, viewpoints, and practices are brought together and expected to work in smoothly functioning cross-functional and multiparty projects. Jay Galbraith describes how American aerospace firms created the matrix structure

(Chapter 3) as a dual-reporting integration mechanism to establish a balance of power between functional and project lines of authority. An integrator understands the orientations of differing or competing internal groups and is able to influence external organizations and people with the authority and power to support or curtail a project—a role performed so well by Bernard Schriever on the Atlas Project.

Members of organically structured projects teams are often physically co-located—working together in the same office throughout a project—to integrate multiple participants and address reciprocal interdependency, as we found in the Atlas Project. In his book on R&D projects, Thomas J. Allen suggested that even the smallest degree of dispersion, such as locating people on different floors of the same building, can undermine the intense interaction and cooperation required in project teams. Close proximity and the regular physical presence of co-workers helps to foster more frequent communication, build trust, forge closer interpersonal relationships and informal interactions, and strengthen social ties among team members. There are often a few key individuals in project teams to whom others frequently turn for information. These 'technological gatekeepers' as Allen called them are skilled in translating and articulating diverse functional languages and communicating technical information across organizational boundaries.

In the 1970s, insights and concepts from contingency theory were used to identify the key characteristics of the project organization. In his book *The Structuring of Organizations* (1979), Henry Mintzberg borrowed the word 'adhocracy' from Alvin Toffler (Chapter 1) to identify the project as a new form of organization which combines people with diverse expertise in transient project teams working to solve complex, ill-structured problems and dissolves when the task is accomplished. This organization is based on an organic structure, unit production, problem-solving innovation, coordination by face-to-face mutual adjustment, and horizontal integration mechanisms. Boundaries between disciplines become increasingly blurred as information flows horizontally and freely between people in cross-functional teams. The selection of team members tends to be based on a person's expertise and their ability to work collaboratively, rather than their position or rank in the managerial hierarchy. The knowledge and experience assembled in the team is the base for creating innovation and continuously developing new knowledge.

Adhocracies can be temporary or permanent. In a temporary adhocracy, a standalone organization is assembled to undertake a project and disbands on completion, such as a single film production, an election campaign for a single candidate, an Olympic body established to build and host a single Games, and the joint venture organization established to coordinate a megaproject such as Boston's Central/Artery Tunnel.

In a permanent adhocracy, multiple projects are embedded in two types of parent organizations. One type—the 'operating adhocracy'—undertakes projects for external clients, such as an architectural practice, engineering consultancy, construction contractor, film producer, or advertising agency. An operating adhocracy never really stabilizes. Strategies emerge and evolve in response to the needs of clients—like Arup's Dongtan project—and the adhocracy adapts continuously as projects change and new ones come along, living from one project to the next and disappearing when it can find no more. To ensure a steady and balanced stream of incoming projects, managers of an operating adhocracy spend a great deal of time developing relationships with potential customers and negotiating contracts with them.

Another type of permanent entity—the 'administrative adhocracy'—undertakes projects only to serve itself, not external clients. Operational tasks are cut off from the rest of the parent organization, so that the administrative core is organized in project teams and free to focus on problem-solving and innovation. For example, much of the R&D and overall systems integration work on the Apollo programme was conducted in-house by NASA, but the development of components and subsystems and provision of services and expertise was contracted out to a network of external suppliers.

## New thinking about project organizing

The adaptive and innovative capacity of Mintzberg's adhocracy depends on smoothly functioning project teams, which vary in composition, size, and scope. Some projects are undertaken by people who already know each other in small in-house project teams. Others are composed of many individuals from around the world with different backgrounds and perspectives, as illustrated by Arup's Dongtan project. Many large projects are broken down into smaller subprojects, each undertaken by a separate multiparty team. The construction in London of the new Heathrow Terminal 5, for example, was organized as a programme divided into 16 major projects and 147 subprojects, with the smallest valued at £1 million, to large projects, such as the £300 million Heathrow Express underground railway station. Each subproject was undertaken by a multiparty integrated project team comprising members from the client and contractor organizations (Chapter 6).

Recent research suggests that the classic studies placed too much emphasis on the organic-adaptive nature of project teams. Project teams often combine organic and mechanistic, and co-located and dispersed elements. Some teams have the flexibility required to cope with dynamically changing environments, while others are relatively stable structures.

In a study of product development projects undertaken by American, European, and Asian computer firms, Kathleen Eisenhardt and Behnam Tabrizi identified two contrasting models for accelerating the pace of development. A 'compression' strategy is designed to simplify and compress the time taken to complete sequential steps in a well-known and clearly defined process. An 'experiential' strategy of adaptation relies on improvisation, flexibility, and trial-and-error learning to deal with an uncertain and fast-changing process. The study found that successful new product development calls for a subtle blend of these mechanistic and organic processes. Multifunctional teams led by powerful project leaders use planned milestones to compress time and set the pace, but also depend on improvisation and real-time learning through design iterations and testing when conditions change unexpectedly.

Using insights from contingency theory, Amy Edmondson distinguishes between stable and flexible project teams. Stable project teams bring people together with the right combination of skills and experience and have time to build trust to accomplish simple and predictable tasks for existing customers and well-understood situations. Membership is clearly defined: each person or group knows which task to perform and no one has to cross disciplinary boundaries, deal with unexpected events, or do entirely new types of work.

Flexible project teams, by contrast, are required in complex, uncertain, and fast-changing situations, such as product design, research, rescue operations, and strategy development. New groupings of people and organizations—including highly experienced as well as novice team members—are assembled to tackle unique, one-off problems, time and time again. People from different disciplines and other external specialists work in multiple, co-located teams that vary in duration, have constantly shifting membership, and pursue moving targets. Because work is temporary and cuts across functional, geographical, and organizational boundaries, members of a project team have little time to build trust and grow accustomed to each other's working styles, strengths, and weaknesses. There is a need to sort tasks by level of interdependence, but also for coordination by mutual adjustment to keep plans flexible. Project teams learn and execute at the same time, pace their activities to meet deadlines in a limited period of time, and respond to problems and innovative opportunities when they arise.

In a process Edmondson calls 'teaming', flexible teams depend on leaders who can emphasize purpose, build psychological safety, tolerate the inevitable failures that come with experimentation, and embrace conflict and miscommunication that arise when shifting and diverse groups of people with different values and competing priorities start working together. Arup's project to design and build the Water Cube aquatics centre for the Beijing 2008 Olympics illustrates how teaming works. This complex task could not be accomplished by traditional project management planning and efforts to divide up tasks into sequential phases. The team brought together people from twenty disciplines in four countries and external specialists working in collaborative groupings that were formed and dissolved in response to many unforeseen problems that were identified and resolved as the work progressed.

An increasing number of firms are organizing global projects over distance, using digital communications (e.g. email, voice, mobile, and web-based services) and periodic face-to-face meetings to coordinate tasks and forge collaboration amongst team members (Chapter 5). Firms like IBM, General Electric, and SAP have created competency centres to bring together people with relevant expertise from multiple locations to perform specific tasks in spatially dispersed project teams. Members of dispersed teams are geographically spread across cities, countries, and continents, come from different disciplinary backgrounds, speak different languages, and live in different countries with different values, interests, and beliefs.

Collaborating in spatially dispersed teams can be more difficult than in a co-located office. Physical distance can be a hindrance to togetherness and familiarity, resulting in reduced trust, an inability to find a common ground, and difficulties in coordination and cooperation. Members of a dispersed project—or 'virtual' team—may have to adapt work patterns and reorganize schedules to accommodate differences in time zones. If team members are regularly unavailable to discuss problems or clarify how tasks have to be adjusted to resolve them, situations easily addressed in face-to-face meetings can unravel, resulting in frustration, disagreement, and conflict.

In some global industries, such as software development, spatially distributed teams have been known to outperform teams that are co-located. Teams in the same building often underestimate the barriers to collaboration, such as the inconvenience of having to climb a flight of stairs to meet a co-worker. By contrast, software teams that are spread around the world are often more aware of difficulties involved in collaborating and make extra efforts to improve communication and interaction. Periodic face-to-face group meetings help to build team cohesion, develop a shared understanding of the task at hand, and support informal communication. Informal interactions, such as 'going out for a beer with team members', help to establish the common ground and 'rules of the road' before starting a virtual collaboration.

## Contingent dimensions of projects

Building on contingency arguments, many scholars now recognize that projects differ greatly in their degree of uncertainty, complexity, and urgency and suggest that distinctive forms of organization, process, and managerial approach are required to manage each of these dimensions. Arthur Stinchcombe's and Carol Heimer's in-depth study of North Sea oil and gas projects was one of the first attempts at applying contingency theory to large-scale projects. They recognized that the highly uncertain and unexpected situations frequently encountered in one-off projects have to be resolved by innovative and adaptive processes, but emphasized that projects incorporate many features we associate with permanent, mechanistic, and stable structures. Contracts between multiple parties in projects incorporate some of the functions managerial hierarchies are set up to achieve, such as incentives and controls to address uncertain and changing conditions.

Uncertainty refers to the state of information about the project's goal, task, and environment, which is often poorly understood and inadequate particularly at the start, as we saw in the Manhattan Project. Uncertainties can be foreseeable and unforeseeable, each of which requires a different project management approach.

A 'foreseen uncertainty' is an event or risk—or 'known unknown'—that can be identified while planning for a project. Risk management is the technique used to identify, evaluate, and control uncertainties that might be avoided or mitigated. Risk registers (i.e. a record of identified risks) are completed before executing a project to identify the technical events (e.g. test or interface problems), partner selection, customer requirements (changes in scope), and other risks. Handling risks means simply accepting them as an unavoidable nuisance or taking preventive action to avoid them, including contingency plans (with reserve funding and time buffers) with instructions for dealing with them if and when they occur.

An 'unforeseen uncertainty' refers to an event, impact, or unanticipated interaction that cannot be identified at the start. Sometimes called 'unknown unknowns', this type of uncertainty occurs frequently in any project that develops new technology, opens up a new or partially understood market, or has to tackle an unanticipated crisis or disaster. Traditional risk management tools are unable to cope with breakthrough projects or projects undertaken in fast-paced competitive environments where unforeseen uncertainty is unavoidable or seen as a risk worth taking, such as Arup's futuristic eco-city design for Dongtan.

Projects have to cope with a variety of economic, institutional, and ecological uncertainties classified by their source and impact. Technological and market uncertainties are singled out by Aaron Shenhar and Dov Dvir as the most widespread, persistent, and challenging unpredictable and unknown factors affecting the goal and tasks undertaken in projects. There are four types of technological uncertainty—low-tech, medium-tech, hi-tech, and super-high-tech projects. Each is associated with how much new technology is incorporated into the final product and the process used to produce it (see Chapter 5 on the use of digital technology to develop the Boeing 777 aeroplane). Projects incorporating significant amounts of new technology (e.g. defence, computer, and aerospace projects) require greater interaction among team members, numerous design cycles, iterative learning, and prototyping. The more new technology employed or developed on a project, the greater the likelihood of cost, time, and quality overruns, and risk of not achieving planned performance objectives.

Market novelty is the uncertainty about the goal or outcome a project is set up to achieve. It refers to the extent to which buyers are familiar with the product and its potential uses and able to articulate their requirements for new or improved products. For example, the fashions and tastes of air travellers—such as demand for low-budget airlines or long-haul flights—are reflected in the airlines' requirements for new planes which are designed and produced by Boeing and Airbus. Building on classification of innovation discussed at length in Chapter 5, Shenhar and Dvir distinguish between derivative, platform, and breakthrough projects. The newer the product, the more difficult it is to identify what customers need and define their requirements during the design stage of a project.

In projects established to develop a major advance in technology or create a new market, traditional risk management techniques would encourage the team to 'get back to the plan', when in practice they need to learn new things, adjust tasks, and change direction. Rather than attempting to tackle unexpected situations by more rigorous application of planning and risk management, Christoph Loch and his co-authors recommend that teams should rely on a combination of 'flexibility and learning'. When too many unknowns exist to allow accurate forecasts of risks, project goals, formal plans, scheduled tasks, and ongoing processes have to be adjusted as new information becomes available and the organization learns more about the project and how it interacts with the environment. As shown in the Manhattan and Atlas projects (Chapter 3), unforeseen uncertainties can be reduced by engaging in multiple and parallel trials to gather valuable information before selecting among alternatives. The costs of repeated tests and experiments may be less than the cost of deciding on a single technology at the outset, which subsequently faces major difficulties not originally envisaged or which becomes outdated when the product is launched.

Flexibility and learning may help managers distinguish between different types of projects according to the degree of uncertainty and adjust their management approach to deal with it. As Sylvain Lenfle and Christoph Loch show in their insightful study of the Manhattan Project, the need for such adaptive processes is apparent not just for different types of projects, but also within large, complex projects. A strategy of targeted flexibility can be used to break down large projects into distinct subprojects to address different pieces of uncertainty. Specific structures, processes, and risk management techniques are required to cope with foreseeable (contingency planning and instructions) and unforeseeable pieces of uncertainty (parallel trials and iterative learning). The London 2012 Olympics project, for example, employed a variety of contracts to target the uncertainty associated with the construction of different venues. Collaborative risk-sharing contracts were relied upon to deal with more uncertain projects (e.g. the distinctive Zaha Hadid designed Aquatics Centre), whereas fixed-price contracts were used for routine and predictable ones (e.g. temporary venues comprising standardized and reusable components).

The structure of a project organization reflects the complexity of the product or system it produces, as we saw in the Atlas Project. The product or outcome of each project involves numerous interconnected parts, components, subsystems, and entire systems, including physical artefacts (e.g. hardware and software) and intangible services (e.g. logistics, maintenance, and operations). Studies have distinguished between projects based on their increasing degree of complexity, ranging from materials, components, and product assemblies to more complex platforms, systems, and 'system of systems' projects. Increasing complexity calls for more elaborate forms of organization and processes (such as a modular design strategy) to cope with the challenge of integrating multiple components, managing interfaces between subprojects, and dealing with reciprocal interdependency (Box 6).

In their three-part classification of project complexity, Shenhar and Dvir suggest that complexity affects interdependencies among tasks and shapes the organization required to manage each project. A relatively simple assembly project is a single component, service, or product with a complex assembly (e.g. a radio base station in a mobile communications network) which is often conducted in-house by a small product development team. A system project consists of components and subsystems, often part of a platform, with multiple functions that together meet a specific operational requirement, such as the development of a new computer, car, or aeroplane. Managed by a large prime contractor with in-house systems integration capabilities (Chapter 3), a central project or programme office is often established to coordinate the technical efforts of the network of in-house functional groups and external suppliers involved in each system project. The most complex array—or system of systems—project consists of a large collection of systems, each serving their own

## Box 6 Modularity and systems integration

Electronics-based components produced for the Atlas Project (Chapter 3) often came in black metal boxes with clearly defined interfaces so that it was not necessary to open the 'black box' when assembling the system. Inspired by a similar design strategy, many complex projects in construction, oil and gas, aerospace, and nuclear power plants are composed of modular components with standardized interfaces to simplify the process of construction and integration. Modular components can be produced with greater precision and more cheaply in offsite factories, tested in trial runs, and then assembled onsite like a model kit. For example, 'The Shard', London's 310-metre building designed by Renzo Piano, used prefabricated and pre-assembled modular components and steel structures, which were tested off site prior to their installation on a congested site above the London Bridge railway station.

Modular components are designed to be mixed and matched—rather like Lego bricks—with minimal uncertainty and coordinated via arm's-length market transactions without relying on the conscious intervention of a systems integrator. The seamless inter-firm project coordination promised by modularity is, however, rarely achieved in practice. In their studies of complex projects, Stefano Brusoni and Andrea Prencipe found that firms with capabilities in systems integration are required to oversee the overall design and development of each individual module, accommodate numerous component interactions and adjustments, and tighten the links amongst suppliers of components.

specific purpose, that work together to achieve a common goal, such as a new airport, urban development, or nationwide mobile network. A large systems integrator organization—such as a standalone client organization or joint venture delivery partner—is usually established to deal with financial, legal, and political issues and coordinate and schedule multiple contractors within a large programme.

Projects can be classified according to their urgency, depending on how much time there is available to complete the task and what happens if the time goals are not met. The pace and sequencing of tasks can be driven by chronological time—calendar and clock time—including contracts and time-lines to demarcate and coordinate who does what and when in a project. Pace can be driven by events—predefined deadlines and milestones—to maintain a sense of urgency and focus attention on keeping within the time allocated to complete the project. Predefined milestones establish specific dates when certain tasks should be accomplished or completed more rapidly before moving to the next stage, such as the completion of a design freeze in a product development project. Lars Lindkvist and his co-authors found that the project team responsible for introducing Ericsson's first mobile communications system in Japan had to accept an incredibly tight deadline. In what was considered an 'impossible task', the team dramatically shortened the time taken to deliver the project after they shifted from a sequential to a new 'fountain model' of concurrent development driven by a very clear goal (delivering a fully operational system by 1 April 1994), unambiguous deadlines, and frequent milestones.

In their four-part classification of project pace, Shenhar and Dvir emphasize that the more urgent the project, the greater the need for autonomy, rapid decision making, and senior management involvement. Regular projects—such as many public construction works or organizational change programmes—are endeavours where some time delay may be tolerated. Fast-competitive projects found in most industries and profit-driven organizations, by contrast, have to respond rapidly to market opportunities, build new lines of business, and create a strategic advantage. Time-critical projects are those that are constrained by a window of opportunity (e.g. buildings for the Millennium celebrations) or must be completed by a specified date (e.g. major events in the sporting calendar such as the Olympic Games or FIFA World Cup). Missing the deadline results in project failure. Blitz projects are formed to deal with the most urgent problems—natural disasters, emergencies, or crisis situations—as quickly as possible, such as the successful rescue of the 33 Chilean miners trapped 700 metres underground for 69 days in 2010. They require more autonomy and resources than any other project to deal with emergent and on-the-spot situations that must be handled almost instantaneously and move rapidly and flexibly to save lives, protect property, and restore order to chaotic situations.

In recent years, several influential scholars have attempted to develop conceptual frameworks that address the contingent dimensions of projects. In their book *Managing the Unknown* (2006), Christoph Loch, Arnoud DeMeyer, and Michael Pich identify different approaches for managing projects in technology and market environments ranging from simple and predictable to novel and unknown. A contingency theory of project management appears in research articles by Shenhar and Dvir and is brought together in their book *Reinventing Project Management* (2007). They argue that there is no one-size-fits-all structure or process suitable for all projects. Some projects are simple and predictable, while many are complex, uncertain, and strongly shaped by the dynamics of the environment.

In Chapter 5 we consider how project management was transformed in the 1980s and 1990s to manage innovation in increasingly competitive global markets.

# Chapter 5
# Lean, heavy, and disruptive projects

The world market for cars was dominated during most of the 20th century by a handful of giant mass production enterprises—Ford, General Motors, and Chrysler in the United States and Volkswagen, Renault, Fiat, BMW, Daimler-Benz, and a few others in Europe. By the 1980s, however, the Western monopoly of the global automotive industry was under threat. Japanese car manufacturers Honda and Toyota had discovered a way of developing and producing an enormous variety of new models in high volume at less expense and more rapidly than their Western counterparts. In a study of product development projects in the world motor industry undertaken between 1983 and 1987, Kim Clark and Takahiro Fujimoto found that a new Japanese car required on average 1.7 million engineering hours and 46 months from first design to customer delivery, whereas it took Western producers 3 million engineering hours and 60 months. Japan's producers were 'lean' because each new product development project was developed with less than half the number of people and in nearly half the time.

## Lean product development

In the 1980s all car manufacturers, Japanese and Western, used some form of matrix to organize their product development projects (Chapter 3). Experts from different functional units—marketing, engineering (power train, body chassis, and process), and manufacturing—had to collaborate intensively in projects to develop a new car. Each firm had a range of different models, components, and factories that had to be shared. When a new product was developed, the division leading the endeavour had to interact with other divisions and component suppliers that manufactured the shared parts. In practice, however, a Japanese matrix bore little or no resemblance to a Western one. In *The Machine that Changed the World* (1990)—the book that introduced the idea of lean production—James Womack, Daniel Jones, and Daniel Roos distinguished between the traditional Western and revolutionary new Japanese approach to product development.

The 'mass production' development approach used by Western producers is illustrated by General Motors in the 1980s. In a sequential development process (Chapter 4), the project was 'handed over the wall' from one functional department to the next during its life and worked upon by different and fragmented groups along the way. The parties involved had to reach thousands of decisions on specifications, performance, and appearance including the target market, price, most appealing features, and physical dimensions of the car. Engineers then had to work out precise specifications for each part and which parts could be obtained from other GM products. Hirotaka Takeuchi and Ikujiro Nonaka likened this approach to the passing of the baton in a relay race. Similar to NASA's 'phased program planning' (Chapter 3), the product moves through highly structured phases: concept development, feasibility testing, product design, development, pilot, production, and product launch.

GM appointed a programme manager to lead and coordinate members of the project team on short-term loan from functional departments. In a weak position to champion the project within the firm, GM's programme managers did not have the authority needed to insist that their orders were obeyed. Acting more like coordinators than managers, they were often reluctant to confront conflicts and struggled to convince members and functional groups to cooperate. When they urged engineering departments and others to commit to design decisions or move faster, they were met with promises rather than action. The communication required to solve problems was often poor because the design process was sequential and dispersed, rather than being co-located at team headquarters. The number of people involved in design decisions was small at the start, growing to a peak as the project proceeded to product launch, when far too many new people were brought in to solve problems that should have been addressed at the outset.

The 'lean' approach was created by Honda and Toyota to develop a wider range of products faster and with fewer errors than their Western counterparts. Development work was subdivided to address the demands of different geographical markets around the world. Once the product plan and specifications were set, dedicated members of the project team worked rapidly with no interruptions to achieve the overall goal, collaborating with the functional departments when necessary.

A project leader—Honda's Large Project Leader or Toyota's 'shusa'—was appointed to head the development of each new model, with the authority to acquire resources and manage, rather than simply coordinate, the development process. Although Japanese producers also used a matrix structure, people were borrowed from the functional departments and transferred for the life of each project. They worked in a tightly knit team—with far fewer staff than Western projects—under the control of the 'heavyweight project manager' (see 'Team structures and leaders'). A collaborative problem-solving approach was fostered by the continuity of team membership and shared experience developed while working together on past projects. Communication among members and different disciplines was greatest at the start of the design process when all the relevant expertise was brought together. The heavyweight project manager's job was to encourage members to confront trade-offs and resolve conflicts over resources. Motivated by the project's guiding vision, individual members signed formal pledges to do what everyone agreed upon as a team.

Japanese firms in other consumer goods industries such as Fuji-Xerox and Canon developed an adaptive 'overlay' approach for developing new products in overlapping (or concurrent) phases—adding flexibility to the acceleration in pace provided by lean. Using the overlay approach, teams can absorb new information and engage in an iterative and adaptive process of trial-and-error learning to narrow down the number of alternatives they must consider—similar to the use of concurrency on the Atlas Project (Chapter 3).

Over the past two decades, lean development has spread to many industries experiencing rapid product obsolescence and shorter product life cycles, such as consumer electronics and other fast-paced environments. It has been adopted by unit producers, such as aerospace, construction, and film making (e.g. Pixar), where concurrent product development and cooperative relationships are used to generate new ideas, drive performance, and communicate any desired changes while the project is under way.

## Lean development supported by digital technology

By the 1990s, fast, flexible, and lean development processes were increasingly used in conjunction with digital technologies—computer-aided-design (CAD), computer-aided-manufacturing (CAM), and telecommunication systems—to coordinate co-located and dispersed teams involved in the design, production, integration, and testing of new products.

The Boeing 777, for example, was the first commercial aeroplane designed entirely using computers. Originally conceived in 1988, the design of Boeing's new long-range, wide-body, twin-engine aeroplane with fly-by-wire computer controls was decided upon in March 1990. After a period of development and extensive testing, the first 777 aeroplane entered service with United Airlines on 7 June 1995. On Boeing's previous development projects, physical drawings had been thrown over the wall between spatially and organizationally separate design and manufacturing teams. On the 777 project, by contrast, every engineer had access to digital information and three-dimensional designs were often exchanged back and forth online between closely interacting teams. Rather than wait until physical drawings were copied and checked for compatibility, an engineer on the 777 project could use the computer to call up all the parts and identify interferences or 'clashes' when they were fitted together (Box 7).

In his biography of the 777 project, Karl Sabbagh found that in 'the fiercely competitive world of plane-making, it is project management that Boeing hope will give their plane the edge over Airbus and McDonnell Douglas'. The development of the 777 was led by two of Boeing's most powerful and experienced project managers. Alan Mulally, who would later become Chief Executive of Ford, ran the project during the most intense phases of design and manufacture after the previous manager, Phil Conduit, left to become Boeing's Chief Executive. Boeing's 777 digital design technology worked well because it was embedded in a highly collaborative and problem-solving project organization. Under Mulally's leadership, Boeing established an approach called 'Working Together' to encourage engineers to meet face to face, exchange ideas of mutual interest, resolve conflicts, build trust, and develop a shared understanding about what they were trying to create (Figure 8). Boeing also adopted the collaborative 'design-build' project teams pioneered in Japan, so that airline customers and external suppliers were involved in early design decisions.

The availability of digital technologies—CAD, CAM, and network-based broadband communication delivered by web

### Box 7 Boeing's 'paperless plane'

Computer-aided design had been used in automotive manufacturing, civil engineering, and architecture as a drawing tool, but never on the scale implemented by Boeing. Two linked computer systems were used to design, assemble, and test a simulation of the 777 aeroplane: Computer-Aided Three dimensional Interactive Application (CATIA) and Electronic Preassembly in the CATIA. CATIA was developed for the aerospace industry by Dassault and in collaboration with IBM. Using this paperless system, engineers could zoom in on one part and zoom out and see how that part fitted in a whole plane composed of four million parts. Boeing's Everett, Washington, factory, the main design location for the 777, was equipped with 2,200 computer terminals connected to IBM mainframe computers. Eventually members of the project had access to over 7,000 workstations dispersed around the world in over seventeen time zones. A dedicated private data network was laid across the Pacific Ocean from Washington to Japan, where the Japanese Aerospace Industry consortium of companies was responsible for designing 20 per cent of the fuselage structure. All the 238 project teams, each comprising up to 40 engineers, had access to computer data. The CAD programme supplied the CAM system with digital data required to produce components of the fuselage. The system provided a complete digital model of the component parts of the 777 which maintenance staff needed when the plane was in service.

browsers and stored in 'the cloud'—over the past two decades coincided with the adoption of lean and more collaborative ways of managing projects. Digital technologies have spread from aerospace to more traditional sectors like construction to assist with the design, construction, integration, as well as the 'virtual' testing of components and systems.

8. The phrase 'Working Together', a management style that contributed to the smooth running of the project, is used as the name of the first Boeing 777.

Frank Gehry, for example, purchased CATIA aerospace software (used on the Boeing 777 project) from IBM in 1991 to design and build the Guggenheim Museum in Bilbao, northern Spain. The building contains gallery spaces for the exhibition of works of internationally recognized contemporary artists. It would have been impossible to design and build such a complex construct without the aid of computers. With its loose arrangement of curved shapes designed to catch the light, the building was constructed with a steel frame to form crumpled shapes, covered in glass, limestone, and titanium-coated tiles that could adapt to the curves of the exterior building. The steel and titanium components were first manufactured and cut to shape with greater precision under factory conditions and then assembled on the site. Based on a detailed and realistic cost estimate before commencing, the project was successfully delivered on time and within budget. Since the museum opened on 18 October 1997, the benefits of this spectacular and awe-inspiring building have far exceeded the costs of the project. It has revived a provincial city by establishing it on the map of global art and architecture, making it a popular place that tourists from around the world want to visit.

The Guggenheim project marked the beginning of Gehry's shift from a traditional to a digitally adapted design practice. Digital tools and processes support collaborative project teams involved in the design and construction of avant-garde, inspirational buildings. A digital model is a 'single source of information' for each project and used as a 'projective argument' for discussions with the client. In a process that Gehry describes as 'fast and adaptable', the digital model is used to explore and test numerous possibilities, experiment with rapid prototyping techniques (where physical models are produced from a 3D digital model), suggest new directions, and continue to make adjustments, if needed, until late stages of a project. Every interdependent part, emerging problem, and changing priority of a project can be seen with a high degree of precision and controlled and managed in real time. Placing architecture at the centre of a collaborative process with clients, engineering consultants, and contractors, Gehry believes that digital tools can help re-establish the role of the architect as 'master builder' in a future (Chapter 1) when all buildings and cities will be designed and built using digital tools, much like the Boeing 777.

## Innovation projects

Developing new products and taking an innovative idea from concept to reality is often said to resemble a 'funnel'. Starting with a broad range of inputs, the process gradually refines and selects from among them, and creates a few development projects that converge on a specific product that addresses a stable customer need for an incremental improvement or opens up new and highly uncertain markets for radically new products or services.

In their book *Revolutionizing Product Development* (1992), Steven Wheelwright and Kim Clark developed a classification of development projects according to the degree of novelty in products and processes on a continuum from incremental to radical innovation. There are three types of commercial product development projects. Derivative projects involve incremental innovation and range from cost-reductions to enhancements of existing products and processes. They require fewer development resources than other projects because the customer's requirements are well known and specifications set at an early stage. At the other end of the spectrum, breakthrough projects are based on radical innovation because they introduce entirely novel processes or untried products leading to the creation of entirely new markets and industries. Breakthrough projects require significantly more resources and greater autonomy to decide how to design radically new products and processes. Situated in the middle of the incremental–radical innovation continuum, platform projects develop new products and processes (sharing standardized, modular, and common components) for existing customers and known markets.

Apple provides an example of a company almost exclusively focused on breakthrough innovation. On many projects, Apple's former CEO, Steve Jobs, had a knack of creating wonderfully designed things people were not aware they needed, but then found they could not live without. Apple's transformation into one of the world's most successful firms began with a breakthrough project: the iPod music player, unveiled on 23 October 2001. Apple disrupted the music industry by changing the way people listen to, make, and buy music. Although Apple's design adopted existing MP3 technology, the iPod was a breakthrough because it worked in tandem with iTunes software, allowing users to manage their own music, pictures, video, text, and other features. It created Apple's digital hub for other breakthrough projects, including the iPhone and iPad. Jobs encouraged development teams to focus on novel ideas and was

Lean, heavy, and disruptive projects

notoriously impatient with those who stuck to the plan and made compromises in order to get the product out on time and on budget. As Isaacson points out in his biography of Apple's CEO, on the iPhone, Apple store, and other projects, Jobs 'pressed the "pause" button as they neared completion and decided to make major revisions'.

Unlike Apple, few companies have serial breakthrough projects in their portfolio. Commercial airliner manufacturers, for example, establish platform projects to launch each new family of products, such as Boeing's models from the 707 to the most recent 787 plane. Between each generation of product, changes occur in both the customer requirements a product must address and the technologies it uses to satisfy these needs. Boeing undertakes derivative projects to provide enhancements and 'stretch design' improvements that represent the series of modifications within a given model. The 767 designers, for example, stretched the design to accommodate the airlines' requests for more seats, making the plane 14 metres (46 feet) longer.

The other two categories of projects are R&D and alliance and partnership projects. R&D projects convert ideas into new products, services, and processes. They create new knowledge of materials, technologies, and services that are eventually incorporated in new commercial development projects. Because the process and outcome of an R&D project is highly uncertain, firms have different expectations about the resources required to support them than for commercial development projects. Alliance and partnership projects are formed with multiple external parties for any type of R&D or derivative, platform, or breakthrough development projects. In recent years, many firms—Xerox, IBM, Intel, Procter & Gamble, and others—have shifted from a closed model of innovation where R&D and product development projects were largely undertaken in-house to an increasingly open model which leverages internal and external sources of ideas to commercialize a new offering.

## Portfolio management

A certain amount of slack in an organization is said to advance innovation by providing the time and space needed to experiment with new and uncertain ideas that might not otherwise attract support when resources are scarce. Innovation is costly and creating too much slack can absorb a firm's valuable resources. A portfolio approach provides a top–down, strategic way of managing innovation and allocating scarce resources to families of sequentially related product development projects. Firms use portfolios to evaluate and map a set of projects into different categories based on their novelty, identify how projects are sequenced over time in waves, and compress the time taken to execute them individually and collectively. The most innovative projects—platforms and breakthroughs—require greater resources, redundancy, and slack to cope with longer and more uncertain development cycles. By mapping the project types and identifying gaps in the product development strategy, managers of portfolios can identify which new projects should be added to the mix, when to add them, and when to terminate them. They can also identify the capabilities and develop the skills that individual members, teams, and project leaders need to plan and execute them.

Strategies used to circumvent strict portfolio evaluation criteria include various bottom-up, small-scale projects scattered throughout an organization. Requiring only limited resources, these projects can be undertaken covertly within existing business units and often without senior management ever being aware of them. Under-the-table, unofficial 'bootlegging projects'—sometimes embarked on with the tacit support of senior management—are an important source of innovation and entrepreneurship that may later become officially accepted and absorbed by mainstream product development activities. Today many executives have 'side projects' to experiment with an idea, develop a hobby, learn new skills, or create a start-up business free from the constraints of the mainstream organization. Google, for example, is well known for encouraging its employees to develop side projects as part of their day-to-day jobs. Many businesses—Twitter, Craigslist, Flat Planet, and Groupon—started out as side projects.

## Team structures and leaders

Wheelwright and Clark developed a well-known classification of four types of project team structures used for product development and innovation in many industries. In the 'functional team structure', tasks are subdivided at the outset into separate activities performed independently by functional groups. The project moves sequentially, although often not smoothly, from one function to the next. When there is limited overlap and interaction amongst team members, functional groups often develop their own habits, routines, and mindsets and face difficulties forming tightly knit cooperative teams with other groups.

In the 'lightweight team structure', members also reside physically in their functional disciplines, but each group designates a liaison manager as its representative on the project coordinating committee. In this matrix form of organization, the manager is said to be lightweight because he or she has less status in the organization, and key resources and power remain under the control of the functional managers. However, there is now at least one manager who looks across the functions to ensure that members of the team are kept informed about any cross-functional issues and interdependent tasks are performed in a timely manner.

In the 'heavyweight team structure', members borrowed from the functional groups are dedicated and physically co-located with the heavyweight project leader. As the Honda, Toyota, and Boeing examples showed, the project leader is a heavyweight because he or she is a senior manager in the organization, often having more expertise, experience, and status than the functional managers. Physical co-location is preferable to online digital communications because problems that arise in real time are best dealt with directly in face-to-face meetings, rather than having to wait for an episodic meeting to occur or use online communication to initiate cross-functional problem-solving. The core team is responsible for subdividing tasks, scheduling the project, and adjusting tasks when circumstances change. A heavyweight team requires a distinctive style of leadership to galvanize and motivate the team, while championing the basic concept being developed by the project—the role performed by Mulally on the 777 project. The heavyweight project manager is able to understand the needs of the customer and market, speak the language of the different functional groups, coordinate and integrate their work, and identify and resolve any conflicts that inevitably arise when groups with different expertise, behaviour, and priorities are expected to work together.

Faced with unforeseen circumstances or opportunities, the heavyweight team is able to develop new knowledge, reallocate resources, and reconfigure tasks to get the work accomplished in the best possible way. Clark and Fujimoto suggested that this structure is most effective for platform projects. American car producers in the mid-1980s using functional or lightweight team structures employed approximately 1,500 engineers in full-time work over several months, whereas Japanese platform projects with heavyweight managers employed only 250 engineers working full-time for the same period.

In the 'autonomous team structure', people from the various functions are also co-located as an integrated team but now with their own home, often in a separate building, for the duration of the project. The project leader, also a heavyweight, has full control over the resources and people provided by the functional groups and is sole evaluator of the performance of individual team members. Sometimes known as a 'tiger team', an autonomous project has a 'clean sheet of paper': it does not have to follow established policies and can make almost any changes required to accomplish the project goal. Members interact informally by mutual adjustment in organically structured teams. Lockheed Martin, the American aerospace and defence company, pioneered what is known as a 'skunk work' organization during the Cold War. It created this autonomous structure to house the cross-functional capabilities required to develop new high-technology projects, such as the U-2 spy-plane, SR-71 Blackbird, and F-117 Stealth Fighter, at a distance from the firm's mainstream organization and unencumbered by established rules and procedures.

## The balancing act

Undertaking projects to serve existing customers or create new markets entails a difficult balancing act. Using the metaphor of a stream, Rosabeth Moss Kanter suggests that an organization can maintain projects—'swim with the stream'—it is already committed to in its mainstream technology and market home base or it can cut a new channel and start a new stream of projects that will be of benefit in the future. Organizations require a certain amount of ambidexterity to know how to exploit their mainstream business, while launching breakthrough projects to explore and open up new market opportunities.

Derivative or platform projects in a firm's mainstream business develop incremental enhancements and new products for existing clients with stable preferences and predictable needs in existing markets. When projects depend on familiar technologies, plans and schedules can be developed before action is taken. Firms have a history and experience base, providing data for predictions about the future, an opportunity for careful planning prior to execution, and the ability to allocate resources to different projects and smooth out activities over the calendar year.

Firms are successful in mainstream markets because they listen to their customers and carefully study market trends before investing in new and improved products. It may seem surprising, for example, but until the 1990s Boeing did not generally seek the advice of the airlines before deciding on a new plane. It would develop the idea of a new plane, design and manufacture it, and then wait for airlines to buy it. Faced with intense competition from Airbus and McDonnell Douglas, changing demand for air travel, and other uncertainties, a new approach was needed. Boeing's 777 project team had to spend time with the airlines to find out what they required in terms of range, size, payload, and economy. Meetings with representatives of the 'Gang of Eight'—United, American, Delta, British Airways, Japan Air Lines, All-Nippon Airways, Qantas, and Cathy Pacific—helped Boeing design the 777.

New sources of revenues must be found when mainstream activities stagnate and decline. But the mainstream is often too slow and bureaucratic to compete in volatile markets or cope with rapid product obsolescence. Past investments in resources and commitments—budgets, schedules, role definitions, and expectations—made to keep mainstream projects flowing also make it difficult for them to change direction. Projects carried out by established R&D departments often fail when it comes to creating 'new to the world' products, which do not satisfy the performance requirements of existing customers, as Eastman Kodak, the camera manufacturer, found when it fatally delayed the switch from film to digital technology, which marked the beginning of the company's eventual demise and the rise of Fujitsu, Canon, and others.

Breakthrough projects initiate new streams of innovation. They imagine new possibilities, create entirely new offerings, and disrupt established industries. Because they have little or no experience base in the new technology and there are no current customers to listen to, forecasts about user requirements are difficult to produce, project schedules are usually unrealistic, and costs are likely to overrun. Action must be taken before plans can be developed and tasks have to be adjusted to deal with technical problems and unforeseen events while the project is under way. Existing knowledge is applied where possible, but new knowledge is required to make sense of poorly understood technologies and unknown customer requirements. As Kanter explains:

> Multiple approaches, flexibility, and speed are required for innovation because of the advance of new ideas through random and often highly intuitive insights and because of the discovery of unanticipated problems. Project teams need to work unencumbered by formal plans, board approval, and other 'bureaucratic delays', that might act as constraints against the change of direction.

Because breakthrough projects compete directly with the mainstream for resources, attention, and loyalty, senior management in the parent organization may become nervous about delegating too much control to the autonomous team and its leader. Too often, there is a risk that an autonomous team goes off on a tangent and creates difficulties for the parent organization. It may become too focused on the priorities of the individual project, rather than the needs of the wider organization (Chapter 6). Keeping breakthrough projects separate poses less of a threat to vested interests and helps to create the new culture, entrepreneurialism, and autonomy required to nurture and develop new ideas without being overly constrained by the dictates of established business fiefdoms or cumbersome bureaucratic procedures.

The autonomy required when launching breakthrough projects is illustrated by the development of the IBM Personal Computer (PC) in 1981. IBM established an autonomous team as an independent cross-functional structure called 'Project Chess' led by Bill Lowe. Located in Boca Raton, Florida, the project was far removed from the firm's headquarters and R&D department. This so-called 'renegade team' had a mandate to do whatever was required to develop the personal computer. At the same time, IBM's mainstream project called Datamaster, which continued with the established policy of producing components in-house, was stuck in its fourth year of development with no end in sight. A willingness to break the rules, including buying in components and software (e.g. the operating system) from external suppliers, enabled Project Chess to develop and bring the PC to market in just one year.

## Achieving breakthroughs

The most effective breakthrough project teams—like Project Chess—are structurally independent from the existing organization, but supported by top management and tightly integrated into the wider corporate structure. They share resources with traditional units, but being physically and organizationally separate ensures that the new project's processes, values, and approach are not overwhelmed by bureaucratic procedures. With so much responsibility and power delegated to the breakthrough project team, special integration mechanisms have to be put in place to maintain close contact between the team and parent organization. Senior management needs to retain the ability to guide the project, with a strong executive sponsor acting as a coach and mentor for the heavyweight manager and core team. If the members of the senior management team or other functional heads have concerns or require more information about the progress of the project, these can be communicated through the executive sponsor.

Breakthroughs are difficult to accomplish in well-established industries and those dominated by a few large firms likes cars, aeroplanes, mobile phones, and construction. In the early 1990s, for example, innovation in the car industry involved well-understood technologies and demand for its products was growing continuously. James Womack and his co-authors asked whether car producers were able to pass the 'final test' of applying the lean approach to breakthrough innovation: the creation of navigation and congestion-avoidance systems, autonomous driver-less cars, hydrogen and electric vehicles needed to address society's demands for motor-vehicle technology that does not contribute to rising levels of carbon emissions and the pollution of our cities.

Clayton Christensen identified the electric vehicle as the car industry's potentially disruptive technology and recommended that car manufacturers create a small, independent project organization separated from the mainstream, such as GM's Saturn Division, to nurture and commercialize the new technology. While a few firms started to develop electric cars (GM and Renault-Nissan), most focused on improving their existing products or developing hybrids, such as the Toyota Prius (Box 8).

A start-up from outside the industry—the first in the United States since Chrysler was established in 1925—challenged the mainstream manufacturers by producing the first all-electric car. Tesla Motors was founded by Martin Eberhard and Marc Tarpenning in 2003 and financed by serial entrepreneur Elon Musk who became Tesla's CEO. The Tesla Roadster, the first electric sports car, was introduced in 2008, but it was the Tesla Model S introduced in 2012 which launched the firm as an independent volume producer of electric cars. Powered by a battery pack, guided by an on-board computer with an Internet connection, dependent on downloaded software updates, and supported by a network of charging stations, the Model S is considered the 'automotive equivalent to an iPhone' because it can be plugged in and recharged at night. In a recent biography, Musk explains that the established car producers were reluctant to develop all-electric cars because they 'are so derivative. They want to see it work somewhere else before they will approve the project and move forward.' Tesla had to compete with the core capability of every car manufacturer in the world to achieve Musk's vision. The car that began technological disruption of the industry was developed at rapid pace by a small, autonomous project team of experienced engineers with its own office in a corner of Musk's SpaceX factory to 'add some separation and secrecy to what they

**Box 8  Disruptive technology**

Clayton Christensen suggests that listening to customers helps firms know which 'sustaining technologies' are required to improve the performance of established products that mainstream customers have traditionally valued. At the end of the 20th century, for example, the automotive industry continued to invest in products that their customers wanted: cars fuelled by petrol engines, providing high performance at low prices. At the time, no car producer was threatened by electric vehicles and few were contemplating moving into this uncertain market. But there are times when 'not listening to customers' is the right strategy. This occurs when entrepreneurs invest in high-risk 'disruptive technologies'—like the electric or self-driving autonomous car—which existing customers may not want and result in worse performance in the near term, but ultimately promise to open up new, growing, and lucrative markets.

were doing'. Led by a 'free-spirited, creative' car designer named Franz von Holzhausen, the Model S team had to deal with Musk's demands for numerous design changes, advanced vehicle technologies developed in-house, and aggressive time schedule for product delivery.

## Agile project management

An alternative to lean has emerged incorporating some of its adaptive elements but which is even more strongly focused on real-time learning, improvisation, and iterative development. Originally developed for software projects, the 'agile' methodology offers a radical alternative to the traditional standard waterfall model of project management (Chapter 4) and its emphasis on an early design and specification freeze, a fixed scope, sequential phases of planning and execution, and limited customer interaction. Those advocating an agile approach believe that the traditional reliance on rigid front-end planning processes and formal contracts can result in various 'downstream pathologies' such as a lack of flexibility when conditions change, excessive rework, dissatisfied clients, and an inability to adjust in real time to changing circumstances while a project is under way. As we saw in Chapter 1, for example, Motorola's Iridium project developed the full potential of satellite phone technology, only to find that the rapid expansion of terrestrial mobile communications had largely eliminated the need for it while the project was under way.

Relatively stable environments are amenable to front-end planning and scheduling, whereas a changing and uncertain environment requires agile methods so that planning and replanning is spread out across the development life cycle. Agile is an iterative and incremental 'rolling wave' process designed to facilitate flexibility and responsiveness to abruptly changing technology and market conditions. Agile methods require the minimum use of documentation, continuous design iterations so that the design freeze is delayed until the last responsible moment, frequent customer and stakeholder interaction, and a modified lightweight project team structure. An agile approach shares many of the adaptive, real-time 'teaming' processes discussed in Chapter 4. Adjustments are made 'on the fly' to deal with abruptly changing conditions and plans are altered as new information about customer requirements and technologies becomes available during the execution of a project. Growing evidence suggests that agile contributes to the success of software and IT projects, and may be of value for projects undertaken in hi-tech and more traditional industries.

In Chapter 6, we use examples of some of the infrastructure megaprojects undertaken in London over the past decade to illustrate some of the different ways of organizing projects in the 21st century.

# Chapter 6
# London's megaproject ecology

The Jubilee Line Extension project of the London Underground—a 10-mile (16-kilometre) tube line with cavernous stations—was built to connect London's West End with the office metropolis at Canary Wharf and south and east areas of the city. This time-critical project was supposed to open as a complete system in time to carry millions of passengers to London's Millennium Dome for the millennium celebrations. Based on a fixed-price contract, it was scheduled for completion in March 1997 at a cost of £2.1 billion (an earlier estimate in 1989 was £900 million). It was designed to incorporate the most advanced radio-based, moving block signalling system technology to allow the trains to run closely together, much faster and more safely. It represented the future of travel in the world's congested cities. Construction of the extension started in December 1993 but difficulties with tunnelling and signalling forced the project to abandon the new signalling technology, delayed the completion date, and significantly raised the final cost. Some contractors submitted low-cost tenders on the expectation that they could recoup the money and earn additional profits by submitting over £500 million of claims for changes to the specification and unexpected problems encountered during construction. To resolve these problems, the London Underground was removed from the management of the project in 1998 and replaced by Bechtel, the American engineering and construction firm. The project eventually cost £3.5 billion and was opened in three stages from May to December 1999.

The Jubilee Line is one of a long list of UK megaprojects in the 1980s, 1990s and early 2000s—the Channel Tunnel, Millennium Dome, Scottish Parliament Building, Swanwick Air Traffic Control, and many others—that were overdue and over budget. In a review of the Jubilee Line project, Bechtel concluded that British clients and contractors were incapable of managing large-scale infrastructure projects.

In the late 1990s, BAA (formerly British Airports Authority)—the owner and operator of major UK airports—was preparing to build the £4.3 billion fifth terminal (T5) for British Airways at London's Heathrow Airport (Figure 9). Richard Rogers won the competition to design T5 in 1989, construction started in July 2002, and the terminal opened in March 2008. Sir John Egan, BAA's Chief

9. **Heathrow Terminal 5 during construction.**

Executive in the 1990s, was aware of the UK construction industry's poor track record in delivering projects and concerned that any significant cost overrun on T5 'could bankrupt the company'. BAA decided to examine every major UK construction project over the previous decade and every international airport that had opened during the previous fifteen years (e.g. Denver and Charles de Gaulle) to find out why megaprojects so often failed.

The answer was surprisingly simple. Clients assumed that future conditions could be foreseen in low-cost bids and accounted for in a fixed-price contract that transferred all risks to the contractor and allowed no room for changes in circumstances (see NASA's view of fixed-price contracts in Chapter 3). When problems arose, there was no collaborative mechanism to resolve them. Disputes between client and contractor frequently ended up in court, delaying the project. BAA knew from its own experience with a fixed-price contract in the mid-1990s—the delayed Heathrow Express railway from the airport to Paddington station—that the risk of delivering a project could not be contracted out to a construction company. If T5 was delivered using the traditional model, BAA estimated that the project would be £1 billion over budget, a year late, and result in six deaths during construction. BAA's insight was that in complex and uncertain projects the client ultimately always bears the risks when things go wrong and it concluded that a radically new 'project delivery model' (the contractual and organizational relationship between client and contractors) was required for T5.

The T5 project was established as an autonomous structure led by a heavyweight team of managers with experience gained in other industries (e.g. automotive, nuclear power, and aerospace) and other complex projects (e.g. GSK's UK research facility and Hong Kong International Airport). This core team 'changed the rules of the game' by creating a new flexible contract called the 'T5 Agreement' based on two principles: the client would bear the risks involved in constructing T5 and work collaboratively with contractors in co-located integrated project teams. Contractors had their costs reimbursed and were incentivized to innovate and improve performance by bonuses for doing better than previously agreed 'target costs' and completion dates. Any profits earned were shared among team members. In contrast to the traditional delivery model, the T5 process was flexible and adaptive to deal with unforeseen events and embrace opportunities to innovate that could not be anticipated at the start:

> Conventional project logic seeks to predefine all requirements and banish change once the project has started. Yet flexibility and adaptability are key objectives for T5. Conventional processes and solutions are therefore not tenable. It will require flexibility of approach: flexibility of solutions; latest responsible decision making.

> (*T5 Delivery Handbook*, 1999)

Despite the disrupted opening (Chapter 1), the T5 project was delivered on time and within budget. One year after opening, T5 was voted the world's best airport terminal by passengers. It has radically transformed how megaprojects in the UK are delivered and started an industry-wide narrative about the need for flexibility, collaboration, and innovation. Individuals, teams, and organizations working on T5 carried many of the new ideas and innovative practices with them when they went to work on other megaprojects in London, such as the construction of the £6.8 billion London 2012 Olympics venues and infrastructure, the £14.8 billion Crossrail urban railway system traversing east–west across London, and the £4.2 billion Thames Tideway Tunnel scheme to replace London's ageing Victorian sewer system (Box 9).

As this brief introduction to London's megaprojects illustrates, it is important to understand the context within which projects are initiated and unfold over time. It raises many questions that cannot be answered by project management's traditional preoccupation

## Box 9  Inside the world of a megaproject

London's Crossrail project illustrates what it's like to work on one of these massive endeavours. The project is constructing a new railway—the Elizabeth Line—from Reading and Heathrow in the west via 21 km of twin-bore tunnels under central London to Shenfield and Abbey Wood in the east, including ten new and thirty upgraded stations. Many of Crossrail's tunnels (Figure 10) have been excavated and constructed close to existing tube lines. At its closest point, one of Crossrail's tunnels is only 37 cm (15 inches) from the Northern Line tunnel.

One station is underneath the junction between Oxford Street (Europe's busiest shopping street) and Charing Cross Road where a small army of construction workers, electricians, engineers, and project managers have been working to complete the £1 billion transformation of Tottenham Court Road Station. The station and two ticket halls provides an interchange between the Elizabeth Line and existing Northern and Central lines. The 250-metre (825-foot) platform and station located 24 metres below ground is about the length of Wembley Football Stadium. Construction work has been undertaken in front of the Centre Point multi-storey office building in a protected conservation area with heritage listed buildings, businesses, shops, restaurants, and other amenities. Components and prefabricated structures had to be delivered to the site and excavated materials removed with as little disruption as possible to central London. Many passengers using London's Northern and Central lines through the existing Tottenham Court Road Station were unaware of what was going on behind a hoarding in front of the Crossrail building works. When complete, more than 200,000 passengers are expected to pass through the new station every day.

10. Crossrail's tunnelling machine makes breakthrough into the City of London, 40 metres below ground under Liverpool Street Station.

with the 'lonely project', such as: How do individuals, teams, and organizations involved in projects learn from the past? How do they develop their knowledge and prepare for the future?

## No project is an island

Over the past two decades, researchers have provided insights, frameworks, and perspectives on how organizations work together in projects and how projects are embedded in organizations. This research first emerged in Scandinavia in the early 1990s, possibly because these countries have a disproportionately large number of project-based firms in complex engineering industries—such as Ericsson, ABB, Saab, Skanska, Statoil, and Nokia—with close ties to local universities. In what became known as the 'Scandinavian School of Project Studies', project management (Chapter 3), organizational theory (Chapter 4), innovation management (Chapter 5), and other streams of literature were used to undertake in-depth studies of how projects evolve in different contexts.

While its roots were in Scandinavia, the field of project studies expanded in the late 1990s when scholars elsewhere in the world began to discover that many firms and industries are project based. These studies shared the view that traditional writings on project management were too narrowly concerned with producing handbooks on how to manage a project, programme, or portfolio, rather than how projects shape—and are shaped by—the wider development of organizations, industries, and society. Matts Engwall expressed it well when he said that 'no project is an island': what goes on inside a project must be understood in relation to previous, current, and future projects, and the wider institutional context within which it is undertaken.

A project is a temporary organization and designed to dissolve when its task is accomplished, whereas a firm is a permanent organization which is established to grow, prosper, and survive indefinitely. Jörg Sydow and his co-authors suggest that this temporary and permanent context creates the two fundamental tensions or dilemmas associated with project-based organizing.

The 'autonomy versus integration' dilemma is between the autonomous requirements of each project and the need to integrate projects in the wider organization. The focused, fast, and autonomous work undertaken in a particular project serves to create new knowledge and innovation for each client (Chapter 5), but may not align with the strategic priorities of the parent organization within which the project is embedded. BAA recognized this tension when the T5 project was established as a standalone organization with autonomy and resources required to manage such a complex programme of work, but with a direct line of reporting to the executive team to ensure that the project was tightly integrated into Heathrow's corporate activities.

The 'doing versus learning' dilemma is between creating new knowledge to address the immediate demands of a project and using the learning gained to improve the performance of projects undertaken in future by the parent organization. In the traditional project management literature, projects are generally treated as unique, non-recurring, and undertaken in isolation from previous or future projects. This 'every project is unique' mindset encourages organizations to believe that there is little point in capturing the learning gained in one project and repeating successful practices on subsequent projects. Consequently, firms often suffer from organizational amnesia when it comes to transferring knowledge from one project to the next and to the wider organization (Box 10).

The two dilemmas are interwoven in practice because, as Sydow and his co-authors point out, being focused means that team members may be less interested in things taking place outside the project; being fast means that people have little time to reflect on their work and record lessons learnt; and being autonomous means that the project team may develop into a silo of learning,

## Box 10  Unique and repetitive projects

Projects involve a spectrum of tasks ranging from unique to repetitive. A unique task is for a one-time situation and requires visionary, flexible, creative actions, and real-time learning. A repetitive task has been performed many times in the past (standardized procedures such as bidding, cost control, and risk management) with established clients and will be undertaken repeatedly in the future. People know what to do, how to do it, and share similar experiences and interpretations of the situation. We can only really understand whether a project as a whole is unique or repetitive by placing it in the wider historical context. Some projects really are unique undertakings if they represent an entirely new experience for the parent organization, whereas many others are repetitive because they show little deviation from projects performed in the past.

forcing others to 'reinvent the wheel' and restricting the flow of knowledge to other projects and the firm as a whole.

It is now recognized that no single species of organization—such as the adhocracy—captures the variety of organizations involved in projects. In their book *Managing and Working in Project Society* (2015), Rolf Lundin and his co-authors identify several different forms of project organization and discuss how they differ from those that prevailed during the industrial age. Here we refer to a simple matrix originally developed by Jonas Söderlund to highlight some of the distinctive temporary and permanent forms of project-based organizing (Figure 11). By distinguishing between single and multiple projects and between single and multiple organizations (e.g. firms and government agencies), the matrix helps us identify four broad categories of project organizing: single-project organizations, project-based organizations, project networks, and project ecologies. All four exist in some form or another in most industries and encompass a variety of firms, government agencies, joint ventures, public–private partnerships, and other structures.

|  | One organization | Many organizations |
|---|---|---|
| **One project** | Single-project organization | Project network |
| **Many projects** | Project-based organization | Project ecology |

11. Forms of project organizing.

## Single-project organizations

A single-project organization is established as a one-time legal or financial entity to achieve a specific goal and designed to dissolve when the task has been accomplished. It inherits its strategic purpose and funding and is not usually required to generate further revenues until the task is completed—although additional injections of money may be needed when the project is under way. When an aircraft carrier, movie, hospital, or high-speed railway link is completed, the single-project organization ceases to exist. Some can last for as little as a few weeks or months (e.g. a feature film), but organizations with a duration of ten years or more are not uncommon in large public infrastructure and military projects.

The single-project organization has little time to develop the 'organizational memory', routines, and capabilities that firms like Microsoft, Sony, and Google rely upon to survive, grow, and prosper in a changing competitive environment. Any knowledge and learning acquired and developed during the project generally disappears when the organization is disbanded on completion of its task. There is also much less time to cultivate personal relationships and build trust that people develop in firms over years and decades. Yet studies of independent film producers—an extreme example of a single-project organization—have shown that people can develop 'swift trust' to compensate for working for the organizational equivalent of a 'one-night stand'. Unlike the major studios (e.g. Disney), an independent film company is established to make a single movie and disbands when the film is released. Members of a film crew assembled to produce the movie are able to trust each other and coordinate complex interdependent tasks because they have clearly defined expertise and professional roles (e.g. production, photography, and set design). Each member of the project knows their role, has performed a specialized task repeatedly in the past, and is able to do so again when working with new and familiar crew members.

Various forms of single-project organizations have been created to manage large public infrastructure projects in London including public–private partnerships (PPP), special-purpose vehicles (SPV), client bodies, and delivery partners. As we saw in Chapter 1, a number of consortiums have been awarded PPP contracts to design, build, finance, operate, and maintain London's tube lines, railways, and hospitals. Rail Link Engineering (an incorporated contract between Arup, Bechtel, Halcrow, and Systra) was formed as an SPV in 1996 to manage the design and construction of High-Speed 1 (HS1)—the 109-kilometre (65-mile) high-speed railway between the Channel Tunnel and London St Pancras station. Established as a fully autonomous legal entity, the risks associated with an SPV can be isolated and considered to pose less of a threat to the sponsor or parent organization than would the establishment of a new business unit or division.

The Olympic Delivery Authority (ODA) was created in 2006 by Act of Parliament as a temporary public body accountable to its sponsors—the government and the Greater London Authority. The Act provided the ODA with the legal power and responsibilities to construct the infrastructure and venues for the Games. The ODA, which employed around 220 staff, recognized that a delivery organization could not be established in-house with available resources or in the time available, so decided to appoint a 'delivery partner' to manage the programme: a private sector consortium called 'CLM' employing over 500 staff at its peak seconded from the three parent firms of CH2M, Laing O'Rourke, and Mace. CLM was selected because the parent firms in this joint venture had proven capabilities in managing previous Olympic construction programmes and large infrastructure projects (including Heathrow Terminal 5). The ODA and CLM reduced significantly in size after the Games started on 27 July 2012 and were eventually dissolved: CLM in March 2013 and the ODA in December 2014.

The Crossrail project could have been undertaken as part of the Transport for London (TfL) programme of activities, but there was a concern that the progress of such a high-profile endeavour might be jeopardized if the wider needs of TfL were to take priority over those of the project. Crossrail Limited was, therefore, established as a separate company to ensure that the people responsible for its delivery were entirely focused on a single task, with a clear remit and clarity of purpose. An integrated programme delivery team of around 1,200 staff was formed including the client (Crossrail Limited) and two delivery partners: a programme partner called Transcend (a joint venture between CH2M, AECOM, and The Nichols Group) and a project delivery partner called Crossrail Central (a joint venture led by Bechtel and supported by Halcrow and Systra) to manage the construction of the complex central section of tunnels. As the project moved towards completion, the operator (Rail for London) became a more active member of the integrated programme delivery team. When the project is completed in 2019, the client and delivery partner organizations will be disbanded.

## Project-based organizations

Many firms depend on projects to create and develop new products and services in competitive and fast-changing markets, but their core business is high-volume operations (Chapter 1). A firm or an organization is 'project-based' when most of its design, development, and productive activities are handled as projects for clients and are embedded in a permanent organization which is expected to remain in business and find new work when each project is completed. In most cases, employees in project-based organizations have relatively stable positions and many have long-term exclusive contracts.

Building on Mintzberg's observation (Chapter 4), we distinguish between two types of project-based organization. Those organized to address their own in-house needs for projects include a number of large private companies (e.g. Shell and BP in the oil and gas industry), government agencies, and publicly funded organizations as diverse as the US Department of Defense, NASA, and TfL. Those serving external clients, by contrast, are widespread in industries that produce customized products and services as one-off units or in small batches. They include capital goods (e.g. defence, aerospace, factory automation systems, rolling stock, nuclear power stations, oil and gas platforms, shipbuilding, software, and telecommunications), creative industries (e.g. film studios, music, video games, and TV production), public infrastructure (e.g. hospitals, roads, railways, and schools), professional services (e.g. advertising and consulting), construction and architecture, and high-value bespoke products (e.g. Formula One racing cars, private jets, and luxury yachts).

Project-based organizations are sometimes nested within the divisions, business units, and subsidiaries of large firms and departments of government. The continuing survival and growth of a diversified firm like Toshiba, the Tokyo-headquartered global corporation, depends on substantial high-volume production operations (e.g. consumer electronics and household appliances) and securing a series of major projects in high-value capital goods (e.g. high-speed rail transportation and nuclear power plants). Government agencies responsible for railways, roads, water, and other utility networks have large organizations to operate and provide services and internal project-based divisions to procure and manage major projects in collaboration with private sector contractors. The London Underground (a subsidiary of TfL), for example, is responsible for operating tube trains and stations and managing major capital projects, such as the construction of new lines or refurbishment of stations.

Frequently found in construction, architecture, and professional services, the activities of a project-based firm are based entirely on managing dozens, hundreds, if not thousands of projects at any particular time. They have to balance the discontinuous requirements of each project and the firm's longer-term strategic business objectives. Bechtel, the large American civil engineering, construction, and project management firm, for example, has been prime contractor on some of the world's largest projects such as the Hoover Dam, San Francisco's Bay Area Rapid Transit system, Boston Central Artery/Tunnel, Channel Tunnel, Jubilee Line Extension, and Crossrail. Employing about 55,000 people to manage about 25,000 projects in 160 countries in 2016, Bechtel has the breadth of capabilities to handle multiple aspects of large-scale projects, including project planning, financing, procurement, design, construction, and management of contractors.

Various structures are used to coordinate projects embedded in project-based firms, ranging from functional (where projects are undertaken by one or more groups or departments) at one extreme to dedicated project-based organizations at the other (Chapter 3). Many, like Arup, have some form of matrix structure to combine functional and project activities. Whereas pure project-based organizations are good at problem-solving, advancing innovation, and focusing on the individual requirements of each client, they are less effective than matrix structures when it comes to coordinating resources, sharing knowledge across projects embedded in the parent organization, and achieving organization-wide efficiency gains. Many organizational units in project-based firms are led by powerful individuals—whom David Gann and his co-authors call 'project barons'—who compete for resources to support their existing and new entrepreneurial initiatives.

When projects are similar and repetitive, a project-based organization can develop the intellectual resources, expertise, and routines required to win, coordinate, and efficiently execute multiple projects in a technology or market base. When project tasks are repeated, organizations with 'project capabilities' can perform tasks more reliably and efficiently. Project capabilities are comprised of tacit knowledge (or personal experience) possessed by members of project teams and the codified (or explicit) knowledge embodied in standardized project management procedures, processes, tools, and guidebooks. When Sir John Egan joined BAA from his previous position as CEO of Jaguar Motors, for example, he found to his surprise that every project in airport construction was 'treated as a blank sheet of paper' and newly assembled teams 'tended to think it through from first principles over and over again'. To discourage managers from treating each project as unique, BAA developed capabilities embodied in a guidebook (based on lean processes used by Japanese car producers) to perform standardized and repeatable time-sequenced tasks, milestones, and stage-gates and deliver cost-effective, profitable projects.

A firm's project capabilities are occasionally reconfigured to keep pace with a changing environment when a 'vanguard project' is created to achieve a breakthrough innovation, as illustrated by Arup's Dongtan project and attempts to grow a sustainable urban design business (Chapter 4). A sign of how technologies and markets will evolve in the future, vanguard projects often reveal the fragility of an organization's existing project capabilities, developed over many years to execute projects for a stable group of clients and markets. Members of a vanguard project explore alternative approaches, engage in trial-and-error learning, and often ignore established procedures to create new offerings, anticipate progress, capture innovative thinking, and develop new project management structures, tools, and processes. Vanguard projects sometimes mark the beginning of a 'project epoch' when a new-type project emerges and takes hold, lasting years or decades, to address the fairly predictable and well-understood requirements of established clients.

In a process of project-capability building, the new knowledge created in a vanguard project may be developed and reused across projects to support a firm's growth in a new market. For example, Heathrow T5 was a vanguard project for Laing O'Rourke, the largest firm by contract value involved in the construction of the new terminal. Working closely with BAA and other suppliers, Laing O'Rourke helped identify, develop, and introduce many innovative processes used to deliver the T5 project such as integrated project team working, digital design technology, project collaboration software, and offsite prefabrication. The capabilities that Laing O'Rourke gained on T5 were developed, honed, and improved further when the firm went on to become the leading contractor and delivery partner on a series of megaprojects in London (e.g. St Pancras railway redevelopment, London 2012 Olympics, and Crossrail) and elsewhere in the world.

## Project networks

Many projects involve some form of collaboration with external parties and the most complex projects have to coordinate large networks—or temporary coalitions—of contractors and subcontractors. The word 'network' conveys the idea that a project consists of many organizations working on a joint task for a defined period of time. It draws attention to the relationships or ties and the frequency, duration, and density of interactions among individual and organizational members of a project.

Project networks are found in a great variety of private and public sectors such as aerospace, oil and gas platforms, defence, university research, advertising, biotechnology, and construction. They range in size from small projects with a few partners to megaprojects like the T5, HS1, London 2012 Olympics, and Crossrail involving dozens of contractors and thousands of subcontractors. They also vary in duration from as little as the days, weeks, or months needed to make a TV documentary to several decades in some major defence systems projects such as the development of the Joint Strike Fighter programme, which began in 1993 and has still not entered service. Organizations often play different roles during the life of a project network. In large civil engineering projects, for example, the client organization, prime contractor, or delivery partner remains in place for the full duration, while other organizations are brought in for specific phases, such as design or construction.

In large project networks, one or more organizations leads the endeavour and coordinates and schedules the activities undertaken by multiple parties. As we have seen in Chapter 3, capabilities in systems integration (a practice pioneered by US defence and aerospace firms) are particularly important in complex projects. A client organization can develop these capabilities in-house, appoint a prime contractor, or work with a delivery partner. The London 2012 Olympics, for example, consisted of more than 70 individual projects managed by principal contractors including design and construction of 14 temporary (e.g. International Broadcast Centre) and permanent buildings (e.g. Olympics Stadium, Velodrome, and Aquatics Centre), 20 km of roads, 26 bridges, 13 km of tunnels, and 80 hectares of parkland and utilities infrastructure. Working closely together, the client (the ODA) and its delivery partner (CLM) coordinated the design, construction, integration, and delivery of the venues and infrastructure. The ODA was responsible for the overall progress of the project and dealing with external stakeholders and neighbours impacted by it. CLM managed the programme and principal contractors responsible for each major venue, coordinated the interfaces between them, integrated them into the Olympic Park infrastructure, and prepared for the staging of the Games.

In addition to these coordination challenges, mechanisms are needed to build cooperation among the participants in a project network. In recent years, sponsors of the UK's large infrastructure projects have attempted to establish more collaborative relationships between clients and contractors. Following BAA's pioneering approach on T5, more enlightened clients no longer rely exclusively on fixed-price contracts for complex projects which penalize contractors for delays, promote adversarial relationships, and often lead to irreconcilable conflict. Like Heathrow Airport, clients are adopting relational contracts that build long-term cooperation with their suppliers, with a balanced mix of incentives and penalties to reduce opportunism and reward innovation and problem-solving. Similar forms of cooperation exist elsewhere in the world such as the 'Integrated Program Team' in the United States and 'Alliancing' in Australia.

On Crossrail, for example, a judicious balance has to be found between the differing objectives, time horizons, and priorities of the client and its contractors. The client delivery organization is focused on the long-term goals of finishing the project on time, safely, and within budget, dealing with external stakeholders, and handing over a 'world-class railway' to the operator, whereas the more immediate priority of each contractor is to complete a discrete piece of work and make a profit. Crossrail has over sixty major contracts with individual firms and joint ventures to construct the railway, such as the £400 million western tunnel contract awarded to the BAM Nuttall, Ferrovial, and Kier (BFK) joint venture. Contracts range in size from as little as £1 million for design services to over £500 million for the largest tunnelling and systems contracts. The client relies on collaborative contracts and various forms of persuasion and personal relationships to motivate the contractors (if necessary talking directly with the contractor's CEO to wield influence) and keep the project on track towards completion. To overcome problems and resolve disputes, members of Crossrail's delivery partner also work onsite with contractors in co-located integrated project teams.

Achieving cooperation is particularly challenging in 'global projects' ranging from activities undertaken in a specific geographical location (e.g. the London 2012 Olympics) to spatially dispersed project teams at multiple locations around the world (e.g. the Boeing 777 project). As firms outsource and internationalize their activities, global projects have become what Richard Scott and his co-authors describe as the 'nexus of inter-organizational cooperation in a global marketplace'. Aligning the interests of participants is difficult in global projects because they are so institutionally complex, culturally diverse, and often conflict-ridden. Participants from various organizational and cultural backgrounds inhabit different 'thought worlds' that often create frictions when teams are co-located. CH2M, for example, found that working in a co-located integrated project team—as it did so successfully during the London 2012 Olympics project—was particularly challenging in the cross-cultural setting of the $5.35 billion project initiated in 2006 to expand and modernize the Panama Canal. Conflicts soon appeared after the local client (Autoridad del Canal de Panamá) hired CH2M, the American-based global engineering firm, to jointly manage the Panama Canal expansion project. Negotiations about who should lead the project and be accountable for the outcome were sometimes tense and difficult to resolve, in part because the two parties had such different expectations and institutional and cultural backgrounds.

## Project ecologies

The organizations we have been discussing are often participants in industries—as diverse as aerospace, advertising, software, and consulting—that depend on projects to undertake most of their productive activities. Various terms—such as project business network, geographical cluster, and ecosystem—are used to describe the constellation of organizations involved in each other's past, current, and future projects. They may include clients, contractors, subcontractors, consultants, manufacturers, financiers, universities, funding bodies, and other stakeholders. In project-based industries, organizations enter into various forms of collaborative partnerships or arm's-length contractual relationships with participants in some projects, whilst competing to win new contracts and improve their competitive advantage in others. Relationships between entities often alter from one project to the next. For example, suppliers of railway rolling stock, such as Alstom, Bombardier, Toshiba, or Siemens, may be a prime contractor on one urban railway system project and subcontractor on another. Government agencies often play a pivotal role as project sponsor and client in public sector projects (e.g. highways, railways, and healthcare) to ensure that public and private parties work together to achieve public policy objectives.

Learning and capability development is possible in project-based industries because the enduring relationships and trust established among the participants collaborating in projects provide a repository of shared learning and prior experience which can be retrieved when participants work together in the future. The experience gained while working together—known as the 'shadow of the past'—often decides which participants will be selected to work on future projects. The expectations and hope that participants will work together again—known as the 'shadow of the future'—is an incentive to behave and perform well on a current project. BAA, for example, established five-year 'framework agreements' to build constructive relationships with suppliers involved in current and future projects at Heathrow and other airports. Treating its suppliers as long-term partners in a stream of projects reduced BAA's coordination costs and provided suppliers with the stability they needed to develop the capabilities and improve their performance over time.

Gernot Grabher introduced the concept of a 'project ecology' to describe the dense network of personal ties, organizational, and institutional relationships found in geographical clusters of project-based activities, such as the advertising agencies concentrated in the Soho district of London or the vast mobilization of people, firms, and bodies required to plan and build the London 2012 Olympic Games. The four layers of a project ecology—the core team, the firm, epistemic community, and personal networks—provide a deep pool of personal, organizational, and institutional capabilities and memory of project experiences that can be retrieved and mobilized to manage current projects and prepare for the future (Box 11).

Some of the grandest civil engineering projects in living memory have been undertaken in London since the start of the 21st century to renew and expand the city's ageing Victorian

## Box 11  Layers of a project ecology

The core team layer refers to the professional roles and tasks performed by individuals and how they collaborate in project teams. In a 'cumulative ecology', teams remain stable over successive projects to achieve incremental improvements in performance. In a 'disruptive ecology', the composition of the team is altered to combine people with fresh ideas needed to create radical change.

The firm layer refers to the project capabilities (see 'Project-based organizations') which are required to improve performance by repeating practices that worked well in the past. New combinations of technologies and practices are pulled together when innovative solutions are needed to address challenging client demands, such as BAA's T5 project.

The epistemic community layer refers to the knowledge, extending beyond the boundary of the firm, that professionals in client, supplier, or corporate groups establish to share non-confidential information, case studies, and other experiences.

The personal network layer refers to the relationships and ties among individuals that extend beyond projects and business relationships. Often remaining in the project background, this layer is activated when people are called upon to solve specific problems or to provide support and advice when needed.

infrastructure, develop entire urban districts, and build new air and railway transportation links. They include high-profile projects such as HS1, T5, London 2012 Olympics, Crossrail, Thames Tideway Tunnel, High-Speed 2 (the multi-billion-pound high-speed railway from London Euston via Birmingham to Leeds and Manchester). The expanding network of individuals, teams, contractors, and clients working on these projects and circulating between them has helped to establish London's thriving megaproject ecology and worldwide reputation for innovative project delivery models.

With head offices in and around London, architecture, consultancy, construction, programme management, and civil engineering firms—such as Rogers Stirk Harbour + Partners, Arup, Balfour Beatty, Mace, Costain, CH2M, and Laing O'Rourke—are located in close proximity to each other. Because of their heavy dependence on government infrastructure contracts, senior executives in these firms have cultivated close relationships with project sponsors, government officials, and political leaders. They are the first to hear about new proposals and are in a strong position to bid for new work, often in collaboration with one of their local partners. Firms that have successfully developed their capabilities and reputation on one megaproject tend to reappear in different guises in the future. Laing O'Rourke, for example, was the largest contractor on T5, London 2012's delivery partner, the contractor appointed to build Crossrail's Tottenham Court Road Station, and part of the consortium building the central section of the Thames Tideway Tunnel. Core teams in firms and client bodies often migrate from one project to the next. For example, after completing its work for London 2012, the ODA's entire procurement team went on to work for Crossrail.

Many individuals—at all levels from senior executives to project managers and operatives—are 'project nomads', developing knowledge and sharing expertise as they move between London's megaprojects. For example, Andrew Wolstenholme, the project director of T5, went on to become CEO of Crossrail, Andy Mitchell, the programme director of Crossrail, became CEO of the Thames Tideway Tunnel, and Mark Thurston, a senior programme manager on London 2012 and Crossrail, became CEO of High-Speed 2. Often their professional identities are more closely tied to the project than to the permanent organization that employs them. Managers working for CLM, London 2012's delivery partner, had to get used to 'wearing two hats': they knew that they would eventually rejoin their parent firms, but identified closely with the project while it was under way. Personal ties and relations between individuals who have worked together in the past permeate each new megaproject, encouraging the circulation of knowledge, ideas, and successful practices.

Several of London's megaprojects have recently promoted the idea of creating a systematic and formal approach to harness innovation to complete projects more efficiently and create better outcomes—something achieved informally on the Erie Canal project (Chapter 2). In 2013, Crossrail established an innovation programme encouraging contractors, suppliers, and other stakeholders in the project to develop, implement, and share new ideas, technologies, and practices An in-house team managed the innovation programme and established a database to capture all the innovative ideas, proposals, and solutions submitted by members of the project. In October 2016, the CEOs of Crossrail and the Thames Tideway Tunnel projects used their personal networks and relationships to form a client-led epistemic community called the 'Infrastructure Industry Innovation Platform' supported by major contractors, a government funding body, and leading universities. To prevent innovation from occurring in isolation on each megaproject—as it had in the past—the platform (which builds on a database and collaborative approach originally created for Crossrail) was established to share new ideas, practices, and technologies with other megaprojects in London and elsewhere in the UK.

In Chapter 7 we consider whether these new and emerging forms of project organization will be able to deal with the major challenges societies are facing in the 21st century.

# Chapter 7
# Back to the future

Project management came of age during and after the Second
World War when the systems approach was invented to coordinate
and schedule the development of weapons and aerospace systems.
The traditional, systems-based model, formalized in the late 1960s
and 1970s by professional bodies to bring coherence, standardized
procedures and discipline to the management of projects, was
based on the expectation that markets and technologies were
well understood and projects could be carefully prepared to
accommodate stable and predictable conditions. The assumption
behind this model, that all projects can be managed in a similar
way, has been questioned in recent books and articles that urge
us to rethink, reinvent, and reconstruct project management.
Few of today's projects are predictable and unchanging. In most
cases, plans have to be realistic and flexible to address a future that
cannot be fully known at the outset and adjustable and responsive
to unexpected, novel, and fast-changing conditions arising when a
project is under way. It is now recognized that an adaptive model
of project management supported by digital technologies is required
for the complex, innovative, and unpredictable projects of the
21st century. Yet the idea that projects are shaped by the dynamics
of the environment within which they are planned and executed
is not a new one. The leaders of America's early weapons systems
projects—Groves, Schriever, Ramo, Raborn, and Webb—understood
that the extent of uncertainty, complexity, and urgency varies for

different kinds of projects and each project has to be managed in a flexible and adaptive way. Until recently it seems project management had forgotten its roots.

## Wicked problems

The trend towards project-based organizing is increasing in the 21st century as managers recognize that innovation is the norm in competitive global markets and organizations expect to have to manage a continuing stream of projects. Large-scale organizations are increasingly infiltrated by transient project organizations, groups, and teams that spring up in their midst and then disappear. Organizations that are good at learning from the past, building project capabilities, and working with partners in adaptive, collaborative teams will be better prepared for the future. But will existing project management structures, processes, and tools be able to cope with the difficult challenges now facing societies, such as an ageing population, poverty, terrorism, the migration and refugee crisis, and other issues?

Perhaps the most significant and challenging 'wicked problems'—difficult to define with no clear solutions—of our age result from the combination of rapid urbanization and climate change. The rise of mass production, the car and aeroplane, and a pattern of urbanization based on cheap energy powered by fossil fuels (about 80 per cent of global energy demand in 2014) set us on a path of industrialization over the past 200 years that has fundamentally changed our climate system. Current predictions suggest that at the end of the 21st century, the warming effect of greenhouse gases such as carbon dioxide and methane will create a climate that will be very different from pre-industrial conditions. Uncertainties about our future climate—arising from the complexity of the climate system and the social, political, and economic responses to it—mean that project organizations of the future might have to be even more innovative, flexible, and fast-paced.

The number of people living in cities is expected to rise to 70 per cent of the global population in 2050, from 50 per cent in 2015. A study by McKinsey Global Institute in 2013 estimates that $57 trillion will be spent on investment in the world's infrastructure between 2013 and 2030. Many infrastructure megaprojects are being initiated and executed to keep pace with the unprecedented acceleration of urbanization in newly industrializing countries like China and India. In cities like London, Berlin, and New York, they are needed to replace the ageing buildings, urban developments, and fragmented infrastructures of a past industrial age. They are needed to design and build the ecologically sustainable 'smart city' of the future using digital sensors and monitoring instruments to control transportation, communications, water, and other utilities, and make energy supply more adaptive to changing demand.

Megaprojects in densely populated urban areas might be more challenging than the systems projects of the Cold War. Although the Apollo programme was complex and uncertain, for example, it was a closed system with almost unlimited resources to achieve a clear and unwavering goal (to land a man safely on the Moon by the end of the decade), largely protected from political interference and other social, economic, and environmental pressures. Megaprojects in cities—like the Boston Big Dig and the London 2012 Olympics—are open systems. They have porous boundaries that extend beyond the system and have to accommodate multiple stakeholders with diverging, often ambiguous and conflicting interests.

Our new and reconstructed cities and infrastructures will have to be designed to be resilient to climate change and responsive when the unexpected happens, such as Japan's Fukushima nuclear accident in 2011. It is highly unlikely that a monolithic Manhattan-style project designed to achieve a single goal will be able to cope with the pervasive, diffuse, and continuously evolving problems associated with mitigating and adapting to climate change. Thomas Hughes suggested that multiple, diverse, and geographically dispersed 'eco-technological projects'—carbon capture and storage, low-cost solar battery, flood risk, tidal energy, and eco-city projects, for example—will be required to achieve the transition towards a post-industrial and ecologically sustainable society powered by low-carbon and renewable energy sources.

We end this book by considering how projects of the future might be equipped to respond to these societal challenges and the relentless pressure to innovate and compete in global markets. Many years ago, Alvin Toffler predicted that adaptive project organizations, with authority and responsibility distributed horizontally among self-motivated and knowledgeable members of problem-solving teams, would challenge and ultimately replace top–down, regimented bureaucracy as societies make the transition to a post-industrial age. Government agencies, firms, and individuals have found it difficult to adjust to this new style of organization and the transition has taken longer and may not be quite as far reaching as Toffler expected. Some of the examples and case studies described in this book provide an indication of what tomorrow's projects might look like.

## Post-industrial projects

In this post-industrial future, project success will no longer be measured solely by how well the team or organization meet time, budget, and specified requirements. It will depend on whether the operational outcome creates exceptional value for sponsors, customers, operators, and users. The Gehry-designed Guggenheim Museum project in Bilbao did much more than construct an iconic building on time and within budget. It revitalized a declining industrial city. Apple's success in creating the iPod and iTunes platform changed how people listen to music and created one of the world's most successful firms. Many firms and government agencies are finding that bids specifying the required operational performance of an IT system, hospital, or railway create better and more innovative outcomes. For example, invitations to tender for a specified number of trains will produce a range of prices, but may not stimulate innovation. In contrast, demands for 'train availability'—as we saw in the case of Alstom—may result in a variety of proposals outlining novel ways to build, operate, finance, and maintain a fleet of trains over many years.

Highly capable sponsors and client organizations will spend time at the start defining the project goal and selecting the best way of achieving it. Learning systematically from previous projects helps to calibrate the risks involved, reach informed judgements about how to address them, and produce more realistic schedule and cost estimates. Faced with the uncertainties involved in building the fifth terminal at London's Heathrow Airport, BAA learned lessons from previous construction and airport projects and decided to create a flexible delivery model. It was based on an overarching flexible contract and depended on collaborative teams being able to solve emergent problems and embrace new opportunities that could not be anticipated at the outset. The London 2012 delivery model, by contrast, used a variety of contracts to target the pieces of uncertainty involved in constructing the mix of standardized and bespoke buildings and structures in the Olympic Park.

During this front-end definition period, the sponsor or parent organization will develop a compelling vision showing how the project meets the needs of existing customers or creates a new market opportunity. Operators and users will be more fully engaged at an early stage to ensure that their requirements, concerns, and priorities are fully addressed in the design of the eventual outcome. Boeing, for example, listened closely to the needs and priorities of eight major airlines to define their requirements and shape the design of the 777 aircraft. But as Elon Musk knows so well, there are times when not listening to existing customers is important. Until recently, for example, car manufacturers were reluctant to develop electric and autonomous vehicle technologies that they believed customers had no desire to purchase. The breakthrough came when the all-electric Tesla car was developed by the industry's first start company since the 1920s. As we have seen, firms competing in fast-changing markets—Apple, Microsoft, and Google—have a balanced portfolio of projects to know how to sustain existing markets and when to open up new ones.

Organizations will have dynamic and flexible teams with the capability to solve problems, innovate, and adapt as circumstances change during the planning and execution phases of a project. Project leaders will be adept at building collaborative teams and overcoming the conflicts and creative tensions that often arise when diverse groups of people with different ideas, cultural values, personalities, and competing priorities start working together. Members of Arup's Dongtan and Beijing Water Cube projects had to learn how to work together in multidisciplinary and multicultural teams—in co-located offices and distributed across continents—that emerged and dissolved in response to the changing needs of demanding clients and unexpected problems that were identified as the work progressed. Lean and agile processes may spread to industries where project teams competing in fast-changing, innovative markets have to develop alternative solutions in parallel, work concurrently, and adapt in real time to the feedback from frequent interactions with customers and executive sponsors.

In the past, megaprojects sometimes incorporated new technology in the design of an infrastructure system (e.g. advanced signalling technology on London's Jubilee Line), but rarely experimented with new ideas, practices, and technologies once the project was under way. Innovation during execution was considered an unnecessary downside risk associated with delays and cost overruns. Tomorrow's sponsors and clients, by contrast, will embrace innovation as an upside opportunity to design better outcomes and complete megaprojects more efficiently. They will know that performance can be improved by using existing knowledge and adopting proven technologies that worked well elsewhere. But they will recognize that the uncertainties involved in experimenting with new technologies and practices can be minimized prior to their introduction by undertaking trials to develop, test, rehearse, and learn about alternative solutions. The innovation programme established by Crossrail to create, share, and implement new and existing technologies, ideas, and practices, for example, is now being applied on other megaprojects in London and elsewhere.

The systems integrator of the future will have to design and integrate increasingly complex and interdependent infrastructure systems. Many complex projects—the construction of high-rise buildings and nuclear power plants, for instance—will be modular, using flexible combinations of standardized components produced more cheaply and with greater precision in offsite factories and assembled more safely and efficiently when brought together onsite. Each part of a project—components, subsystems, and systems—will be designed to work as an integrated whole and achieve targets for sustainable low-carbon and efficient operational performance. Arup does this when it delineates how the social and technical components and systems of an ecologically sustainable or smart city—such as water, energy, transport, governance, culture, education, telecommunications, and housing—will interact when the entire system of systems becomes operational. The integrator will be more fully engaged with stakeholders inside and outside the systems they are building. On several of London's megaprojects, a client organization provides a single point of contact for all external relationships with government agencies, local authorities, utilities, businesses, communities, and other stakeholders, while a delivery partner focuses inwardly on managing the programme of interdependent activities undertaken by a large network of contractors and subcontractors.

Supported by digital technology, tomorrow's projects will be alive with the information and data required to coordinate the design, construction, handover, and operation of products and systems and respond in real time to any changes in circumstances. Co-located and geographically dispersed virtual teams sharing the same digital model can visualize the final design of complex products, detect interference and clashes between components prior to their integration, test virtual prototypes, and identify the latest moment a design can be changed before moving to fabrication and construction. The usefulness of digital technology extends to the operation and maintenance of an asset by creating a database showing the exact location of components such as the cabling, heating, and cooling systems of a building. Frank Gehry is using his own Digital Project software to control construction costs in a collaborative process where the traditional boundaries between designer, constructor, and user continue to blur. In future, projects might use 'augmented reality' headset technology that is able to supplement the real world by laying computer-generated images on top of it. Equipped with smart glasses, designers can inspect a product from different vantage points, lay three-dimensional images onto it, and rearrange the position of virtual components. AECOM, the global firm of architects and engineers, for example, uses the HoloLens headset produced by Microsoft to help designers walk around and review the digital representation of a building with complex geometry.

For the individual working in projects, the post-industrial future brings new threats and opportunities. Many organizations will be filled with transient teams and extremely mobile individuals. Relationships with colleagues will be less permanent, more temporary than in the past. People will develop quick and intense relationships on each temporary endeavour, and learn to bear the loss of more enduring ones. They must get used to being frequently reassigned and shuffled about from one project to another. With each new change, individuals must reorient themselves. Each change brings the need for new learning and may strain the adaptability of the individual, creating social and psychological tensions. But others may thrive in this temporary and fast-changing world. Whereas careers were once defined by loyalty to one or more permanent organizations, a growing number of people will happily move from one project to the next throughout their working lives. As Toffler predicted, projects will be attractive to individuals who want to work in challenging and creative environments where they can 'play with problems' and are encouraged to innovate. They will begin to think about their work, daily activities, and even their personal ambitions as projects.

# Further reading

## Chapter 1: Introduction

A. Davies, T. Brady, and M. Hobday, 'Charting a path toward integrated solutions', *MIT Sloan Management Review*, Spring (2006), 39–48.

D. Defoe, *An Essay Upon Projects* (Rockville, Md.: Arc Manor, 1697; repr. 2008).

*The Economist*, 'Project management: overdue and over budget, over and over again', 11 June (2005), 65–6.

B. Flyvbjerg, 'What you should know about megaprojects and why: an overview', *Project Management Journal*, 45(2) (2014), 6–19.

P. Hall, *Great Planning Disasters* (Harmondsworth: Penguin Books, 1980).

T. Heatherwick, *Thomas Heatherwick: Making* (London: Thames & Hudson, 2012).

T. P. Hughes, *Rescuing Prometheus* (New York: Pantheon Books, 1998).

R. A. Lundin, N. Arvidsson, T. Brady, E. Ekstedt, C. Midler, and J. Sydow, *Managing and Working in Project Society: Institutional Challenges of Temporary Organizations* (Cambridge: Cambridge University Press, 2015).

P. W. G. Morris and G. H. Hough, *The Anatomy of Major Projects* (Chichester: John Wiley & Sons, 1987).

T. Peters and R. H. Waterman, *In Search of Excellence: Lessons from America's Best-Run Companies* (New York: Harper & Row, 1982).

W. A. Randolph and B. Z. Posner, 'What every manager needs to know about project management', *Sloan Management Review*, 65 (1988), 65–73.

P. Scranton, 'Projects as a focus for historical analysis: surveying the landscape', *History and Technology*, 30(4) (2014), 354–73.

A. J. Shenhar and D. Dvir, *Reinventing Project Management: The Diamond Approach to Successful Growth and Innovation* (Boston: Harvard Business School Press, 2007).

A. Toffler, *Future Shock* (New York: Bantam Books, 1970).

A. Toffler, *The Third Wave* (New York: Bantam Books, 1980).

A. Toffler, *The Adaptive Corporation* (London: Pan Books, 1985).

## Chapter 2: America's venture into the unknown

P. L. Bernstein, *Wedding the Waters: The Erie Canal and the Making of a Great Nation* (New York: W. W. Norton & Company, 2005).

B. Flyvbjerg, 'What you should know about megaprojects and why: an overview', *Project Management Journal*, 45(2) (2014), 6–19.

B. Flyvbjerg, N. Bruzelius, and W. Rothengatter, *Megaprojects and Risk: An Anatomy of Ambition* (Cambridge: Cambridge University Press, 2003).

A. O. Hirschman, *Development Projects Observed* (Washington, DC: The Brookings Institution, 1967).

G. Koeppel, *Bond of Union: Building the Erie Canal and the American Empire* (Cambridge, Mass.: Da Capo Press, 2009).

R. Miller and D. R. Lessard, *The Strategic Management of Large Engineering Projects: Shaping Institutions, Risks, and Governance* (Cambridge, Mass.: The MIT Press, 2000).

P. W. G. Morris, *The Management of Projects* (London: Thomas Telford, 1994).

J. Ross and B. M. Staw, 'Organizational escalation and exit: lessons from the Shoreham Nuclear Power Plant', *Academy of Management Journal*, 36(4) (1993), 701–32.

Z. Shapira and D. J. Berndt, 'Managing grand-scale construction projects: a risk-taking perspective', *Research in Organizational Behavior*, 19 (1997), 303–60.

R. E. West, *Erie Water West: A History of the Erie Canal, 1792–1854* (Lexington, Ky: University Press of Kentucky, 1966).

## Chapter 3: From Manhattan to the Moon

T. P. Hughes, *American Genesis: A History of the American Genius for Invention* (Harmondsworth: Penguin Books, 1989).

T. P. Hughes, *Rescuing Prometheus* (New York: Pantheon Books, 1998).

S. B. Johnson, 'Three approaches to big technology: operations research, systems engineering, and project management', *Technology and Culture*, 38(4) (1997), 891–919.

S. B. Johnson, *The Secret of Apollo: Systems Management in American and European Space Programs* (Baltimore: Johns Hopkins University Press, 2002).

S. Lenfle and C. Loch, 'Lost roots: how project management came to emphasize control over flexibility and novelty', *California Management Review*, 53(1) (2010), 32–55.

P. W. G. Morris, *Reconstructing Project Management* (Chichester: Wiley-Blackwell, 2013).

S. Ramo, *The Business of Science: Winning and Losing in the High-Tech Age* (New York: Hill and Wang, 1988).

H. M. Sapolsky, *The Polaris System Development: Bureaucratic and Programmatic Success in Government* (Cambridge, Mass.: Harvard University Press, 1972).

L. R. Sayles and M. K. Chandler, *Managing Large Systems: Organizations for the Future* (New Brunswick, NJ: Transaction Publications, 1971).

J. E. Webb, *Space Age Management: The Large-Scale Approach* (New York: McGraw-Hill Company, 1969).

## Chapter 4: Arup's adhocracy and projects in theory

T. J. Allen, *Managing the Flow of Technology* (Cambridge, Mass.: The MIT Press, 1984).

W. Bennis, *Beyond Bureaucracy: Essays on the Development and Evolution of Human Organization* (San Francisco: Jossey-Bass Publishers, 1966).

S. Brusoni and A. Prencipe, 'Unpacking the black box of modularity: technology, products and organization', *Industrial and Corporate Change*, 10(1) (2001), 179–205.

T. Burns and G. M. Stalker, *The Management of Innovation* (Oxford: Oxford University Press, 1961).

A. De Meyer, C. Loch, and M. T. Pich, 'Managing project uncertainty', *Sloan Management Review*, 43(2) (2002), 6–67.

*The Economist*, 'A Chinese eco-city. City of Dreams', 21 March (2009), 68–9.

A. Edmondson, *Teaming: How Organizations Learn, Innovate, and Compete in the Knowledge Economy* (San Francisco: John Wiley & Sons, 2012).

A. Edmondson, 'Teamwork on the fly', *Harvard Business Review*, April (2012), 72–80.

K. M. Eisenhardt and B. N. Tabrizi, 'Accelerating adaptive processes: product innovation in the global computer industry', *Administrative Science Quarterly*, 40 (1995), 84–110.

J. R. Galbraith, *Designing Complex Organizations* (Reading, Mass.: Addison-Wesley, 1973).

C. J. G. Gersick, 'Pacing strategic change: the case of a new venture', *Academy of Management Journal*, 37(1) (1994), 9–45.

C. Jones and B. Lichtenstein, 'Temporary inter-organizational projects: how temporal and social embeddedness enhance coordination and manage uncertainty', in S. Cropper, C. Huxman, M. Ebers, and P. Smith Ring (eds), *The Oxford Handbook of Inter-Organizational Relations* (Oxford: Oxford University Press, 2008), 231–55.

P. Jones, *Ove Arup: Masterbuilder of the Twentieth Century* (New Haven: Yale University Press, 2006).

P. R. Lawrence and J. W. Lorsch, *Organization and Environment: Managing Differentiation and Integration* (Boston: Harvard Business School Press, 1967).

L. Lindkvist, J. Söderlund, and F. Tell, 'Managing product development projects: on the significance of fountains and deadlines', *Organization Studies*, 19 (1998), 931–51.

C. Loch, A. De Meyer, and M. T. Pich, *Managing the Unknown: A New Approach to Managing High Uncertainty and Risk in Projects* (Hoboken, NJ: John Wiley and Sons, 2006).

H. Mintzberg, *The Structuring of Organizations* (New York: Prentice-Hall, 1979).

A. Prencipe, A. Davies, and M. Hobday, *The Business of Systems Integration* (Oxford: Oxford University Press, 2003).

J. Sapsed and A. Salter, 'Postcards from the edge: local communities, global programs and boundary objects', *Organization Studies*, 25(9) (2005), 1515–34.

L. R. Sayles and M. K. Chandler, *Managing Large Systems: Organizations for the Future* (New Brunswick, NJ: Transaction Publications, 1971).

A. J. Shenhar and D. Dvir, *Reinventing Project Management: The Diamond Approach to Successful Growth and Innovation* (Boston: Harvard Business School Press, 2007).

F. Siebdrat, M. Hoegel, and H. Ernst, 'How to manage virtual teams', *MIT Sloan Management Review*, Summer (2009), 63–8.

A. L. Stinchcombe and C. Heimer, *Organizational Theory and Project Management: Administering Uncertainty in Norwegian Offshore Oil* (Oslo: Norwegian University Press, 1985).

J. D. Thompson, *Organizations in Action: Social Science Bases of Administrative Theory* (New York: McGraw-Hill, 1967).

J. Woodward, *Industrial Organization: Theory and Practice* (Oxford: Oxford University Press, 1965).

W. Wu, A. Davies, and L. Frederiksen, 'The birth of an eco-city business: Arup's Dongtan project', in G. Grabher and J. Thiel (eds), *Self-Induced Shocks: Mega-Projects and Urban Development* (Berlin: Jovis Verlag GmbH, 2015), 201–20.

## Chapter 5: Lean, heavy, and disruptive projects

C. M. Christensen, *The Innovator's Dilemma: When New Technologies Cause Great Firms to Fail* (Boston: Harvard Business School Press, 1997).

K. B. Clark and T. Fujimoto, *Product Development Performance: Strategy, Organization, and Management in the World Auto Industry* (Cambridge, Mass.: Harvard Business School, 1991).

W. Isaacson, *Steve Jobs* (St Ives: Little Brown, 2011).

R. M. Kanter, *When Elephants Learn to Dance: Mastering the Challenges of Strategy, Management, and Careers in the 1990s* (London: Unwin Paperbacks, 1990).

B. Lindsey, *Digital Gehry: Material Resistance/Digital Construction* (Basel: Birkhäuser, 2001).

C. A. O'Reilly and M. T. Tushman, 'The ambidextrous organization', *Harvard Business Review*, April (2004), 74–833.

K. Sabbagh, *21st Century Jet: The Making of the Boeing 777* (London: Pan Books, 1995).

P. Serrador and J. K. Pinto, 'Does agile work? A quantitative analysis of agile project success', *International Journal of Project Management*, 33 (2015), 1040–51.

H. Takeuchi and I. Nonaka, 'The new new product development game', *Harvard Business Review*, January–February (1986), 137–46.

A. Vance, *Elon Musk: How the Billionaire CEO of SpaceX and Tesla is Shaping our Future* (London: Virgin Books, 2015).

S. C. Wheelwright and K. B. Clark, *Revolutionizing Product Development: Quantum Leaps in Speed, Efficiency, and Quality* (New York: The Free Press, 1992).

J. Whyte and R. Levitt, 'Information management and the management of projects', in P. Morris, J. Pinto, and J. S. Söderlund (eds), *The Oxford Handbook of Project Management* (Oxford: Oxford University Press, 2011), 365–88.

J. P. Womack, D. T. Jones, and D. Roos, *The Machine that Changed the World* (New York: MacMillan Publishing Company, 1990).

## Chapter 6: London's megaproject ecology

K. Artto, A. Davies, J. Kujala, and A. Prencipe, 'The project business: analytical framework and research opportunities', in P. W. G. Morris, J. Pinto, and J. Söderlund (eds), *The Oxford Handbook of Project Management* (Oxford: Oxford University Press, 2011), 133–53.

B. A. Bechky, 'Gaffers, gofers, and grips: role-based coordination in temporary organizations', *Organization Science*, 17(1) (2006), 3–21.

T. Brady and A. Davies, 'Building project capabilities: from exploratory to exploitative learning', *Organization Studies*, 25(9) (2004), 1601–21.

E. Cacciatori, 'Memory objects in project environments: storing, retrieving and adapting learning in project-based firms', *Research Policy*, 37 (2008), 1591–601.

C. Cattani, S. Ferriani, L. Frederiksen, and F. Täube, 'Project-based organizing and strategic management: a long-term research agenda on temporary organizational forms', *Advances in Strategic Management*, 28 (2011), 3–26.

A. Davies and T. Brady, 'Organisational capabilities and learning in complex product systems: towards repeatable solutions', *Research Policy*, 29 (2000), 931–53.

A. Davies and M. Hobday, *The Business of Projects: Managing Innovation in Complex Products and Systems* (Cambridge: Cambridge University Press, 2005).

A. Davies and I. Mackenzie, 'Project complexity and systems integration: constructing the London 2012 Olympics and Paralympics Games', *International Journal of Project Management*, 32 (2014), 773–90.

A. Davies, D. M. Gann, and T. Douglas, 'Innovation in megaprojects: systems integration at London Heathrow Terminal 5', *California Management Review*, 51(2) (2009), 101–25.

A. Davies, S. MacAulay, T. DeBarro, and M. Thurston, 'Making innovation happen in a megaproject: London's Crossrail suburban railway system', *Project Management Journal*, 45(6) (2014), 25–37.

R. J. DeFillippi and M. B. Arthur, 'Paradox in project-based enterprise: the case of film making', *California Management Review*, 40(2) (1998), 125–39.

M. Dodgson, D. Gann, S. MacAulay, and A. Davies, 'Innovation strategy in new transportation systems: the case of Crossrail', *Transportation Research Part A: Policy and Practice*, 77 (2015), 261–75.

M. Engwall, 'No project is an island: linking projects to history and context', *Research Policy*, 32 (2003), 789–808.

D. Gann, A. Salter, M. Dodgson, and N. Phillips, 'Inside the world of the project baron', *MIT Sloan Management Review*, Spring (2012), 63–71.

D. Gann and A. Salter, 'Innovation in project-based, service-enhanced firms: the construction of complex products and systems', *Research Policy*, 29 (2000), 955–72.

N. Gil, 'Developing cooperative project–client relationships: how much to expect from relational contracts', *California Management Review*, 51(2) (2009), 144–69.

G. Grabher, 'Ecologies of creativity: the Village, the Group and the heterarchic organisation of the British advertising industry', *Environment and Planning A*, 33 (2001), 351–74.

G. Grabher and J. Thiel, 'Projects, people, professions: trajectories of learning through a mega-event (the London 2012 case)', *Geoforum*, 65 (2015), 328–37.

M. Hobday, 'The project-based organisation: an ideal form for management of complex products and systems', *Research Policy*, 29 (2000), 871–93.

R. A. Lundin and A. Söderholm, 'A theory of the temporary organization', *Scandinavian Journal of Management*, 11(4) (1995), 437–55.

R. A. Lundin, N. Arvidsson, T. Brady, E. Ekstedt, C. Midler, and J. Sydow, *Managing and Working in Project Society: Institutional Challenges of Temporary Organizations* (Cambridge: Cambridge University Press, 2015).

S. Manning and J. Sydow, 'Projects, paths and practices: sustaining and leveraging project-based relationships', *Industrial and Corporate Change*, 20(5) (2011), 1369–402.

Further reading

C. Midler, '"Projectification" of the firm: the Renault case', *Scandinavian Journal of Management*, 11(4) (1995), 363–75.

P. Morris, J. Pinto, and J. S. Söderlund, *The Oxford Handbook of Project Management* (Oxford: Oxford University Press, 2011).

A. Prencipe and F. Tell, 'Inter-project learning: processes and outcomes of knowledge codification in project-based firms', *Research Policy*, 30 (2001), 1373–94.

A. Schwab and A. S. Miner, 'Learning in hybrid-project systems: the effects of project performance on repeated collaboration', *Academy of Management Journal*, 51(6) (2008), 1117–49.

W. R. Scott, R. E. Levitt, and R. J. Orr, *Global Projects: Institutional and Political Challenges* (Cambridge: Cambridge University Press, 2011).

J. Söderlund and F. Tell, 'The P-form organization and the dynamics of project competence: project epochs in Asea/ABB, 1950–2000', *International Journal of Project Management*, 27 (2009), 101–12.

J. Sydow, L. Lindkvist, and R. DeFillippi, 'Project-based organizations, embeddedness and repositories of knowledge: editorial', *Organization Studies*, 25(9) (2004), 1475–89.

A. H. Van Marrewijk, S. Ybema, K. Smits, S. Clegg, and T. S. Pitsis, 'Clash of the titans: temporal organizing and collaborative dynamics in the Panama Canal megaproject', *Organization Studies*, 37(12) (2016), 1745–69.

R. Whitley, 'Project-based firms: new organizational form or variations on a theme?', *Industrial and Corporate Change*, 15(1) (2006), 77–99.

G. Winch, 'Three domains of project organizing', *International Journal of Project Management*, 32 (2014), 721–31.

## Chapter 7: Back to the future

T. P. Hughes, *Rescuing Prometheus* (New York: Pantheon Books, 1998).

T. P. Hughes, *Human-Built World: How to Think About Technology and Culture* (Chicago: The University of Chicago Press, 2004).

R. E. Levitt, 'Towards Project Management 2.0', *Engineering Project Organization Journal*, September (2011), 197–210.

McKinsey & Company, 'Infrastructure productivity: how to save $1 trillion a year', The McKinsey Global Institute, The McKinsey Infrastructure Practice, January (2013).

H. W. J. Rittel and M. M. Weber, 'Dilemmas in a general theory of planning'. *Policy Sciences*, 4 (1973), 155–69.

# Resources

## Systems-based project management textbook:

D. I. Cleland and W. R. King, *Systems Analysis and Project Management* (New York: McGraw-Hill, 1968).

## Practitioner guide:

Project Management Institute, *A Guide to the Project Management Body of Knowledge (PMBOK® Guide) 5th Edition* (Newton Square, Pa.: Project Management Institute, 2013).

## Recent project management textbooks:

H. Maylor, *Project Management* (Harlow: Prentice Hall, Financial Times, 2005).

J. K. Pinto, *Project Management: Achieving Competitive Advantage* (Boston: Pearson, 2010).

## Project management and strategy:

M. Morgan, R. E. Levitt, and W. Malek, *Executing your Strategy: How to Break it Down and Get it Done* (Boston: Harvard Business School Press, 2007).

## Megaproject management:

B. Flyvbjerg (ed.), *The Oxford Handbook of Megaproject Management* (Oxford: Oxford University Press, 2017).

E. W. Merrow, *Industrial Megaprojects: Concepts, Strategies, and Practices for Success* (Hoboken, NJ: John Wiley & Sons, 2011).

## Case study of the Sydney Opera House:

http://theoperahouseproject.com

# "牛津通识读本"已出书目

| | | |
|---|---|---|
| 古典哲学的趣味 | 福柯 | 地球 |
| 人生的意义 | 缤纷的语言学 | 记忆 |
| 文学理论入门 | 达达和超现实主义 | 法律 |
| 大众经济学 | 佛学概论 | 中国文学 |
| 历史之源 | 维特根斯坦与哲学 | 托克维尔 |
| 设计，无处不在 | 科学哲学 | 休谟 |
| 生活中的心理学 | 印度哲学祛魅 | 分子 |
| 政治的历史与边界 | 克尔凯郭尔 | 法国大革命 |
| 哲学的思与惑 | 科学革命 | 民族主义 |
| 资本主义 | 广告 | 科幻作品 |
| 美国总统制 | 数学 | 罗素 |
| 海德格尔 | 叔本华 | 美国政党与选举 |
| 我们时代的伦理学 | 笛卡尔 | 美国最高法院 |
| 卡夫卡是谁 | 基督教神学 | 纪录片 |
| 考古学的过去与未来 | 犹太人与犹太教 | 大萧条与罗斯福新政 |
| 天文学简史 | 现代日本 | 领导力 |
| 社会学的意识 | 罗兰·巴特 | 无神论 |
| 康德 | 马基雅维里 | 罗马共和国 |
| 尼采 | 全球经济史 | 美国国会 |
| 亚里士多德的世界 | 进化 | 民主 |
| 西方艺术新论 | 性存在 | 英格兰文学 |
| 全球化面面观 | 量子理论 | 现代主义 |
| 简明逻辑学 | 牛顿新传 | 网络 |
| 法哲学：价值与事实 | 国际移民 | 自闭症 |
| 政治哲学与幸福根基 | 哈贝马斯 | 德里达 |
| 选择理论 | 医学伦理 | 浪漫主义 |
| 后殖民主义与世界格局 | 黑格尔 | 批判理论 |

| | | |
|---|---|---|
| 德国文学 | 儿童心理学 | 电影 |
| 戏剧 | 时装 | 俄罗斯文学 |
| 腐败 | 现代拉丁美洲文学 | 古典文学 |
| 医事法 | 卢梭 | 大数据 |
| 癌症 | 隐私 | 洛克 |
| 植物 | 电影音乐 | 幸福 |
| 法语文学 | 抑郁症 | 免疫系统 |
| 微观经济学 | 传染病 | 银行学 |
| 湖泊 | 希腊化时代 | 景观设计学 |
| 拜占庭 | 知识 | 神圣罗马帝国 |
| 司法心理学 | 环境伦理学 | 大流行病 |
| 发展 | 美国革命 | 亚历山大大帝 |
| 农业 | 元素周期表 | 气候 |
| 特洛伊战争 | 人口学 | 第二次世界大战 |
| 巴比伦尼亚 | 社会心理学 | 中世纪 |
| 河流 | 动物 | 工业革命 |
| 战争与技术 | 项目管理 | 传记 |